THIS IS A TRUE STORY

To Robert

I Don't Want My Son to Cry

By Ernest Gregory

First published by Dog Ear Publishing
4011 Vincennes Rd
Indianapolis, IN 46268
www.dogearpublishing.net

ISBN: 978-1-4575-5175-8

This book is printed on acid-free paper.

Printed in the United States of America

Foreword

It was my intention in writing this story to bring to light a remarkable human being and of all who came in contact with her. In relating this story, I also will be making known my own life and the influence of her on me, which will remain with me all of my life. I wish to acknowledge individuals whom I asked for information. They are my Aunt Stella who is now deceased, Mr. Peter Christopher, and Al Lopes. I dedicate this book to Mary Michalreas Grigoropoulos, and my Aunt Stella Tavanis. May they rest in peace where they are buried.

CHAPTER ONE

Malden, Massachusetts

I could hear the siren of the ambulance. I had called for it against my mother's wishes. She had left a trail of blood, from the bedroom to the bathroom. "Sonny, I don't want to go to the hospital. I don't need an ambulance," she said.

A friend of hers had called her. It was Mr. Karas. I told her to hang up as I could hear the ambulance stopping in the front of our house. She hesitated and told him good-bye. "Sonny, I don't need an ambulance and I am not going to the hospital."

I could see the trail of blood from the bedroom to the bathroom. Just then the doorbell rang, I ran down the stairs to open the door. "Hi," the medic said. "You called for an ambulance. "Yes," I said. "This way up the stairs, turn right, and walk straight down to the bedroom. My mother is in there."

She still refused to go, but saw the two medics and she did not give me any more trouble. I grabbed my coat, as they were taking my mother down in a stretcher. We were off to the Massachusetts General Hospital. The sirens were blasting as cars pulled over going through Malden Square, heading up Main Street toward the city of Everett, from there to Sullivan Square and toward City Square in Charlestown, to the corner of Causeway Street in Boston past North Station up toward Cambridge Street. Turning right and just two streets to Fruit Street, passing my old neighborhood of the West End.

It must have taken all of ten minutes to arrive at the hospital. How could I believe that I would be in an ambulance? I thanked the two medics for the service of getting us there in safety.

The Vincent Memorial is part of the Massachusetts General Hospital. My mother had met Dr. John Richardson from one of her friends at a christening she had gone to a few months back. He was the chief gynecologist here at the Vincent Memorial.

The medics had brought her in on a stretcher and transferred her to the hospital stretcher. It wasn't long before we saw Dr. Richardson. "Mary, how nice to see you. I wish it wasn't under these circumstances," he said. After asking her a few questions, he turned to me and said, Listen, son, I want you to go to the waiting room or get something to eat. Your mother will be having some tests done, so it will be a while. I'll keep you informed, okay?"

"Okay," I said, rather tired and worried for the first time since this happened. I went to the waiting room and there I sat. There was a couch there and I sprawled out, I started thinking of the things my mother had told me about her childhood.

My yiayia and papou, as we say in the Greek language for grandmother and grandfather, had come to America from Mani, the most southern part of Greece.

Mani is located in the province Laconia where Sparta is which, is famous for Leonidas and the Three Hundred who helped save Greece from the Persians in ancient times.

My grandmother was a midwife in the old country. She was just like a doctor, and this is what she did in her village. She set bones and sprains, etc.

My grandmother's marriage was arranged or as it was commonly called "a match marriage." She had to have a dowry to set up housekeeping, as was the custom, without it you did not get married.

My grandparents, Sofia and Leonidas Michalareas, arrived in New York City in 1912 accompanied by their seven-year-old son Louis.

There was a large influx of immigrants at that time from Europe. The immigration authorities could not pronounce their name and they were given an abbreviation of their name. They were now known as Mr. and Mrs. Maharis.

Luckily, they had relatives who had preceded them and met them. They settled in the city of Peabody Massachusetts, about eighteen miles from Boston.

Their first house was on Walnut Street. My grandfather's only brothers Panagioti and Mitso followed a month later. The language was very difficult for them because they did not know how to read or write.

My mother was the second of five children. She was the first-born in America, in March of 1916, and named Mary.

At my mother's birth, my grandmother agreed to have a doctor present, although she did not have faith in him. My mother's birth was okay up to a point. The doctor, a Dr. Hammond, a real Yankee said, "she may never walk, as her legs didn't seem as though they were straight enough." My grandmother dismissed the doctor and his remarks.

CHAPTER TWO

Peabody, Massachusetts

Peabody was then known in the United States as the "Leather Capital." There were many leather tanneries in Peabody, and their relatives were already working for them, so it wasn't difficult for them to get jobs.

In 1917 my Uncle Charlie was born followed by my Uncle Harry in 1918, and my Aunt Stella in 1920.

My grandmother and my grandfather, as well as his brothers, were learning English at their jobs in the tannery, and so my grandmother started learning some words from them as well as from her son my Uncle Louie.

My grandmother bought a straw carriage and put my mother in it. In the next few years my grandparents saved enough money to buy a combined store and house. The store was a variety store and the house was in the back. English Street was very close to my grandparent's house. It was here that the Greeks had built a church and named it Saint Vasilios. My grandfather was one of the founders of the church. One day my grandmother decided to leave my mother there in the carriage and come back to get her.

People had left the church. My mother was six years old now and waiting for my grandmother to come back to take her home. It grew dark outside. The only light that there was, came from the kantilia lights. These lights are candle lights in front of the icons at the altar. Suddenly, as my mother remembered telling me what happened, she felt a hand on her head and a voice saying, "Mary, get up and walk."

She was frightened, and whether that had something to do with it, I don't know. She immediately got up out of the carriage and started walking home.

So now she was about three minutes from her house. Everyone was home, my grandfather's brothers, Papou Mitso, and Papou Panagioti. Papou in Greek means grandfather, and out of respect you would call them by this name, as they were your grandfather's brothers. My grandmother was getting ready to go to get Mary at the church when a knock came at the door. "Poios Einai?" (who is it?) My grandmother answered. She opened the door and looked down at this little girl and fainted. My grandfather and the others heard the commotion and came running from the dinner table and quickly lifted her head, and brought her a glass of water and a cold towel to put on her forehead. The look on their faces told the story. They were astonished to see Mary in the doorway. My grandmother opened her eyes and looked up at her, "Mary, how did you get here?" she asked. "Mama, it was dark, and the only light came from the kantilia, the candle lights, in front of the icons. I felt a hand on my head and a voice saying, Mary, get up and walk. Mama, it was like no other thing that could happen to me. I got up out of the straw carriage and started walking." My grandmother said, "We must all go to church and thank the Lord for this wonderful miracle that has happened."

My grandfather's brothers, Mitso and Panagioti, could not believe it. Inside of a week the whole town was talking about what had happened. My mother could now go to school and be like other children.

Mr. Blakely was the principal of Lincoln Elementary School not far from Mary's house. It was here she would go to school. My mother excelled in school, so that she skipped grades. She went from the first to the third, and then third to the fifth. She was an A+ student. She was now nine years old and getting ready for grade seven. One morning a boy stopped to talk to her. "Mary, how is everyone?" "Fine," my mother answered. A busybody neighbor saw them together laughing and talking. The neighbor, Mrs. Zareas, had a house that overlooked my grandmother's yard. She went to my grandmother's house and knocked on the door. Opening the door my grandmother greeted her, "Kali mera, "meaning good day", Aspasia, how are you?" "Sofia, kali mera to you, I am fine." "Sit down and I will give you a cup of coffee." "Thank you, Sofia, I guess I am getting old and my eyes are playing tricks on me." "Nonsense," my grandmother answered back, smiling and pouring a cup of coffee and giving her a piece of baklava. "Does your daughter have a boyfriend?" "What? No," came a sharp reply. "Well, I saw her talking and laughing with a blond headed boy this morning." "We came to America from Etylon, Greece. We had nothing, only decency and respect. My husband, Leonidas, started the church with other members of the community. Now we will be a disgrace, my family and I." All this she said in Greek to her friend Aspasia Zareas. "Thank you, good day to you."

My grandmother was furious. The noon hour came, then 1:00 PM, finally 2:30 PM. Mary would be coming home from school. No sooner had she opened the door and greeted her mother when a slap came across her face. Mary turned again, and another slap came across the other side of her face. Mary was crying so much that she nearly tripped on the stick that my grandmother picked up to start hitting her on the rear of her body. She went off to bed without a word to her mother, as she would not listen to any explanation.

The next day she went off to school without a word to her mother, and again this blond headed boy approached her and said, "Good morning, how are you, Mary, and how is everyone at home?" Not a word came from her mouth. He tried again."Hi Mary." No response, continuing to walk toward the school. Well, this young fellow knew what he was going to do. The end of the school day came. He quickly raced to Walnut Street, and knocked on the door. Opening the door my grandmother was greeted with "yiasou, Theia Sofia," which meant, "hi Aunt Sofia, how are you?"

"Kala Peter" meaning good or well in Greek. Peter was the son of my grandmother's first cousin Helen. Peter would call his mother's first cousin aunt out of respect, as he was taught from childhood. "Tell me, is your daughter so high and mighty that she can't say hello?" "Why do you ask such a question, Peter?" "Well, yesterday at about the same time as today, I met Mary and she said hi and we started talking going to school. I met her today and she passed me by without saying anything. Wow what a change from yesterday," said Peter. My grandmother sat down and looked as if she were in another world. "Is there anything wrong, Aunt Sofia?" "No, no, my boy," she said. Peter kissed her and bade her farewell. "What have I done?" she said to herself. "Mary," my grandmother cried out, "she will never forgive me."

Mary was coming up the walk to the front door. My grandmother heard the front door open and Mary came in and closed the door behind her. "Mary," my grandmother cried out. "Please, Mary, come here" Mary was afraid, but not wanting to suffer the consequences of yesterday's beating, she went to her mother. Sofia grabbed and kissed Mary, crying at the same time, "I don't know how to tell you my daughter. I have hurt you very much. I believed a person, a neighbor who I thought was a friend. She was nothing but a terrible gossiper, an evil woman. I will never allow this to happen again. I ask you to forgive me." She grabbed and kissed her, not wanting to let her go.

Time passed and then one day, my mother, her sister and her brothers brought home a dog, part terrier and part German shepherd. This dog started to follow them home, and they felt sorry for the dog. They didn't tell their mother yet.

That night after supper, my mother's brother Louie said to his mother, "Could we have a dog?" She looked over to her husband, Leonidas, to see his reaction. He showed no sign of disapproval. He said, "Yes. Why not?" It was settled then they could have a dog. My mother's brother Louie would train the dog. They named the dog Kemal. When Kemal would go to the store, he would help them with the groceries. He would carry the eggs home and not break one of them. He was the talk of the neighborhood. Louie was training him very well.

One day when the kids had come home from school and my grandmother had put Kemal's food out in the yard to eat, something terrible happened. They had just sat down to eat supper when they heard a crying sound. They all got up from the table and went to the door. "It sounds like Kemal," my mother said. They opened the door to the yard and saw a terrible sight. Kemal was running around crying and shaking his head back and forth. He could not stop. "What are we going to do?" said my grandmother. "This is a terrible thing," said my grandfather. "Something has to be done," said the rest of the kids.

Soon people came out of their houses to see what was going on. "We must do something," someone said. Someone went for the police. When they arrived, they tried to catch Kemal. Nothing doing. They realized they had to get a veterinarian. The police found one and brought him as fast as they could. Upon seeing Kemal running around the yard and crying and howling, he knew this was no ordinary animal problem. The first thing was to catch Kemal. This they did between the police and the veterinarian and the crowd. The veterinarian opened Kemal's mouth, and discovered something awful. He could see down his throat and there were needles in his throat. "My God" exclaimed the veterinarian, "someone has given this dog needles." The veterinarian looked around and found his food. There were still some needles in the food. "There is nothing I can do," said the veterinarian, "except put him to sleep and his pain and suffering will stop."

My mother and her sister and her brothers could not stop from crying and yelling out. "No, no Kemal. Oh poor Kemal we love you so," said Louie. Everyone's eyes filled up and that everyone was there except one. Aspasia Zareas had not shown her face. My grandmother knew she must have had something to do with this, but could not prove it.

Months had gone by and this tragedy was put behind them. Soon my mother would be getting promoted. My mother had a chance to go on to high school. So Mr. Blakely, the principal of my mother's school, paid a visit to my grandmother and grandfather to ask them to let her go on to high school.

In her broken English she told him, "No, girls do not go to high school. They go to work and help the family." He could not change her mind. So my mother went to work and lucky she did because the Great Depression had arrived.

CHAPTER THREE

A Match Marriage

In 1929 my mother was thirteen years of age and working at two jobs, making thirty-eight dollars a week. My mother's uncles, Mitso and Panagioti, had both been laid off from the leather tannery. My grandfather had his grocery store, but now the grocery store was not bringing in that much money because of the Depression in the United States. So my mother, who worked two jobs a week, was supporting all the family as that money was a lot for a person to be making every week.

The only enjoyment that they had to look forward to was going to the movies. The movie theater was down on Main Street in Peabody. So during the 1930s this was her enjoyment. I remember what my Aunt Stella had told me. "Your mother and I went to the movies one Saturday and we saw a movie titled "Four Sons" with Don Ameche and Alan Baxter. That movie stayed in your mother's mind, because when we left the movie theater, she said, "Stella if I ever get married, I hope God gives me four sons just like in that movie."

In 1935, wrestling matches had come to Peabody. One of the wrestlers was nicknamed Gorgeous George. His real name was Nicholas Theodore. My grandfather had found out that Gorgeous George was Greek and invited him up to the house to meet the family and especially his two daughters. When he came to dinner he explained to my grandfather that he was already married, but he had a friend who was single and Greek and his name was George Grigoropoulos. My grandfather asked if he could bring him to their house the following Sunday. The next week came, and with Mr. Nicholas Theodore came this man named George Grigoropoulos.

He told of how he came to America. He was born in the city of Constantinople, which is now a part of Turkey. He was born in 1902, and in those days Greeks living under the yoke of the barbaric Turks suffered immensely as did the Armenians whom the Turks slaughtered. In fact, one million and a half of them were put to death for no reason at all but to get rid of one of the minorities. He was one of twelve children and a twin. The twin had died in childbirth.

When he was about twelve years old he contacted scarlet fever, and it left him deaf in one ear. His father, whose name was John, was a wealthy man, doing business in Greece, Bulgaria, Russia, and Romania. He had a fleet of ships and he traded in rugs, cheeses, olive oil, and other goods. He could afford to send his children to a French school and there they learned three languages at the same time as well as speaking Turkish.

When the Balkan Wars broke out in 1912, many Greeks had to flee as Turkey was battling Greece, Bulgaria, Montenegro, and Serbia. Then the start of the First World War came in which more fighting and more countries were involved. This time Turkey was allied with Germany and the Austro-Hungary Empire. Some Greeks, who could leave Turkey, left. Instead of leaving for Greece, George, who was fourteen years old, signed up and joined the French Foreign Legion.

He told his mother he had signed up for three years. He deceived her, because on the day he said good-bye to her, on the ship that he was leaving on, he put his hand up, and it was five fingers, meaning five years. He went to North Africa, and fought the Arabs in Algeria and Morocco, and was stationed at various cities, such as Casablanca, Marrakech, Oran, and Constantine.

After completing his enlistment, instead of returning home to Greece where his family was, he joined the merchant marine, and came to the United States where he injured himself. This happened in

1920. The authorities allowed him to stay until his injuries had healed. In the meantime, he met a woman of Irish descent and they got married. It wasn't to last as he had other ideas. But now he was legally in the country.

He met Nicholas Theodore and began assisting him in the wrestling profession. Nicholas Theodore was known professionally as Gorgeous George. Then he met another friend of his. His name was Sam Tsouvalekas. The three men lived in the West End of Boston. Nicholas Theodore had met my grandfather when he fought in a wrestling match in Peabody and my grandfather had told him that he had a daughter who was of marrying age. He said that he had a friend that he would like him to meet. My grandfather invited him to bring his friend to dinner the following Sunday.

Sunday came, and Nicholas Theodore, and his friend George Grigoropoulos came to dinner. George, my father, told my grandfather of how he came to the United States from the time he was discharged from the French Foreign Legion. My grandfather asked him, "Are you still married? Did you get a divorce?" George answered that he did, as he did not consummate the marriage.

My grandfather now looked favorably for his daughter Mary to be courted by George Grigoropoulos. It was the fall of 1935, and a 1936 wedding was planned. They were married in September of 1936.

CHAPTER FOUR

The West End

My mother went to live in the West End of Boston, on Staniford Street. When she arrived at the apartment, she went around and turned all the lights on. George thought she was crazy. Then she told him why. "When I was growing up we could not put lights on for very long because my mother would say, "You're burning too much light. So that is why I am doing this." He thought it was funny and yet he understood.

George soon would leave Nicholas Theodore and the wrestling matches, as it was part time work. He had learned to cook when he was in the French Foreign Legion and now wanted to put it to some use.

In 1938 he opened a restaurant at Bowdon Square in the West End. He named it The Reddy Hot Lunch, and it had one hundred and forty seats, which was a large restaurant for its time.

Then in 1940, who would have thought that certain things would happen? The first was a very good one for I was born, but at the same time the restaurant caught fire and burnt to the ground. In the meantime, we had to move as now the apartment was too small for the three of us.

My mother's brothers and sister all started to get married. My Aunt Stella was the youngest and she was the only one who actually married the man that she fell in love with. She was also the only one of the five to go to high school. When she got married she moved to Somerville, Massachusetts. It was here that my mother would take me so Aunt Stella could take care of me. When we finally moved, it was to 36 Lynde Street.

Our apartment was on the third floor. On the floor above us lived a mother and daughter, Rita and her daughter Gilda. On the street level there was a variety store owned by a man named Hagi Sarkissian. My father and mother got very friendly with him and his wife Sally. Sally could speak Greek fluently. She would stay home and it proved to be very helpful for my mother.

In 1941, after staying home for about a year my mother wanted to get a job. She saw an ad in the local newspaper and went to apply for the job. It was a factory on lower Washington Street. The factory was looking for a few good stitchers to make weekend bags for the servicemen or for men and women in general. The foreman was a man named David Pressman, who interviewed her for the job. My mother said that she really did not know how to stitch on a sewing machine. He agreed to teach her because of her honesty. So thus began a friendship that was to last for over twenty years. In the meantime, my father got a job at a restaurant named the Tasty, on the corner of Howard and Cambridge streets. The burlesque house The Old Howard was on Howard Street.

Here Ann Corio and Gypsy Rose Lee performed on stage. This area was known as Scollay Square; there were plenty of barrooms. Also here were two movie theaters next to each other. One was The Scollay Square Theater and the other was The Rialto, known as The Scratch House. How this theater got that name, I don't know, but all the bums and drunks went in there as it was opened all night. The famous Joe & Nemo restaurant was just a block away where you could get the best hot dogs and burgers in Boston. There was also another place known as the White Tower. Sally would take care of me during the day as my mother worked on her new job.

One day when my mother came home she noticed strange people coming into the building. They were men, some in Navy uniforms, and they proceeded to go up to the next floor. She also noted that the hallway light was not very bright on that floor, so she climbed the stairs to see why. The bulb had been changed; it was red. My God, said my mother to herself. A red light district, this is a house of prostitution. She immediately went down to her apartment and used her telephone, which was just installed, to call the landlord, Mr. Max Baer, to tell him about what was going on the next floor above her apartment.

He came down right away and went straight up to the fourth floor and knocked at the door. Rita opened the door and Mr. Baer said, "What is going on in this apartment?

The police are on their way, they will be here in a few minutes." Looking inside the apartment, he could see men hanging around. Rita knew who had called the landlord and yelled down to my mother who she could see in the hallway. "I'll get you for this, Mary," she said.

"Listen, Rita, I'll wipe the streets with you, so don't threaten me. "You're running a whorehouse here, let me say this in plain English. The other tenants in this building have small children and we don't want them exposed to these sorts of goings on. If you want to run a house of prostitution, go somewhere else to live."

With those remarks Rita slammed the door, but had to reopen it when the police arrived. Max Baer explained that he already spoke to his tenant about running a house of prostitution and he wanted it stopped or he would evict her. The police wrote everything down and went back to the station to file a report. As they left my father came home from the restaurant.

The next day after my mother dropped me off at Sally's house, Sally told her that Hagi told her of what had happened and she supported her all the way. "These things are disgusting to happen with children around," said Sally.

It was an early day for my father to get off from working at the Tasty. It was a warm day, and when he arrived home, he left the front door opened to his apartment. He was home two hours before my mother would be home. He heard the street door open downstairs. He could hear someone coming up the stairs and getting closer to his front door. Suddenly the footsteps stopped. It was Gilda and she turned and said, "Hi, George. Boy is it hot."

My father turned and saw her there. He noticed how big she was for her age and her bust with her blouse opened.

"Hi, Gilda. How are you?" "Fine," she said. "Would you like to come up for a cold drink?" "Sure," my father said. He closed his door and followed her up the stairs looking at her curves. They went into her apartment, and she gave him a cold bottle of beer. No sooner had she passed him the beer in a suggestive way, then she put her hand near his crotch and my father started kissing her all over. The next thing they were undressing and they disappeared under the covers of her bed. My mother came home and put the key in the door to unlock it, but noticed that it was unlocked, even though it was closed. She didn't notice anything strange. Just then my father came in. He had straightened his hair out as it had become messy. "Hi, Mary" he said. "Hi, George" she replied. "How was your day?" "Okay," said my father. On the stairs in the hallway you could hear footsteps as someone was passing and going on to the fourth floor. It wasn't long before my parents could hear the siren coming closer to Lynde Street, and stopping in front of our building.

You could hear the street door from downstairs open, and feet on the stairs.

More than one person. Suddenly, without warning, they stopped in front of our door. A knock came on the door. A voice said, "It's the police. Open the door." My parents looked at each other in amazement. My mother went to the door and opened it.

There were two men detectives from Police Station Three. "I am Detective Santini, and this is Detective Mahoney. We are looking for a George Grigoropoulos. Is that you?" they asked. My father answered, "I am he." "We have a warrant for your arrest." "For what?" my father asked. Detective Santini said, "Having sex with a minor." "What?" my mother yelled.

"You will have to come along with us." said Detective Mahoney. They took my father 's hands and put them behind his back and handcuffed him. Down on the street people wondered why the police were there. People came out of their houses to look. The two detectives with my father came down the stairs and put him in the car. Across the street at number thirty-nine lived a lady named Nellie O'Neil. My mother had befriended her by making her hot meals and taking them to her. Nellie immediately went up and knocked at my mother's door. "Who is it?" crying as she spoke. The voice on the other side of the door said, "It is Nellie. May I come in?" "Yes," my mother said. Upon opening the door, Nellie could see that she had been crying and screaming. "Oh Nellie, what am I going to do?" "Mary, you don't deserve this, you help so many people. Mary I am here to help in any way I can." "Thank you very much, Nellie." "Don't forget I am only across the street, okay," Nellie said. "Good-bye" and she left. My mother picked up the receiver to the telephone and called long distance to Peabody, where my grandparents lived. My grandmother thought it was a stranger on the phone until she heard Greek spoken and then recognized it was Mary. "How are you, my Mary?" Trying to hold back the tears and the emotion in her voice she said, "Something has happened to George. They have put him in jail." My grandmother said, "What? I am taking the next train down there with your father. Don't worry, Mary, we will be there as soon as we can." "Thank you mitera mou," meaning "thank you my mother." With that they ended their conversation, and my mother hung up the phone.

My grandparents took the bus from Peabody to the train station in Salem. They arrived in Boston's North Station that evening. They took a taxicab from North Station to my parent's apartment on Lynde Street. The next morning they all went to the police station.

My father was to go before the judge for arraignment, but it was to be at the Pemberton Square Courthouse, which is behind Scollay Square. They arrived just in time to see the police take him in through the side door. The courtroom was not crowded that morning and his case would be called shortly. Since it was Friday it would be as quick as possible as the weekend was here. The clerk rose and called "All rise" and Judge Hamlin entered the courtroom. My father's case came first. The judge called out his name and asked him to stand. "Mr. Grigoropoulos, are you represented by counsel?" "No, Your Honor," was my father's reply. "Trial date two weeks from today. You understand, Mr. Grigoropoulos, that you must have an attorney two weeks from today as this is a serious matter." "I understand, Your Honor." "Seeing that you have no previous record I release you on personal recognizance. Do you understand? This means that you are free to go; however, if you do not appear for trial a warrant will be issued for your arrest. Do you understand?" "Yes, Your Honor." My father was free to go. My father and mother and my grandparents left the courtroom. My grandparents stayed the night and said to their daughter, "We will be there with you and George. Okay?" For the next two weeks my father worked at his job at the Tasty. If luck was to play into this scenario, I didn't think it could help.

During this time my father and mother hardly spoke. My mother was broken- hearted. You see it was a "match marriage," arranged. The Greek custom was arranged marriages. Now if you had sons in the family and daughters, even if the sons were older, the oldest daughter had to marry first. This is what happened to my mother. The day of the trial came, and it was a day my mother dreaded. It was toward the end of summer that the trial took place. The newspapers, especially the Daily Record and the Boston American had a field day. The courtroom was packed. My father was well known, as he had owned The Reddy Hot Lunch, which had burned down when I was born. Robert Stockpole was my father's lawyer and Gilda's lawyer was a man named John Fenton. I was to stay with my Aunt Stella during the trial. My mother didn't want to speak to my father during the trial because in her heart she knew that he was guilty. This was a trial by jury. The first day of the trial Gilda's lawyer was ready as ever. He brought witnesses to say my father was infatuated with her. My father never believed that he would be in a courtroom. In my mother's mind, never did she think that with all she went through in her life she would be here. She loved my father, but slowly this would fade over time. If my father took the stand, he would lose. He wasn't looking for a cold drink. He looked at her ass going up the stairs and drooled, thinking about getting her in bed. My mother had told my grandmother that she wanted a divorce and wanted to go on with her life. My grandmother scolded her not to get a divorce and that he was a husband of good intentions and that it was this girl Gilda who teased him and tempted him. Besides, people would talk and she would end up being a laughing-stock in the Greek community and her parents would be ridiculed. The trial would not take long. Mr. Fenton put Gilda on the stand to show that she was being a good neighbor by offering him a cold drink and she was not thinking about sex. Mr. Stockpole called Max Baer to the stand to show that Rita had a whorehouse with her daughter, and Rita wanted to get even with my mother for telling the landlord about what was going on upstairs. Mr. Fenton would prove without a doubt that my father wanted to go upstairs and wanted the excuse to try and have sex with her. As more and more was revealed at the trial, my mother got more disgusted and refused to even talk with my father during the trial. The courtroom was standing room only because of the press covering the story and my father was well known because he owned The Reddy Hot Lunch, and it seemed that the whole West End had turned out for the trial. The day had come for the jury to be instructed by Judge Hamlin.

My mother was very depressed, and my father had confessed to my mother that he had done wrong. I know, deep down, my mother loved him. Years later she would tell me so. Later that afternoon the jury had reached a verdict and had returned to the courtroom. The clerk called out "all rise."

"Please be seated," the clerk said. Judge Hamlin turned to the jury and said,

"Members of the jury, have you reached a verdict?" "Yes, Your Honor." "The foreman will read the verdict." The foreman read the verdict. My mother and grandparents looked at the jury, and deep sighs were heard as the foreman read the verdict. "We the jury find the defendant guilty as charged." My mother slumped in her seat screaming and crying with my grandmother and my grandfather trying to console her. My father in the meantime stood motionless as he stood up and the judge instructed him. "Mr. Grigoropoulos, you have been found guilty of the charges brought against you. Do you have anything to say in your behalf?" "No, Your Honor." "I will pronounce sentence on you one week from today. I expect you to be here next week on the twenty-fourth of September. The jury is discharged." The gavel went down and the courtroom gradually cleared. The first to leave were the reporters, as they wanted to make the evening editions. Max Baer approached my mother and said how sorry he was. My mother thanked him very much. My parents and grandparents walked home to Lynde Street. The people of Lynde Street came up to them, expressing regret over what happened. There was nothing to be done now. My grandparents would leave in the morning, taking a morning train to Salem, and then a bus to Peabody. In Peabody, everyone had read the newspapers and heard the news on the radio. The whole town was talking about the trial and its aftermath. The Greeks loved to gossip and this was perfect for them to talk about.

Meanwhile, my father had to tell his boss, the owner of The Tasty, that he would have to leave his job. The boss knew this from reading the newspaper and felt very sorry for what had happened. My mother also explained to her boss that she would have to be in court on September 24th. He understood, as everyone now knew about the trial from the radio and the newspapers. On September 24th, my father made his appearance in court to hear the sentence pronounced on him. Again the courtroom was packed with people. Reporters and spectators had jammed into the courtroom. The clerk called out in a loud voice so all could hear, "all rise," as Judge Hamlin came into the courtroom. "Be seated," said the clerk.

Judge Hamlin turned to my father and asked him to rise. "Do you wish to say anything on your behalf?" "Yes, Your Honor, I do." He turned to my mother and said. "Forgive me for what I have done." My mother turned away from him, trying to console herself, but she could not hold the tears from coming down her face. "I sentence you to one year in the House of Correction at Billerica, Massachusetts." The gavel of Judge Hamlin's went down and the case was closed. The court officer took my father out to start to serve his sentence. My mother returned home and telephoned her boss. Dave Pressman understood and said to her, "Mary, your job is here and I can understand, so take some time off and I'll see you in three or four days. Okay?" "Thank you very much, Dave" she said.

Those were dark days for her. My mother had my grandmother to try to console her. She would go to Peabody and return to work the following week as she had about four days to try and blot this tragedy out of her mind. I would accompany her to Peabody, and when she returned to Boston, Sally would again take care of me Monday through Friday. Fall was upon us and the leaves on the trees started to change color and leave their branches that they had clung to from May. Thanksgiving came, and then December and with it the bombing of Pearl Harbor. The United States was plunged into war with Japan and then the United States declared war on Germany. Things would change drastically for the country. I was a year and half old. By now my father had been in jail for three months. My mother's job was more important than ever. Everyone in the factory where my mother worked would have a job for a long time to come. The factory was near North Station and the Boston Garden. It was not far for my mother to walk to work. The Joseph Corso Bag Company had acquired big contracts from the government and the armed services.

They would be making the weekend nylon bags for all the service men. Blue for the Air Force, green for the Army, and dark blue for the

Navy. Joseph Corso was a smart man. The factory now employed over twenty people. Tony Giggi was the cutter of the nylon fabric, which came in huge rolls. He would cut the patterns and then they would go to the stitchers and they would put loops on where to place the handles, and then they would go to Dave, the foreman, who would be working on a big stitching machine putting the sides together and the bottoms. Someone else would take them and rivet the handles and the bottoms with brass colored studs. Then the bags were finally placed in cartons to be shipped to the service men. My mother returned to work, and winter turned to spring, and then summer came. Finally, September arrived, and my father would be getting out of jail.

CHAPTER FIVE

Uncle Vasili

During the time that my father was incarcerated, my mother could not go up to see him too often, as it was very difficult to do that. My Uncle Nick, my Aunt Stella's husband, had a car and left it for my aunt as he was drafted into the army and was stationed in Europe.

With the car available, my mother was able to see my father a few times before the year was up. Now he was getting out of jail. He returned home to Lynde Street and contemplated what he was going to do. Rita and her daughter had moved under pressure from the landlord, Max Baer. My father now had to get a job, but that wasn't too difficult as he returned to The Tasty. In 1943 my brother was born and they nicknamed him Butchie, as he was not baptized. My nickname was Sonny, I was not baptized either. My mother now had to split us up. I was taken care of by Sally Sarkessian, and my brother by my Aunt Stella or by my grandmother. It was now 1944, a New Year and the war had been going on now for over three years. The day came when my brother and I would be finally baptized. We both were baptized at the same time. Nicholas Theodore baptized me, as he was my father's best man when he married my mother. I was given the name Anastasios, in English Ernest.

My brother was baptized by George Kotaris, one of my father's friends, and my brother was named Nicholas. Our nicknames however stayed with us, especially me, as Sonny was a very popular name that could be used as a primary name.

The Second World War was raging on in Europe and in the Far East. The allies were now getting ready for a big offensive in Europe. The many ships that came from Europe around this time could not return home. An act of Congress kept the ships from returning to Europe. The passengers and crew were allowed to stay in this country until the end of the war. The ships were from allied countries such as Great Britain and Greece. These two countries were allied with the United States. Great Britain had already started an offensive in Greece with the help of the United States, and a bigger one was coming with the allied landing in Normandy, France. Such was the case one day, when a man came to the door and knocked. It was my father's brother-in-law Vasili, who was married to my father's youngest sister Marianthi in Greece. He had worked on the ship that he came over on, as a chef. He was allowed to stay in this country until the war was over. Now was the opportunity to open a restaurant and that is exactly what my father and Vasili did. They opened the restaurant near the South End and the Greek community.

They called it the Broadway Cafeteria because it was around the corner from Broadway. My mother would go on weekends to help out. It was a busy restaurant. My father knew how to make excellent coffee. One weekend my father was away helping his friend Nicholas Theodore with a wrestling match and my mother was left with Vasili at the restaurant. Vasili said, "Mary, look I'll be back in about a half an hour. Okay?" "Okay, Vasili, make sure." It wasn't busy and he left. An hour went by then two and three. He telephoned my mother at the restaurant, "Mary it's me."

"Where the hell are you? You left me here all by myself." "I am in Peabody, and I'll be there in a little while." Come to find out he was playing cards. This was a pastime of his, and it turned out to be his downfall as well. Vasili lived with us. One day my father was the one to close up the restaurant since each took his turn closing and preparing the menus for the next day. Vasili was home alone when my mother came home from work.

She had picked my brother and me up at Sally's house. My Aunt Stella had dropped of my brother off there to make it easier for my mother. She fed us and within an hour and a half we were put in bed.

CHAPTER SIX

The Grade A Lunch

Vasili started making passes at my mother, but she tried to ignore him. He kept it up, and he was finally near my mother's bedroom when he started to undress. My father came home just in the nick of time. When he saw what was going on, he immediately told him to leave. My father threw him out and said, "We will settle this in the morning as to the status of the restaurant." My mother did nothing to encourage this, and she was shook up about it. The next day at the restaurant there was a big argument and the restaurant was closed. My father's lawyer Mr. Stockpole took care of all the arrangements. The restaurant was sold and the money divided between them. Now my parents could go forward and think of the next restaurant my father could open. The opportunity came to open a restaurant on lower Washington Street. He named it the Grade A Lunch. My Aunt Stella even came in with my parents as a silent partner. It was now 1945 and Franklin Delano Roosevelt had died and Harry Truman had assumed the presidency. The atomic bomb had been invented, and shortened the war in the Far East. It was dropped on Hiroshima, and Nagasaki, Japan. Japan sued for peace. In Europe, Germany had surrendered and peace had come to the world at last. Vasili had to leave the United States as the war was over and anyone left here had to return to their country. My parents gave him clothes, shoes, and many other articles to take back to my father's sisters, who included Marianthi, Vasili's wife, Sultana, and Paraskevi. It was learned later that he sold them to his sister-in-laws to make money. He was a gambler and he wanted the money to gamble again in Piraeus, Greece where he lived.

The restaurant, the Grade A Lunch, was a cafeteria-style restaurant. It was open from 5:00 am till 8:00pm. It meant long hours, but it was worth it. The line of people outside of the restaurant waiting to get in attested to the fact that my father was a very good cook. The menu was changed every day as far as the dinners were concerned.

It was at this time that my father took me to the movies. It was the only time that he ever did. I was seven years old, and he took me to the Rialto Theater next to the Scollay Square Theater. As I mentioned before this theater was where the drunks and the bums would come in and sleep it off. It was open twenty-four hours a day. I only know that there was a cowboy picture playing, "West of Sonora", starring Charles Starrett as the Durango Kid. I can remember what happened, and what I have desperately tried to forget.

Remembering it today only brings back the abuse that I suffered at various times from him. While sitting in the theater, I noticed my father moving his hand over to another man's leg who was sitting beside him and then suddenly seeing him caress his penis and shake it up and down. This is how I was to learn about sex. A seven-year-old to be exposed to this! I tried to block it out of my mind. I would never go to the movies with him again. I was to witness something that bothered me for the second time.

CHAPTER SEVEN

A Shocking Revelation

This was when I walked in on my mother and father having sex, but not as a couple in bed. It was a day that my father did not have to go to the restaurant early, as he had prepared everything the night before. My Aunt Stella would open up the restaurant that morning. I came walking into my parent's bedroom and saw something I never saw before. My father was standing and my mother was lying in bed.

He was putting something in her and it was something from his body. The moment he saw me he yelled at me to get out of here. I did as fast as I could. I was scared of him as he spoke to me in a very angry voice. I started hating "sex" as I learned it was called. I started hating him as I thought he was hurting my mother. These things I would put in the back of my mind, only to recall them years later. I would never forget. My father hired waitresses for the restaurant. My parents fought because my father had his eye on one waitress, and he had bought her uniforms. In those days, the employer did not purchase the uniforms, the employee did. I remember one time when an argument broke out between them, and there was a knife on the table and I thought my father was going to hurt my mother by stabbing her. I cried and screamed so that would not happen. My father's eyes again were roving. He would never stop being a womanizer all his life.

When my mother took me to the movies the first movie I saw was "Song of the South" and I wanted to be just like that boy that was in the movies, Bobby Driscoll. I was fascinated with what was going on. That was one of the best times I had in my childhood, when my mother would take me to the movies. The only other form of entertainment was the radio and I can remember listening to The Shadow, The Phantom, and The Lone Ranger, plus many more such as Captain Midnight, Gangbusters, and The Green Hornet.

In 1947, when I was seven years old, I remembered seeing "The Farmer's Daughter," with Loretta Young who won an academy award for her role in that film. Then there was "Johnny Belinda", and I knew what I wanted to do in my life from that time on.

In 1948, my mother was expecting her third child. It was a boy and my parents named him Leonidas in English Leon. He did not have to wait so long to be baptized. In 1949, my brother Johnny was born, but there was a problem. He was a seven-month term baby. The doctor could not hear the baby's heart beat and so my mother had her fourth son by Cesarean section and the baby boy was found to be all right.

At this time, my Aunt Stella had her second child. She named her Sandra. My aunt could not work at the restaurant, because she had to stay home with her new baby.

So my father hired another waitress named Jean Prescott. My father became a little too friendly. This caused friction with my mother and arguments broke out and sometimes I was in the middle of them. I could hear many things that children should not hear. "George, you son of a bitch, you bastard. I found out that you bought this new waitress uniforms. Are you making passes at her, you bastard?"

"Shut up, Mary, I am not. You'll never change." Arguments then silence. He would get up early and go to the restaurant. The building next door to our building caught fire and was partially torn down. This exposed the side of our building where the buildings had been attached. It was very dangerous for any tenant to live in their apartments. All the tenants went to court, as did the landlord, Max Baer. They tried putting boards nailed to the bricks to hold up the wall, to keep it from collapsing. In the end, we had to move. I would miss my friends, Danny, Joe, and Nelson to play with on my street. We moved to 12 Eaton Street, the top floor. I missed my friends but I was only around the corner from where I had lived. Around the corner there was Green Street, a long street that ran to Bowden Square and then you could walk to Scollay Square.

Chambers Street was the longest street in the West End. It ran from Cambridge Street all the way to Charles Street. Here on Charles Street was the Elizabeth Peabody House, famous for Ruth Roman who performed here before going to Bishop's Dramatic School to become an actress. It took something to get used to, going up four flights of stairs to get to our apartment. The landlady was named Tina Schumann. She lived at 8 Eaton Street, and she also owned 10 Eaton Street. She lived with her daughter Marian. I don't know if she had a husband. I never saw him. It was 1950 now, and my father still had the Grade A Lunch. Again disaster would strike. He mismanaged the business and he and my Aunt Stella had a falling out. At this time my mother was still working at the Joseph Corso Bag Company, which had changed names to the Pressman & Giggi Bag Company

David Pressman had bought the bag company when Joseph Corso wanted to get out of the business of owning a factory and still stay in as a representative of the government for procuring contracts for Pressman & Giggi Bag Company of which David Pressman and Tony Giggi would now be the owners. The factory was moved when the building was taken by eminent domain to build the expressway in Boston. The factory was now located on Chardon Street, very close to Scollay Square. Again violent arguments broke out at 12 Eaton Street. This time I understood more and I remember a lot more. My mother's voice carried. "You can't even pay the phone bill. What are you doing with your money, George?" my mother asked. "You son of a bitch." "Mary, I am warning you shut the hell up." There was a knife on the kitchen table, but he went out, mad as hell. He didn't come home until very late. My father left early as usual for work. He was working for someone again. Things started to be peaceful again. By now my mother had met Joanne and her husband, Gordon, who lived on Leverett Street. They would take care of my two younger brothers. I had been going to school since 1947 at the Winchell School. I would become a latchkey child. I would go to school and come from school and try to clean the house and also fill the oilcan, because this is how we heated the house in the winter, with an oil-burning stove. The oilcans were left out in the hallway. I still have pictures of this and of the apartment on Eaton Street. On Leverett Street there was a place called Andy's Pizzeria. I thought it was the best pizza in the West End. Down below Andy's Pizzeria was a bakery named Gallo's Bakery. Here you bought the freshest bread, baked every day. Walking by I used to love to smell the bread coming out of the oven. Farther down on Leverett Street there was a fork in the street. Here Causeway Street began and you went past the Causeway Cafeteria. Here kosher food was served, the owners being Jewish. You walked down to Causeway Circle where there was a horse fountain to water horses in the 1940s and the 1950s because there were still horse drawn wagons. Everyone did not have electric refrigerators, some people still had iceboxes and the iceman would come in with a big piece of ice and put it in the icebox to keep your milk and other perishables cold. On Causeway Circle there was a bakery named Godfrieds, and here is where you bought the best Danish pastry around. Returning back up to the fork in front of Tim's café, you walked across Leverett Street to an alleyway. Here you could walk through to get to Poplar and Chambers streets. This alley way had the smell of piss. The stink was terrible, and to avoid this alley you turned around and walked back up onto Leverett Street to Green Street. Across Green Street directly in front of you was Lynde Street, where I used to live. On the corner of Green Street was the Green Street Pharmacy, and in the middle of the block was a store named Jack Whites. I used to call this store "Many Whites" as it had a little of everything. I bought comic books there when they were only ten cents or fifteen cents. Further up on the corner of Green and

Chambers Streets was a produce store. Across the street was the Canning Pharmacy, where I would go to buy an ice cream soda, which was about forty-five cents in those days. The Mazers owned the pharmacy, and I was friendly with their son Barry Mazer. Coming out of the pharmacy, you turned left and walked to the corner of McLean and Chambers streets. This was the best street in the West End. St. Joseph's church was, and still is, there today. There was another church in the West End. It was a Polish church and it was located in the other direction toward Cambridge Street. The West End also had three synagogues.

Walking down McLean Street on the left was Saint Joseph's Parochial school.The school abutted Blossom Street and next to it on Blossom Street was the William Blackstone School. The schoolyards were next to each other with only a chain- link fence separating them. Occasionally, I would see my friend Danny Feeney playing in the schoolyard there. While I was growing up I would sometimes go to church and go in the back and wait for Danny. He was an altar boy. He told me that Father Powers was very strict. He would punish you if you made mistakes. The sisters, the nuns, would take you in the dressing room and beat your hands with a bamboo stick if you even had bubblegum in your mouth. Walking up farther from McLean Street and turning right you came to Allen Street. There another friend of mine, Mario, lived. A left from Mclean Street and you would be on Blossom Street, where the William Blackstone Junior High School was.

This schoolyard had two entrances, one on Eaton Street and one on Blossom Street. You could walk through the schoolyard from Eaton Street to Blossom Street.

Also on Blossom was the famous West End House Club, which I was a member of, and is now a part of the Massachusetts General Hospital. There is a plaque on the outside of the building near the entrance that designates that the West End House was there. The West End House played an important part in my life. Long before there were any boys' clubs around, the Elizabeth Peabody House and the West End House were a second home to hundreds of kids in the neighborhood. A few steps up from the West End House was the first school that I went to in 1946. The Winchell School was where I had a strict teacher by the name of Ms. Schoonicoff. I can still see her bending down to tell me to stay in line as we went out to the schoolyard. Sometimes I would walk through the schoolyard of the William Blackstone School to see if some of my friends were there and play ball with them.

Charlie Macaroni had a variety store at the corner of Eaton and North Russell Streets. Here I would go in and buy Italian slush, whether it was lemon or chocolate. The building where we moved was owned by a crafty and troublesome person. Tina Schumann was a person not to be trusted. My mother met most of the families in the building. The first floor was a family named the Robinsons, the second floor was a family named Comperchio, the third floor was the Palechucks, and the last floor before us were the Forcelattis. It wasn't long that my mother realized that we were not in such a good neighborhood. I would learn this in a very short time. My parents paid thirty dollars a month for rent, but this was back in the fifties. Among the other people she met was a woman named Alice. She had beautiful white hair that was so vivid. Across the street was a Chinese man named Jimmy Lee. He would wash and iron shirts. I would get to know him much better because of the mischief I would cause. Next to him was a club where some of the older guys would hang out and shoot pool or play cards. Next door to us at 10 Eaton was a family by the name of Stamos short for Stamatopoulos. One of my friends was named Carmen who lived across the street from me. I would hang around with him. On that side of the street you walked down until you got to the Blackstone schoolyard. Just before that there was an alleyway, where you could go through to McLean Street and the back of St. Joseph's Parochial School you could smell the piss from people taking a leak there. You passed Charlie Macaroni's variety store and walked to Parkman Street. On the corner of Parkman Street and North Russell Street was a store named Klamens, which had the best pickles in Boston. I could look down Parkman Street and see the Winchell School.

Eaton Street, although a small street, was far from being a quiet street. From the top floor you could look out the window and look to the left and see the Blackstone schoolyard, and to the right to the top of Eaton and Chambers streets. My brother Butchie's and my room was in the front of our apartment. We could hear everything going on below. Growing up with all this was exciting. When the ice wagon, stopped I used to go behind the wagon and get some ice chips and put some in my mouth on hot summer days. Gemmato Bros. were the ones that brought us the ice all year long for the icebox and in the winter the range oil to help keep us warm. I can remember when we bought our first refrigerator and we didn't need ice any more. It was a Crosley.

CHAPTER EIGHT

Trouble On Eaton Street

We had ice trays, no more ice. One night after my mother had put us to bed and we started to fall asleep, trouble erupted; down below on the street there was shouting and hollering. I could hear a horn or siren, and sure enough the cops had come. I raised the venetian blinds and looked out the window. "Sonny, what's the matter?" "Butchie, go to sleep." "No I want to see too." My mother came to the living room window, that room was next to ours. I was eleven years old and Butchie was eight years old. We could hear everything clearly. My mother said, "Sonny and Butchie, back to bed.

"Oh, Ma, I want to see, what's going on." I could hear a voice saying, "You bitch, you're an asshole." Who was swearing, I couldn't see, as I was too high up from the street. I heard the siren suddenly of another cop car. "Okay, okay, Alice stop it. We are taking you in for disorderly conduct." "Tina, you bastard, you son of a bitch, you caused this trouble and you called the cops." I then saw a white-haired lady being taken by the police in the paddy wagon to the police station. "That's Alice," someone on the street said. Her yelling and the screaming wouldn't stop until she was out of range.

The other cop said, "Shut up, Alice." "I hate you, Tina." The cop continued, "you're drunk." The cops had been here before. "You goddam, Tina, you're no good." Who knows how she got drunk? I did not know it at the time, but someone had given Alice money to buy liquor.

They finally took her away in the paddy wagon to sleep it off at the police station on Joy Street. We could finally go back to sleep.

At the Winchell school, one teacher that I had in the second grade was named Mrs. O'Neil. She had white hair just like Alice. She was very nice, and I did very well in the second grade. My father now was in another restaurant, having lost the Grade A Lunch. I never saw my father until the evening. My mother worked until 5:00 pm. She would pick my two younger brothers up at Joanne and Gordon's house. These two people, husband and wife, were very good friends of my mother. She had met them from Sally Sarkissian.

With the birth of my younger brother John, my mother's wish of having four boys had come true. It was difficult coming home, because I had my key and I guess my mother thought I could take care of myself until she came home at 5 :00 pm. On one occasion my mother's friends Joanne and Gordon could not take care of my two brothers. Leon was taken care of by Sally Sarkissian and I took care of my brother Johnny. I had Johnny on the bed changing his diaper. I had forgotten to take my house keys with me and locked myself out, while filling the oilcan in the hallway. The building that we lived in was attached to the one next door. So I went next door to the top floor and knocked on the door hoping the people were home. "I am sorry to bother you, I got locked out, and my little brother is on the bed, and I am afraid that he may fall off the bed. Oh God help me," I said. "May I climb out your window so I can get in the window next door?" She said, "Okay, be careful." I thanked her very much. I climbed out onto the fire escape trying not to look down. I pushed on the window, hoping that it wasn't locked. I could see my baby brother Johnny kicking his feet and moving his hands, I was lucky the window was unlocked, and I got in and saved my brother from falling off the bed. I really was scared. On one of my mother's visit to Peabody, my grandfather had given me a silver dollar. I can remember holding it in my hand. It was bigger than a quarter and much heavier. On another visit my grandfather had called my mother into his bedroom, because he had become ill, and he wanted to talk to my mother privately. He told her as I remember her telling me years later, that after he was gone the two daughters-in-law

would try to extort money from my grandmother by scheming and conniving to get their husbands to do it. This was to happen, but not until my grandfather had passed away.

CHAPTER NINE

My Grandfather's Funeral

In 1950 my grandfather passed away. My mother got Sally to watch my brothers and I would go with my mother to Peabody. This was something I never experienced, and I was dumbfounded that my grandfather would not be here anymore. Death, what is that, and you never come back?

At the wake and the funeral people kept asking why I was there. I was too young to understand all this. The service at Saint Vasilios was in Greek and I was ignorant of it. I knew more of the Catholic faith than I knew of the Orthodox faith. The procession from the church didn't go too far, Harmony Grove Cemetery was only a few streets away.

Inside the Walnut Street gate is where my grandfather would be buried. There with the trees on each side he was laid to rest. I looked at my mother dressed in black. I don't remember my father staying too long as he was more concerned with his restaurant, than with his father-in-law.

What my grandfather had predicted would now come true. In 1953, my grandmother decided to sell the two houses and the grocery store. Zolotas Plumbing bought them all for thirteen thousand dollars, a lot of money back in 1953. My grandmother bought two houses on Wallis Street in Peabody. Not even a week went by when the squabbling started among the relatives. I can remember quite well the arguments because I usually accompanied my mother to Peabody to see my grandmother. My grandmother lived in the second house, at

60 A Wallis Street in the back of the first, facing a big yard that separated both houses.

My grandmother rented the second floor to an old lady named Irene Kefalas. She was a nice old lady. She knew very little English, like my grandmother. My Uncle Charlie and Aunt Helen lived in the first house at 60 Wallis Street. My Uncle Harry and his wife Aunt Ellen were saying they should get some help. "Your mother has all that money," she said. My grandmother gave them a few thousand dollars. Uncle Harry bought a two-family house in Peabody and an asphalt business. He was doing residential and commercial asphalt covering, such as yards, driveways, etc. Trouble started when he could not get along with his tenant in the two -family where he lived. My aunt and uncle by now had two boys, Andrew and Jimmy. They were both blond headed boys. My aunt had changed her religion from Protestant to Greek Orthodox. Meanwhile my Uncle Charlie and his wife started having children. My Aunt Helen figured by having more children she would get more help from my grandmother. It seemed that almost every year that they would have a baby. They ended up having seven children, five boys and two girls. My Uncle Harry and Aunt Ellen had four children. My Uncle Louie and Aunt Penny had three. My Aunt Stella and Uncle Nick had two children.

Altogether there were twenty cousins including my brothers and me. My grandmother wanted to give them all some money with the exception of my Uncle Charlie, who would get the house that he lived in. My Uncle Harry already got money for the asphalt paving business. My Uncle Louie got some money to purchase a house in Dracut, Massachusetts. My Aunt Stella got some help as she had purchased a house in Medford, Massachusetts. My mother refused to take any money. She was able to take care of us and she did not want to take anything from her mother.

I can remember my mother crying one time that I accompanied her and my father to Peabody. There was trouble with the two daughters-in-law, they mistreated my grandmother. I turned to my father and said, something like, "Why don't you do something, she is crying?" He didn't interfere and I did not like him for that. There were times when I was a teenager and I would go to Peabody to give some money to my Uncle Charlie from my mother so the people wouldn't come and take his furniture. He could not keep up with the payments; he was laid off from his job. This happened in 1954 at about the same time my father opened a restaurant in South Boston, between D and E Streets on Broadway. It was called The New York Cafeteria. It was across the street from the biggest nightclub in New England, Blinstrubs. This nightclub had one thousand seats. I can remember working after school at my father's restaurant. He had a soda fountain and I learned how to make ice -cream sodas and frappes as well as cheeseburgers and other light foods. My brother Johnny's godfather, George Kehalas, used to make the donuts.

We sold them for forty-five cents a dozen. I can remember the waitresses coming over from Blinstrubs, the nightclub and saying to my father, "George, you make the best coffee." My father acknowledged this, and said thank you. A woman who owned a barroom a few doors down would come into the restaurant when I was there and talked to my father in Polish. She would then ask me for a cup of coffee. She liked my father's coffee and wished he would share the secret of how to make it. It had been nine years since the Second World War ended. Europe had been divided. The Iron Curtain had fallen in Central Europe. The Communists had control of half of Europe. They were trying to take over Greece, as they had done in most of the Balkan Peninsula. Yugoslavia had Tito and his brand of Communism independent of Russian Communism. Greece had broken out in civil war between the communists and the monarchists.

President Truman had proclaimed The Truman Doctrine to save Greece from Communism. At this time the U.S. Congress passed the Displaced Persons Act. This law had to do with anyone coming from a country that was fighting communism, to be able to come to the United States, without a sponsor.

Greece at that time was fighting a civil war for five years, since 1946. Turkey had remained neutral in the Second World War and had been on the side of the Axis powers in the First World War. Turkey was never a good ally of the United States. Even today that country is a belligerent country, and respecting human rights means nothing to them.

They will not admit to massacring over a million and half Armenians before the First World War. They also massacred three hundred thousand Greeks and burned the city of Smyrna. The people had to jump into the Aegean Sea to try to escape the fire, and not to be burned alive. Aristotle Onassis, one of the worlds' richest men, came from Smyrna and escaped the flames.

CHAPTER TEN

A New Guest in the House

"Mary, please come to Peabody." "Ma, I'm coming just as soon as I can. I'll take the train in the afternoon just as soon as I can get in touch with Stella to see if she can take care of the kids." Friday after work, my mother got in touch with Aunt Stella, and she was able to take the kids and bring them over to her house in Somerville. She told Stella that my father was working all weekend. "Thanks, Stella," my mother said. My mother went off to North Station to get the afternoon train to Salem and then a bus to Peabody to my grandmother's house. The bus stopped at Kellor Street and when she got off the bus, she walked down Kellor Street to my grandmother's house. Kellor Street was a short street and a big dip just like a valley. She had my brother Johnny, the baby, with her. Taking care of three boys was difficult enough for my aunt, let alone trying to take care of a fourth. My mother walked into this alleyway next to the store. Then she climbed the stairs and knocked on the door. "I am so glad you have come," my grandmother said, as she opened the door.

"Sonny, Butchie, and Leo are at Stella's house in Somerville. I brought the baby with me." My mother looked in the kitchen and saw this young girl sitting at the table, crying. She put the baby in the crib in the bedroom my grandmother kept for when the grandchildren came to visit. After she gave my baby brother a bottle of milk, he went off to sleep. My mother came back into the kitchen and sat down with her mother and this girl crying. My grandmother turned to my mother and said, "Well, Tina Batsinelas came to see me."

"How is she?" my mother asked, smiling. "Fine," my grandmother said. My grandmother then introduced her to this girl named Olympia Paxinidou. Of course all this was in Greek, as the girl did not speak English. My grandmother continued, "Well, this girl came to the United States under the Displaced Persons Act that was passed by the United States Congress in 1950, to help refugees fleeing communism. The American Hellenic Educational Association, an organization helped to settle these refugees in America with Greek families. A.H.E.P.A. as it was known by its initials, had contacted Tina Batsinelas because she had done some charitable work for them in the past. Tina took her into her home, but because she has two grown boys, she got her a room on Kellor Street. She told me she couldn't do any more for her."

"Look, ma, I'll take her to Boston with me in the morning." Olympia looked at my mother and thanked her very much for her kindness. "You will stay the night with us and tomorrow go and pack your things and bring them here and we will leave together. "Okay?" The next morning there was a knock on the door to my grandmother's house.

My mother answered the door. "Tina Batsinelas, how are you? It's nice to see you." "Mary, it's nice to see you too. I see that you have met Olympia." "Yes," my mother answered. "Mary, I want you to know that I did all I could for her. I have my two sons, grown men, and it is not right for me to keep her in my house. You know she is expecting a child, and the talk would spread that one of my sons had sex with her and is the father of the baby. This town is ripe for this kind of gossip and they won't let go of this if it came out that way." "I understand. Tina, don't worry. I am taking her with me.

We will be leaving on the afternoon train for Boston from Salem," my mother said. Just then Olympia returned with her suitcase and greeted Tina and thanked her for all she had done for her. My mother fed my baby brother Johnny to make sure he was all set. She kissed my grandmother good- bye, as did Olympia and Tina My grandmother said, "Wait, I'll get your brother Charlie to drive you to the train in Salem." Charlie had come home from work early and his car was out in front of the house on Walnut Street.

My grandmother called Charlie on the telephone and asked him to take his sister to the train station. In the meantime, Tina said good-bye to everyone and wished Olympia good luck. Uncle Charlie came down from upstairs from his house and greeted his sister and was introduced to Olympia. Again, my mother embraced and kissed her mother, and said good-bye. My Uncle Charlie got them to the train station in Salem and said good- bye to them. It wasn't long before they arrived at North Station. From here my mother got a taxicab to get to Eaton Street, which was only five minutes away by taxicab. My brothers would stay the night at my Aunt Stella's house.

At home my mother made room in the dining room and put a cot there so Olympia could sleep. Of course my father learned about all of this when he came home from work. He would say this is wonderful, but he really didn't like the situation at all.

When the three of us came home from my grandmother's house, I did not know how long Olympia would be staying with us. I didn't know that she was pregnant. I did not know where babies came from at the time. I was eleven years old and I would try to listen when big people would talk to learn what was going on. I was very naive, more so than most kids my age. This was a new experience for me. I learned some Greek from my grandmother and I hoped, Olympia would understand me. She knew only a few words in English.

My mother would teach her how to stitch on the sewing machine so she could get a job at Dave's place or another factory. A few more months went by and Olympia was now in her sixth month of her pregnancy. As I could understand, she did not want this baby. I can remember listening from my bedroom and from little Greek that I understood she wanted to give this baby up when it was born. Olympia was a young, dark-haired, beautiful girl. Of course this was all said in Greek and I understood some of what was going on. "Mary, someday I will want to have a husband and a family, but not now." This is where my Aunt Stella came into the picture. My mother asked her if she knew of a family who could not have children. Stella did. Doris and Nick were a childless couple and jumped at the chance to adopt a baby, especially a Greek baby. I was almost twelve years old now. The time came and the baby was born, and papers were signed, and money passed hands. In the end, Olympia had given up her baby for two hundred dollars.

Olympia continued to work as a stitcher as my mother had taught her, and on the weekends she and my mother would go to my father's restaurant and help out. At the restaurant, Olympia met a man, a very good -looking man by the name of Tommy Sullivan. He was crazy about her. He would do anything for her. He worked as a longshoreman and in his spare time he was a boxer. He had a beautiful build. I met him when he came calling to try and go out with Olympia on a date. All this time Olympia was going to the International Institute of Boston where immigrants were being helped to learn English. She learned English very well. Tommy had a drinking problem, and on one of the visits to my house to see Olympia, he invited me and the three of us went to an AA meeting in Medford, Massachusetts. It was right after this date that she told him that she did not care for him as he did for her, and that she wanted to marry a Greek man. He was broken-hearted and would have done almost anything to win her love for him. I never saw him until two months after that he came to my father's restaurant and I served him a cup of coffee. "How is Olympia?", he asked. I answered, "Fine." "Tell her I was asking for her," he said. I told him I would and he left after having a cup of coffee.

How much could he tell a twelve-year-old? I went to the back room to play the jukebox and then to start to peel potatoes so my father would have them ready for tomorrow's menu. On Fridays, I could stay later at the restaurant because I did not have to go school the next day. When I would see my mother on Friday with Olympia

I knew it was time to go home and help with my brothers. Joanne and Gordon would bring the boys home to Eaton Street and I would take care of them feeding them and putting them to bed. I knew it was a help to my mother and I was glad to do it.

One day I picked up the paper, The Daily Record, and there it was in the paper, "Tommy Sullivan dies," murdered by longshoremen. I never exactly knew the whole story. All I knew was a middleweight champion had died and I was dumbfounded that a professional boxer had died. I don't remember Olympia saying much when she learned of it. She would look at my mother and me. I was melancholy as he was a jovial fellow with his blue eyes and blond hair. I will always remember the first the Alcoholics Anonymous meeting that I went to with him. Time would pass and with it the memory of Tommy Sullivan. I would remember him and left it at that, as I was just a kid. If I asked too many questions I was told to shut up. I knew he would have done cartwheels if Olympia had wanted him to do that. He would have done anything. "I wish she would just love me, I'll always love her," he would say. Now his life was snuffed out. He had been murdered by organized crime and the case was never solved. I thought to myself because he wasn't Greek that she would not get serious with him. It was over now, his murder ended it.

I enjoyed going to my father's restaurant after school selling donuts, making ice- cream- sodas, banana splits etc. The restaurant had a big back room with wooden booths. Oh, how I loved it. There in this backroom was a jukebox, a Wurlitzer with the lights going around. One dime played a song of your choice and three plays could be had for a quarter. I would put in a quarter for three plays. Listen to Kay Starr sing, "Wheel of Fortune," The Mills Brothers sing "Glow Worm," or Tony Bennett sing his third hit, "Rags to Riches." My father's restaurant in South Boston was doing very well and we were the first to have a television set. My friends that lived on the second floor would come up to see some programs such as serials and Beat the Clock with Bud Collyer and Strike It Rich with Warren Hull. The television set cost four hundred dollars in those days and you could not get a bigger size screen than twelve inches. It was a combination television, phonograph, and radio and a cabinet to store records below. I also remember watching I Remember Mama, with Peggy Wood. My mother wouldn't let me watch Man Against Crime because of the guns and the violence, but sometimes I would sneak out of my bedroom and put the television on and watch it.

In 1955 I was fifteen years old and many things were happening in the world. Joseph McCarthy was investigating the film industry, looking for Communists he thought were plotting to overthrow the government of the United States. Ronald Reagan testified behind closed doors and named names. He was president of the Screen Actors Guild, and had access to everyone's information. Many people lost their jobs and would never be employed in the film industry again.

My mother became friendly with Anna Compercio, as I was friendly with two of her sons, Henry and Junior. Henry would come up and watch television, and would not want to go home when his mother would call him to come downstairs. Summer had come and gone and Fall arrived One day close to Christmas, my mother had met Anna just outside of the front door going into the building and Anna looked very glum. My mother asked her how everything was and she said, "All right." It wasn't really; her husband had been laid off from his job as a printer.

Christmas was almost here and it looked rather bleak for them. Talking with Anna, my mother found out what Anna's kids wanted for Christmas, not to mention what was in her heart and her husband's. My mother then and there decided to buy them all Christmas presents. So a few days before Christmas my mother came down the stairs in the building where we lived and knocked on the door. Anna opened the door and shouted, "Mary, what have you done?" "Merry Christmas to you and your family." Anna couldn't compose herself, and started crying, grabbing my mother and hugging her. "As long as

I live, Mary, I will never forget what you did for us." With that, my mother kissed and hugged Anna, and wished her a Merry Christmas and left.

My mother got friendly with a woman named Alice. Now Alice was a maid, working for Tina Schuman our landlady. She had a bed for her in the cellar, as I could see the bed, when I went by 8 Eaton Street, looking through the window in the cellar. Alice had seen how my mother stood up against Tina. "Hi Mary," "Hi Alice, how are you?" Replying to my mother, she said, "Mary, Tina is very mean to me." She won't give me anything to eat. "She is starving me." "What?" my mother said. My mother took this as a cause to confront Tina. Tina Schumann hadn't fixed the window frame on our front window, and we were holding it up with a baseball bat. You could hear the bang on the front door at 8 Eaton Street. "Tina, I want to talk to you," as she went to confront her. "What the hell are you doing to Alice?" my mother asked. "I am not starving Alice," Tina fired back. "By the way, Anna Comperchio told me, that I told you, that Anna is a whore for having seven kids."

"What are you doing telling Anna Comperchio that she is a whore because she has so many kids? You lying bastard," with that she made her go to her door and yelled for Anna Compercio. Anna came to her window. "Okay, tell her Tina, before I wipe the streets with you." "I am sorry I called you a whore for having so many kids, and blaming Mary, for having said it." Anna left the window and came running down the stairs and opened the door to the street. "Mary, I am so sorry" as she approached Tina Schumann and Alice and my mother. "Never will I believe anything that she says again. I promise you." Someone living on the street called the police. The police cruiser pulled up in front of number 8 Eaton Street, and the police asked, "What's the trouble?" "Nothing officer" Tina answered back. "It's my fault officer," said Tina Schumann. "It's all right now." "You're sure?" asked the police officer, looking at her straight in the eye.

He remembered Tina Schumann from the other night with the trouble with her maid Alice. Tina left after the police and Anna and Alice thanked my mother for all that she had done for them.

I was going through difficult times, as I hardly knew my father was around as he worked fourteen to sixteen hours a day. Sunday was the only day we got to see each other. It was just as well, as he really did not help me one bit. He never asked me how I was doing in school. The times that I worked after school at the restaurant, I was lucky to be able to talk to him, and he never asked me about my interests.

In 1957, Olympia received a letter from her sister Dorathea saying that she was getting ready for her trip to the United States. The United States embassy had informed her that all the papers were in order and she could set sail at any time. Upon receipt of this letter Olympia responded and told her to take the ship the Queen Fredericka to the United States as soon as she could book passage.

The Winchell School and the Peter Faneuil School, these were the two schools I attended in the West End. The third school was the William Blackstone, which was later torn down. The Winchell School now belongs to the Massachusetts General Hospital. The Peter Faneuil School is still there, but closed on Joy Street near where Police Station

Three used to be. There were two clubhouses that I became a member of. One was the West End House on Blossom Street. The other was the Elizabeth Peabody House on Charles Street next to the Massachusetts General Hospital.

In the forties the actress Ruth Roman lived in the West End. Her mother was Jewish and her father was Italian. Her last name was Romano and she dropped the last letter and became known as Ruth Roman. She had gone to school to become an actress and she was a member of the Elizabeth Peabody House. In the nineteen fifties, I became a member of the Elizabeth Peabody House. I would eventually join the dance committee, and organize the Friday night dances, which I loved to do. I continued to go to Mass at Saint Joseph's church on Sunday. One Sunday, I came home and told my mother, that I would change my religion from Greek Orthodox to Roman Catholic when I became of legal age of twenty-one. The uproar from my mother and Olympia was devastating. I had hardly ever gone to the Greek Church, and did not understand it. In the Greek Church the Mass is said in pure Greek because the majority of the parishioners understood Greek better than English. The other reason was the Greek Church was not close-by. It was forty minutes by subway.

With Olympia living with us, she started telling me a lot of history, and how these two churches were one at one time in history. Soon I bought books on this subject, and started to learn more. I did not know enough Greek at the time. Although I spoke some Greek, it wasn't enough to understand the liturgy in church. Olympia was a great help as I spoke more and learned more as she lived with us. At about this time my father received a phone call from Mr. Paraskeva Travlos who had just returned from Greece. He was the head chef at the Athens-Olympia restaurant on Stuart Street in Boston. This restaurant was well established in the theater district in Boston. In his conversation with my father, he had spoken of my father's sister whom he had met in Greece. It so happened that Mr. Travlos had come from the island of Kefallonia and my father's brother-in-law came from the same island. My father's sister, whose name was Marianthi, asked about my father and if he knew him. Mr. Travlos said he did. My father met up with Mr. Travlos and he gave him a picture of his sister with a Christmas card. When I saw my father on Sunday, he showed me the Christmas card and the picture. I asked him if I could keep the Christmas card and the picture. My father said, "yes."

In the picture there were two women, and my father was surprised as he saw his other sister named Paraskevi, who was shorter than his sister Marianthi. There was writing on the card and I asked my father to translate it for me.

He did and also the writing on the back of the picture. I started thinking that if I wanted to learn this language, and know what was going on in church to understand everything, I must learn Greek fluently. I could hear my father saying to my mother how Paraskevas Travlos brought this Christmas card and picture from Greece. Paraskevas had met my father's sister Marianthi and her husband, Vasili, as he knew him many years before. My mother and father remember Vasili quite well as he was a troublemaker when he was here in Boston living with my parents. I barely remember him, as I was about five years old when he returned to Greece, at the end of the war.

The next day, I left with Olympia for New York City to meet and bring back Dorathea, Olympia's sister. I had a chance to explore this big city by myself, and I did so by walking up Fifth Avenue and coming to a bookstore named Schoenoffs. I went in and started to browse. To my delight, I found a book entitled "The Complete Book Of Marvels." I purchased it. It had a ton of information on many subjects, things man had built plus natural wonders. I then walked some more and returned to the hotel. The next day the morning was spent meeting the ship the Queen Fredericka and waiting for Olympia's sister Dorathea to come through customs. After waiting for well over an hour, Dorathea saw her sister and began waving to her and me. I would be meeting her for the first time. I had seen pictures of her that Olympia had showed me.

We returned to Boston that afternoon, and now the problem would be to see where her sister would sleep. She got settled in all right and we got another cot for her to sleep on. Olympia had been with us for almost five years. Dorathea became a member of the International Institute of Boston and started to learn English. Then one night after Dorathea had learned to come home by herself, my mother and I noticed black marks around her arms near her shoulders.

My mother asked her about them. She said that she had bruised herself by banging into the bathroom door, not realizing that the door closed automatically. I suppose my mother believed her. This happened again and now the story changed that a man was after her when she left the Institute on Beacon Street to walk home. She lied to my mother. My mother realized that she had done something wrong in bringing this girl to the United States, as she was being manhandled. One night my mother confronted Olympia and asked her straight out, "Is your sister a whore?" Olympia looked with surprise that my mother would say such a thing. Again, my mother asked her the same question and no response came from Olympia. "Well," my mother said, "I want you and your sister to leave my house as soon as you can." Enough said, and we all were silent.

There was no doubt in my mother's mind that Dorathea wanted to be manhandled. We had no idea that she was this type of a girl. The next day I went to school as usual and did not see them leave. Neither did my mother. I was sad Olympia left, as I had learned a lot from her.

CHAPTER ELEVEN

Learning Greek & The Bat on the Head

I really wanted to learn Greek and after school I took the Metropolitan Transit Authority, the subway, to The Greek Cathedral, The Annunciation, that is on the corner of Ruggles and Parker Streets in Boston.

Back then there were no Orange or Blue Lines. You knew how to go where you wanted to or you asked. I wanted to enroll in the class, but it was a month before graduation. I decided right then and there to buy some books on learning Greek. I can tell you it is one of the hardest languages in the world. It has five Es and two Os and two Ss. There are twenty-four letters in the alphabet. I started writing little by little; it was very hard, letters totally different from English. I was determined that if I was learning this language I would learn it correctly or not at all. I started to write to Aunt Marianthi.

They all went to the best school my father's father could afford. Aunt Marianthi made me increase my vocabulary. Any word that I did not know, I wrote down on index cards and used it in conversation and in thinking to myself. I bought a dictionary called the Divry Dictionary, which helped me a lot. It is now out of print. This lexicon has proved to be very valuable for correct spelling. I could now read and write this noble tongue. So I now could correspond practically weekly with Aunt Marianthi in Piraeus, Greece. I learned Greek the right way, not the slang way. I mastered the language.

My brother Butchie had gotten into trouble with the Guardino Family as he hung around with their son and he was not a good influence on him. The trouble was that Harry Guardino and my brother played hooky from school and stole things from Jack White's variety store. They were caught. My mother had to go to court, naturally embarrassed.

Luckily though, the decision was made to change the environment. So off my brother went to live with our grandmother in Peabody. Here he would go to regular school and also Greek School. He had to learn Greek for our grandmother knew only Greek. The few English words she knew were goddam child, and umbrella.

One day my brother Johnny, who had been playing in the schoolyard, came running home, yelling and screaming. "Sonny help me," he said.

When I saw the wound he had in his arm, I gasped. It was deep, very deep. I ran for bandages. Not even ten seconds had passed before we rushed to the emergency room of the Massachusetts General Hospital, which was walking distance from my house. Johnny needed twenty stitches to close the wound in his arm. When my mother came home she gasped when I told her what had happened. "Sonny, I am glad you knew what to do." "I sure did, Mom." I said. "Maybe Johnny you would have been much worse." "All I know is I remember him coming home crying and calling for me, 'Sonny I'm hurt.' So I am glad I was there to help my brother."

During the fifties I loved the movies, and going to them in my spare time. This was the only entertainment we had until my parents purchased our first twelve-inch television set. During this time, I would go to various movie theaters in Boston, walking across Cambridge Street to Joy Street, which is on the Beacon Hill side and walking up Joy Street until the end and then crossing Beacon Street near the State House.

I walked through the Boston Common toward Boylston and Tremont streets. Here just a little further you could see the Metropolitan

Theatre as it was known back then, it is now known as The Wang Center. Here I saw my first science fiction movie and it scared the hell out of me. It was "The Thing" starring Toby McGuire. James Arness played The Thing. It was well done and scary. More and more people bought television sets and stayed at home. The Hollywood studios had to do something or else they would close up. So 3D movies came along and you had to wear the glasses.

I saw all the 3D movies. Then something happened that would change movies forever. A Frenchman invented the CinemaScope lens and 20th Century Fox studios under Spyros Skouras was the first studio to use the new process and history was made and the studios received the shot in the arm that they needed. The first movie was "The Robe" and the screen was twice the size of the normal screen. The other studios immediately got on the bandwagon.

Walt Disney on the other hand had "Cinderella," and he counted on this, as he would have to close down his studio if this were a flop. He made five million dollars and this was back in 1952. I remember waiting in line at the RKO Keith's Memorial on Washington Street. Actually the RKO had two entrances to buy tickets. One was on Tremont Street and the other one was on Washington Street. The line of people went out the door on Washington Street and around to another theater named The Laugh Movie Theater. On the Boylston Street side, they went up for another block. I stood in line on Washington Street and this theater was very elaborate as it had some very ornate work on the inside. Today this theater is known as Opera House. The Boston Ballet performs there, and every year they perform the Nutcracker. The Laugh Movie Theater was one of my favorite theaters as I saw the original L'l Abner, the 1940 version. Next to The Laugh Movie Theater was the Paramount Theater, which is now boarded up.

On Pinckney Street on Beacon Hill a bizarre crime was committed. Suzanne Clift, the niece of the late actor Montgomery Clift, had a lover from Brazil. He jilted her and she found out. While he was staying with her, they had sex and he went off to sleep. While he was sleeping she cut his penis off. He awoke in pain and rushed to the hospital. She, of course, was arrested but was released on her on her own recognizance.

She managed to find out where this other girl lived that he was seeing, and mailed his penis to her. At the trial she stated all this to the jury and was given ten years probation. It was shocking and scandalous and in all the newspapers, the Boston American and The Daily Record.

We had new neighbors at 12 Eaton Street; they were the Palechucks, who moved in on the third floor. The Forcellatis moved in on the fourth floor. As I mentioned before Tina Schumann was a stingy self-centered woman. Many times the police were called to her house. Well, my mother had told her repeatedly that she should mind her own business as she had a big mouth. How many times when I walked by her house at 8 Eaton Street I could see her maid Alice's bed in the cellar, when she could have easily given her a room on one of the floors in her boarding house.

Our three windows in the front of the house looked out on to Eaton Street, which was a small street. I can remember when the Forcellattis moved in. They had a son named Joey, the same age as my brother Johnny.

Now it so happened that one of the windows in the front of the house in the living room was coming apart. It was so old that my mother put a baseball bat to hold up the frame so the huge pane of glass from the window would not fall five stories below and kill someone. My mother had called Tina Schumann and told her about this weeks earlier, but she never sent anyone to repair it. My mother was looking out the window, at my brother Johnny and his friend Joey playing in the street. The bat was on a small platform, as it was one and half inches short from the top. A small platform was needed to make up for the space in between the bat and the window. My mother leaned as she folded her arms and accidentally moved the bat.

My mother yelled to Johnny and Joey to get out of the way. The bat went down and it came down hard onto Joey's head. The screaming and crying that followed turned the street into a mob scene with people running everywhere and from around the corner from both Chambers Street and North Russell Street. Joanne Forcellatti ran down the stairs, crying.

The police arrived and called for a backup. One police cruiser sped off with Joey and his mother headed for the Massachusetts General Hospital's emergency room. The biggest concern was his head to be all right and that there was no brain damage because of the force of the impact. Joanne, his mother, had called her husband, Fred, at work to come as quick as he could. Meantime, back on Eaton Street my mother told the police how it happened. "Who owns this house?" the police officer asked. "Tina Schumann," my mother answered. There she was looking out the window. She was mean as ever. She didn't want to hear about the accident. It was her fault. "What are you going to do about this?" the police officer asked. "This boy Joey Forcelatti could have died and also could have brain damage." "You're so cheap, you bastard. Don't think you can get away with this. Joey's mother is ready to get a lawyer and it will be ever so easy to prove you were responsible," said my mother. Tina responded. "Mary, please listen, I'll fix it right away." "I hope so," my mother said looking her straight in the eye. My mother went upstairs, and I did too, and as I followed my mother I kept an eye on my brothers. Up the stairs came Joey's mother Joanne. "Mary, I know that you're not to blame for what happened." "Listen Joanne I spoke to Tina and I gave her a good piece of my mind. She is having the windows fixed. This only took a few months and an accident like this has to occur," my mother said. "Why so selfish? All she cares about is money, not to spend it but to take it in for herself," said my mother. Joanne said good night and went down stairs to her apartment. Within days the window was fixed.

"Sonny, Sonny help." I heard my name and I heard the footsteps of my youngest brother Johnny on the stairs. "What is it?" I said. "Something is in my eye."

Well when I saw it just a hair above the pupil, there was something and the outer part had turned red. Back again to the Massachusetts General Hospital and to the emergency room. The doctors would have to ever so gently take out what was in his eye above the pupil. We went next door to eye infirmary emergency room. I held his hand and turned away as I didn't have the stomach to watch. That night I told my mother all that had happened. I could see the worried look on her face. Leo was more fortunate as he didn't care about getting into that kind of mischief. He belonged to a club and therefore when you belong to a club like the West End House there are more activities and you weren't on the street. Johnny was a little too young to join the same club.

CHAPTER TWELVE

Getting into Mischief

In 1956 I turned sixteen years of age. Of course I was wild, not as wild as my brother but wild enough. Across the street in the cellar of a building was Ming's laundry. Here my friends and I would stand in front of his window and look at him in the cellar.

We would start to make fun of him by putting our index fingers to our teeth. We had found out this was a bad sign for the Chinese. He came running out of his shop with a knife chasing us down Eaton Street around the corner past Charlie Macaroni's variety store, past the corner of Parkman Street, and then past Klamans; then we stopped in front of the synagogue. Ming stopped chasing us a block earlier. Here sitting in the courtyard of the synagogue was a man named Kabashnick. He was a cantor for the synagogue He was singing. He had a remarkable voice. At that time, I didn't know what a cantor was. I knew nothing of the Hebrew Language or religion. He was a big man. I can still see him with his topcoat, and his short beard, and double chin. Well my best friend, Danny Feeney, and I started making fun of him. I called him crazy. All of a sudden in his very heavy accent, he said, "Get out of here or I will get you my boy." I answered, "I am not your boy. No, I won't go, you can't make me, so there." I said.

"Okay, I am going to get you." He answered, "No, you can't, hah, hah, Kabashnick." I said it again. "Just then he got up from where he was sitting and started running toward us. Danny yelled, "Run for it." We ran for our lives. Nelson and Roger who were with us and a couple of others ran for it. He was after me, for I had called him crazy. We ran down North Russell Street and up Eaton Street. I was a very fast runner. Kabashnick was a very fast runner. I ran past my house at 12 Eaton Street.

Mrs. Schumann our landlady was looking out the window, so she saw me run past her house.

I reached the top of Eaton Street, as did all my friends. We then decided very quickly to run down Chambers Street toward Cambridge Street. Kabashnick was still in pursuit. He yelled at us as he was running. "I am going to catch you boy."

We ran past the Polish church and immediately stopped and I said, "Let's go into this church." Here I knew we would be safe. I did not know anything about the Jewish religion. We took a chance to go into the church. Maybe he would not go in there, because he was Jewish. There were a few candles lit, but we did not see anyone.

The Polish church was attached to other buildings on either side of it. Well, Kabashnick ended his running. He did not see us go in the church. He started walking away up to the corner of Chambers Street and Eaton Street. Great, we were safe. Danny came out from behind the doorway. "Sonny, he's gone. We're safe," he said. "Yeah he's gone, he turned the corner." I said. "You want to buy some balloons?" I remarked, to the three friends. "Okay," they all said. Many Whites was a store that had everything.

There was candy on the counter on the left when you came in the front door. The other side was milk and bread. The farther back you went you came upon the funny books as I used to call the comic books. I came there every weekend to purchase new comic books. My favorites were Batman, L'l Abner, Mandrake the Magician, and The Phantom, Prince Valiant, and The Lone Ranger. I would be back to see if new comic books came in. For a nickel we bought a lot of balloons, but how would we fill them up? It came to me wow.

"Danny, the horse trough in front of Godfried's bakery down on Causeway Street." I said. So away we went, turning down Leverett Street, passing Maxi's meat market on one side and on the other side

Sally Sarkissian's house. Farther down the street we passed Gallo's Bakery with the smell of fresh bread. Andy's Pizzeria was just upstairs from Gallo's Bakery. We then past the Jewish cafeteria on the right and then on the left was Tim's Café and here Causeway Street began and Leverett Street continued on toward Charles Street. We now came upon the horse trough sitting on an island in front of Godfried's Bakery. We quickly filled the dozen or so balloons we had and headed up Chardon Street towards Green Street. Halfway up the street was a mission were drunks and derelicts came in to get off the street. We waited and watched. The opportunity came. We went up to the door, opened it and threw the balloons in. We took off and ran up Green Street and then right toward Chambers Street. Wow we thought. "You want to come up my house?" I said to him. He replied, "No, it's getting late, I'll see you tomorrow after school." It was 7:00 pm and I had to get home too.

After school I would go some days and help my father at the restaurant in South Boston, other days I would take care of my brothers to try and help my mother. I had been going to the Peter Faneuil School after the Winchell and I had to go across Cambridge Street and up Joy Street and I came to the Peter Faneuil School. I went to the Winchell School up to and including the fourth grade. Then came The Peter Faneuil School. Then came the William Blackstone School on Blossom Street with a back entrance to Eaton and North Russell streets I could now go out the door, walk about 150 feet and be in the schoolyard of the "Blacky" as we use to call it. Here I would go from the seventh to the ninth grade and we had different teachers for different subjects. My homeroom teacher in the seventh grade was Ms. Corcoran. I also had her for American history, and I liked this subject very much. I excelled in drawing maps and got an A+ for the maps. French class was an eccentric Ms. Quinn. She told us she would take us to France when the fare went down to a dollar. What a goofball she was. I was to study French for five years and enjoyed it. In the eighth grade I had Ms. Deegan for homeroom and for music. I can recall Joseph Russo, who put a small roll of gum on her piano stool.

Even with her glasses on she didn't see the gum. Well she sat down and when she got up, everyone started laughing. "Well," she said, "Let me know what's going on, so I can join in too."

"Nothing, nothing," a bunch of us said, as the bell rang and the classroom emptied out. Students went over to tell her that she had gum on her skirt. The look was the look of fire in her eyes, for it was too late to bring the class back. The ninth grade brought me in contact with Ms. Schlafman. She walked with a cane and had black hair and glasses. On the blackboard way on the upper left was a place reserved for students who made the honor roll. Their names were written there. I was on the honor roll for the last two years at the Blackstone School.

CHAPTER THIRTEEN

372 Lawrence Road

My Aunt Stella, when she married her husband Nicholas Kazanis, first lived in Somerville on Walnut Street where a murder occurred. I never knew anything about who was murdered as she tried never to talk about it when I was around. Then she moved to another part of Somerville called The Ten Hills.

In the early 1950s, to be precise 1952, they were driving in the city of Medford and came upon an exclusive area known as the Lawrence Estates. The main road there is Lawrence Road. Here they passed 372 Lawrence Road, it happened to be at Christmastime.

Residents who lived here would have contests to see which houses were the best decorated at Christmastime. This particular house was built around 1928, and the first owners were the Hesses. Later on a doctor by the name of Dr. Butters bought it.

When my aunt and uncle drove by this house, it was all lit up. There was a Santa Claus climbing down the chimney. Two huge signs that spelled out Merry Christmas were on display on the upper floor on the outside. It just so happened that the house was up for sale. "That's the house I want you to buy for me," said my aunt to my uncle. On seeing the inside it was full of gumwood. The Gumwood tree is found in the South Sea Islands, and is very expensive to import to the United States. It had a huge center entrance, French doors to the dining room and the living room, plus a sunporch. The kitchen was a working kitchen as the doctor had a maid and no one ate in the kitchen.

The meals were prepared in the kitchen and were served in the dining room. On the kitchen wall were five buzzers for the bedrooms upstairs, plus there was one buzzer in the dining room on the floor. The asking price was sixteen thousand, nine hundred dollars plus an option of six months to buy the land next to it, for five thousand dollars.

Dr. Butters was also selling the furniture, for an additional five thousand dollars.

There was a huge Grandfather's clock very high and grand, striking on the hour and the half hour in the hall, next to the staircase, for which he wanted an additional three thousand dollars. So my aunt and uncle bought the house for Twenty-one thousand dollars, including the furniture, but excluding the grandfather's clock.

My aunt had wanted to purchase this piece of land, but what happened in those six months is why the deal fell through, and the doctor would not wait any longer. My uncle was a truck driver for M&M trucking, and he lost his license for a whole year. My uncle was caught drinking as he was driving home from work. He went to court and the judge suspended his license for one year. My aunt went to work. She worked for one year on two jobs so as not to fall behind on their mortgage payments. Something did happen and it is exactly, what you would think. She was starting to fall behind on her mortgage payments. My Aunt Stella got very frustrated and left her house and no one could find her. Only my mother knew where she was. My Uncle came to see my mother, and she consoled him as I remember him lying on our couch in the living room in our house in the West End. My grandmother found out about was going on, and gave my mother five hundred dollars to give to her sister to save the house so she would not be late on her mortgage payments. So the option to buy the land next to their house expired and Dr. Butters sold the land and a house was built on it, which stands today. Gone was the time of playing croquet on the lawn as they had the mallets and the area for it but not anymore.

CHAPTER FOURTEEN

The Peter Faneuil School & Bedwetting

I was now attending the Peter Faneuil School across Cambridge Street in the West End. It was a few steps past the police station. Here was a very strict teacher named Ms. Megner. Ms. Megner was a fifth, grade teacher.

Ms. Megner was short and pudgy with black hair. If you crossed her, she would make you pay dearly. The coatroom aligned next to a row of desks, so you could hear the whip as she swung the bamboo stick on to someone's hands.

When John Passatoro answered her back, she would have none of that. Into the coatroom, she would say. She followed him into the coatroom with a bamboo stick in her hands. You could hear the screams and the yells coming from there. My eyes opened and I was gasping for my saliva to work down my throat, as I did not want to cough.

In those days, teachers abused their authority. If a teacher did this today, he or she would not be a teacher for very long.

One day I stayed over at my friend Danny's house. I tried to hide the sheets as I had wet the bed. The cat discovered them and the cat had given me away. I was sorry, and I told this to Danny's mother. She understood. Meantime Danny's father Mr. Feeney worked for the electric company and he had a side job playing piano at one of the nightclubs in Boston. One evening he would play the piano at home and he played Heart Of My Heart. I learned the words and joined in. It was great and I had a lot of fun.

One Saturday I was going over to hang around with my best friend, Danny Feeney. Suddenly when I turned the corner on to Chambers Street, there was an ambulance at 41 Chambers Street. This is where Danny lived. I ran down the street to his house as fast as I could. I met Danny at the door of his building. He said his mother had died. I looked dumbfounded for I liked his mother very much. I went to the funeral and tried to console him.

After about a year, his father remarried. He was a very good-looking man, and he had met this woman, Irene, who had come to his house before, as she was an acquaintance of his late wife. She worked as a telephone operator, and I met her once when she had visited Danny's mother. No sooner had three months gone by, and his father had a fatal heart attack. Danny had two older brothers, George Jr. and Walter.

His brother Walter asked him if he wanted to come and live with him in Vermont. He said, he would, and that would mean that I would not see him for a long time. George Feeney Jr. was not able to help his younger brother since he had a drinking problem. I can remember saying good-bye. It was not easy; I was losing my best friend.

"Good-bye," I said as I wiped a tear and hugged him. I would not see him for at least seven years. This would be at his wedding in Vermont. I was happy for him.

I graduated from the Blackstone School in 1957 and went on to Boston Latin School, which was a demanding school, as it had monthly report cards. No time for really anything except studies, and homework in at least five subjects. Mr. Greenhalge was my math teacher. Mr. Sam Weiner, "Sleepy Sam" as they called him, for ancient Greek, and Mr. Scully for French, just to name a few. For the next few years I was in school and home, occasionally trying to see a movie.

During this time, I wrote to the Walt Disney Studios and I started having correspondence with Mr. Joseph Getty. He kept me informed of what was going on at the studio. With the television that my father had bought I was able to watch Walt Disney every week. In 1957 the stereo phonograph was invented. The Walt Disney Studios was working on Sleeping Beauty that would not be released for a few years. On Walt Disney's program that I tried not to miss every week, he tried something new as he pushed stereo sound. He teamed up with local radio stations across the country and with our own WGBH radio station in Boston. This was done to experience stereo sound so natural coming into people's homes. While he showed us a segment of his new animated film, Sleeping Beauty he had the television audience experience stereo sound for the first time. You tuned in to Walt Disney' program on television and then set your radio to station WGBH. It was simulcast so the television audience could now hear stereo sound for the first time in their homes. Of course we lost out as the audience viewed the program in black and white. Color t.v.was years away, and very expensive.

CHAPTER FIFTEEN

Pressman & Giggi Bag Company

In the meantime, I started working at the Pressman & Giggi Bag Company where my mother was employed. Tony Giggi and David Pressman were partners as they had bought the business from Joseph Corso, and moved the factory across the street. You opened the door to the factory, and stepped right into the office, and the secretary, Virginia Giggi, who was Tony's daughter, greeted you. Dave, who was my mother's foreman before he and Tony bought the business from Joseph Corsco, worked on a line machine. This machine stitched all the sides together, except for the bottom piece that he stitched together later. Then I would take them, and put the brass studs on the bottom of the bags in each corner.

My mother could do the work of three people, as she knew practically every job except cutting the fabric, which Tony, at an oversized table, would do. The other women who worked there were Francis Savino, Carmella Mastrangelo, Mary Addrisi, Mary Bright, and Louise Rizzotto. There were three Marys, so not to confuse which one you were talking to, we would say Big Mary for my mother, Medium Mary, for Mary Bright, and Little Mary for Mary Adrissi.

I would greet Francis Savino in Italian, Bon giorno, qui diche. With the exception of Carmella Mastrangelo and Mary Bright, Francis, Little Mary, and Louise all lived in the North End, which was very close to the West End. The residents in the North End were predominately Italian. The residents in the West End were Irish, Jewish, and Italian.

The West End had three Jewish synagogues and two Catholic churches. Besides my mother and myself, there was one other person who also came from the West End.

Her name was Ann DiStasi. She lived on Lynde Street and two buildings down from us before we moved from there. The factory was in full production.

I would do my homework after school, and then go to the factory, and work a few hours. Sometimes, I would work until eight o'clock at night and then go home with my mother. I would talk to the stitchers while I was working. Little Mary did not have children and she was a godmother to one of Louise's children. Louise was known as Lulu and that is what she wanted to be known by at the factory and with friends. Little Mary liked Frank Sinatra a lot and would go to where he was performing, even if it meant she would have to go out of state on the weekends.

When the work at the factory got slow my mother would go to Massachusetts Leather Products so no stitchers would get laid off. Massachusetts Leather Products was located near South Station in Boston. One day Mr. Pearlstein of Massachusetts Leather Products had placed an ad in the three daily newspapers: The Boston Globe, The Boston American, and The Daily Record. A woman named Sophie Panos, short in stature, came in to apply for the job and she was hired. She would do the entire trimming for the eyeglass cases once all the stitching was done by the stitchers. This was a bigger factory and had more workers.

That same week she asked around to see if there were any people of Greek descent working here. "Yes," said Katherine Muzzi. "Mary the Greek, she is over there," was Katherine Muzzi's answer. Well this woman went right over to my mother.

"Hi," she said, with a great big smile. "My name is Sophie Panos and I come from Cambridge."

"I'm Mary the Greek," my mother said, smiling back at her. So there developed a lasting friendship between my mother and Sophie.

In my spare time on the weekends I became a member of the Elizabeth Peabody House located next to the Massachusetts General Hospital on Charles Street. I became a member of the dance committee. The dance committee was in charge of running the dances on a Friday night. On the dance committee was a girl named Cookie Sarro. She wore a kerchief around her head. Later I learned she had contracted scarlet fever and had lost her hair. On Fridays and Saturdays, I would attend the dances at the Elizabeth Peabody House, and would not come home until very late in the evening, sometimes spilling over until the next morning. I would help clean up after the dance, as I was one of the members of the dance committee.

CHAPTER SIXTEEN

Another Brothel

The family on the first floor moved out and in came hookers and pimps. One day I asked my father, "There is a light downstairs and it's a red bulb, what does that mean?"

Well I guess my education into sex was happening. He said, "It's a signal for one and all especially males to come and get it. This is a prostitution house to come and get laid." As naïve as ever, I looked at my father, and I realized that the time I caught him in the bedroom with my mother, he was having sex with her and never explained what he was doing. I thought he was hurting her for putting something in her, and I hated him for that.

One Saturday about 12:30 in the morning I came down Eaton Street and tried to open the door to get into the building where I lived. I could not open the door for something or someone was blocking me from doing so. The lights had been turned off, so I could not see who was there. Finally, someone had lit a cigarette and I saw a whole line of men standing, waiting to get in on the first floor so they could get laid.

Most of these men were sailors. It seemed the entire navy emptied out of the ships in Boston. I finally made it up to my apartment on the fifth floor. Everyone was asleep.

The next morning before going to school I told my mother what had happened. My mother went to the telephone and called Tina Schumann, the landlady. "Tina what the hell did you do here? You bitch, you bastard, I am trying to raise my family as are the other tenants living in your building. "I'll come down there and wipe the streets with you." "Mary I did not know," was Tina Schumann's answer. My mother replied, "Bullshit, you're a liar." With that my mother slammed the receiver hard onto the telephone base. I left for school, as my mother left for work.

Coming down the stairs Anna Comperchio was saying so long to her husband Tony as we were passing by. My mother greeted Anna and her husband. As Tony went down the stairs, Anna turned to my mother and said, "This is awful Mary isn't it?"

My mother responded, "Yes it is. I called her and blasted her for what's going on here. All she cares about is the damn money, not for us who have to live here." "Good, I am glad you gave it to her, Mary." Anna said. "That bitch, we are trying to raise our kids and this daughter of a bitch does this thing."

As the door to the building slammed shut, and my mother walked past Tina's house at 8 Eaton Street, Alice came up the stairs from the cellar where she had been sleeping. She called out to my mother and said, "Mary I am so glad you called her because I could her talking to you last night, that rotten bitch. It's disgusting what she does for the friggin dollar. I heard part of the conversation as she woke me up when she was yelling to you on the phone," said Alice, to my mother.

"I would like to walk right into her house and take her out here and wipe the streets with that daughter of a bitch." My mother was furious and when she got mad there was no stopping her. Tina Schumann didn't even come to the window, as she usually did to see what was going on on our street.

"Well the League of Decency will hear about this as there are minor kids in this building, and they don't have to be subjected to this house of sex," my mother said to Alice.

It didn't take long for action to take place. Within a few days people came from City Hall and looked and saw the red bulb. They said nothing but a few days later a letter was sent to Tina Schumann demanding she take action or else they would go to court and she would lose. Tina knew this and took action and raised the rent and said they could not display a red bulb in the hallway to show this was a whorehouse. So now the pressure was on them. Within a month they moved out.

No sooner had they moved out, when she rented the apartment to gypsies. They paid their rent on time for the first few months, then they fell behind. Now, when she demanded her rent they took matters in their own hands and beat her up. She got what she deserved. The cops were called of course. The gypsies resisted, by kicking the cops.

It took six cops to subdue them, finally putting them in the wagon to go off to jail. When my mother heard about it she said, "Good I am glad she got it up her ass. No one around there felt sorry for her."

CHAPTER SEVENTEEN
The Demolition of the West End

The Boston newspapers started carrying stories that the West End was going to be torn down. There were twenty-two hundred families in the West End. John B. Hynes was the mayor of Boston. He didn't care. There was something there for him and another man named Rappaport. This was a land grab in the true sense of the words. It was called taking the land by eminent domain. They used the law for their monetary advantage. They would say it's blight, and actually the houses were in very good upkeep. Very few were deteriorating. No politician came to the rescue of twenty-two hundred families who lived there. They did not visit a lot of properties to see how well they were kept up. Only Tina Schumann was a slum landlady. You have that today in some sections of Boston. As the closing of the decade came upon us it was true.

Pushing the eminent domain law through the legislature to legalize what he was doing was then sanctioned by the next mayor of Boston. Two assess. Talk of helping people move, plus compensating them with money, was a farce. Not enough by any means.

It was 1959 and with it the last year for the West End. Everyone had gotten notices; we were one of the last holdouts at 12 Eaton Street. Everyone in the building was gone. The streets were barren except for a very few.

The neighborhood had died. What memories from this small neighborhood. A few famous people came from here. I can remember someone telling me one of the best singers from the West End was

Buddy Clark; his career was cut short by an airplane tragedy in 1949. Ruth Roman, the actress, who visited Boston in the early sixties, was saddened at the demolition of the West End. Finally, there was Jerry Colonna who was a comedian and toured with Bob Hope when Bob Hope would go and entertain the troops overseas.

One of his relatives practices law in Medford, Mass. The wrecking crane was just up the street from our house. The West End was a ghost town with a few people such as us remaining, and getting ready to move. What a horrible nightmare. Uprooting thousands of people. Humanity never ceases to amaze me, as people do not feel for other people.

Secretly my mother had been saving money with the help of her boss David Pressman. He belonged to the Hebrew Free Loan Association. Here my mother could borrow money and repay it without paying interest. She did not tell my father, as he had fallen deeply in debt. Creditors were after him. He never bought me a pair of stockings and as for taking me to the movies it was that harrowing abuse of which I will never forget. It is something that has remained with me to this day of the sexual abuse that he inflicted on me and can never leave me.

I can never forget an experience as such and I buried it inside of me for many years. I never told anyone, not even my mother. My thought was if ever I was to get married and have children of my own they would never experience what had happened to me in my childhood.

CHAPTER EIGHTEEN

Moving to Malden, Massachusetts

Dave knew of a family named Mendell who had their home up for sale. Well, one evening Dave, my mother, and I went to see the Mendell family. There was Jean and her husband, Tony. They had one son, Steve Mendell. I did not know this at the time, but Dave had grown very fond of my mother. She had become sort of a silent partner with Dave at the factory. He would do other things to help her. He would take her to Connecticut to see this old friend of hers named Sofia Tsatsakis. She was the only woman my grandmother let her associate with when she was growing up in Peabody.

My mother had saved three thousand dollars and the house was selling for seventeen thousand, nine hundred dollars.

My mother did not put the house in her name, as she feared my father's bad credit would have made it difficult for us to buy a house. My mother took the money she had saved and she gave it to Dave. He then purchased the house and put it in his name. This enabled us to move from where we were and my father could not touch the house. Thank God.

My mother again would come to the aid of people. This time it was a friend of my grandmother's. This woman named Julia Pazatakis had a job in Boston and was looking for additional work so my mother brought her to Dave's factory and she worked there doing trimming and packing. Julia Pazatakis worked from one o'clock, in the afternoon until closing time at six o'clock at night. Julia would come to our house in the West End and sleep until midnight. Julia would walk over to Cambridge Street, then up Joy Street through the Boston Common to the RKO Keith Memorial Theater and work all night cleaning the movie theater. In the morning she would take the train from North Station and go home to Salem where she lived. Julia wanted to repay my mother for all she had done for her.

My mother gave Julia a thousand dollars to buy the furniture for our new house. The furniture was put in Julia's name, so my father and his business dealings would not hurt us getting three new bedroom sets, a dining room set, and a kitchen set. The living room set would come later.

Julia would come to our house three times a week in the West End and then to our new house in Malden. Dave's factory had gotten very busy again so my mother left Massachusetts Leather Products, to return full time with Dave.

Norman Pearlstein was going to lay off Sophie Panos. When my mother heard about it she walked right in to the office. "Listen, Norman, if you are laying her off, I am walking the hell out of here and I won't be back when you get busy again and need me."

"Mary, wait," Norman, said.

"Listen, Norman, it wasn't so long ago that you hired her. All of a sudden you want to let her go."

"Mary, okay, I won't lay her off." Norman replied.

When Sophie heard about this she could not thank my mother enough.

"Sophie, I am going to try and help you out. First I will help you lose weight."

CHAPTER NINETEEN

Matchmaking

Just before we moved to Clark Street in Malden in the summer of August 1959, my mother went to visit my grandmother. There she met the three men that my grandmother had taken in. One was George Velkos, a tall man with jet-black hair, who looked like Charles De Gaulle of France. My mother invited him to come to Boston to our house and meet Sophie. Sophie by now had lost weight and she was no longer overweight. She was slim and many people who saw her could not believe it was the same person. So George Velkos met Sophie at my house and Sophie started dating him.

George did not say that he was married before. He was and the marriage was not consummated. He had married to stay in this country.

Now Julia Pazatakis had a niece named Katina. She was introduced to Evangelis at my grandmother's house and there they started a courtship. Charles, Evangelis's

brother was not in hurry to find a wife as he enjoyed his freedom. Within a year Katina and Evangelis would be married at Saint Vasilios Church on Paleologos Street in Peabody.

Sophie and George dated for a year also and announced plans to wed. She asked my mother if I would be their best man. I was happy to do so. Sophie had been living with her brother in Cambridge on Inman Street. He had a rooming house besides his own apartment. He had come to see where we lived and could not believe it. "Mary you live like this," he said. "Yes George, but we are moving as they are taking the property by eminent domain, for private use."

"I am glad to see that you are moving as climbing four flights of stairs can tire you out fast. This wallpaper is dingy, I can see that your landlady has done nothing to renovate the building, in the past."

The time that Sophie's brother had come to meet us is the day that Sophie and George were getting married.

This was the first time that I would be a best man at a Greek wedding. It wasn't going to be a big wedding as she only invited her closest friends and relatives. The ceremony was, as I remember, quite long. The reception was at her brother's house on Inman Street. He and his family lived downstairs, and besides he was right there for his sister as she was the only one he had. After they married they moved from one room to a three-room apartment.

Again my mother had to go to Peabody, as my grandmother's two daughters-in-law were giving my grandmother a lot of trouble. I mentioned before that my grandfather had a long talk with my mother as he had visualized trouble after he died and made my mother promise to watch and take care of her mother. He knew that the moment my grandmother sold the property she would have plenty of money and that is what they wanted. In 1950 when my grandmother sold all her property she had almost fifteen thousand dollars. Today that is a small sum, but back then it was a lot of money.

My Uncle Harry had married a girl by the name of Ellen. She was English and she changed her religion to Greek Orthodox. They had four children.

My Uncle Charlie had married a girl from New Hampshire, and she was Greek.

She had a child out of wedlock with her stepfather. I never knew all the details, only what I had heard around adults. When you're this young you hear things. I did and kept them locked up inside of me.

I know that they tried to get rid of the child either by putting the child up for adoption or giving the child away. The infant was put up for adoption.

My Uncle Charlie was not a good-looking man, "Who is going to look at me?" he would say. So when he met Helen she was beautiful to him and he did not listen to the rumors about her. My mother had been their maid of honor. She baptized their first child and named it after my grandfather Leonidas. They had six other children, Pericles, John, Steven, and Nicky and two daughters Elizabeth and Sophia.

When my grandmother sold the property on Walnut Street, she bought a big piece of property on Wallis Street in Peabody. This property had two houses and a very big piece of land that could be farmed. The first house faced Wallis Street with the second house in the back. My grandmother lived in the second house. Both houses were two families. My Uncle Charlie lived in the first house and rented the second floor. My grandmother had an elderly lady living upstairs from her. They got along well as neighbors. This was a huge piece of property. No sooner had my grandmother moved, then trouble started. Uncle Harry thought his brother got more than he did as he now saw his brother Charlie with a home. My Uncle Harry though had purchased a two family in Salem, and had an asphalt business started with money my grandmother had given him earlier. Meanwhile my Aunt Helen was having babies one right after the other. They stopped at seven. Uncle Harry could not get along with his tenant and they went to court. It seems his business was going badly too.

My grandmother's tenant, Mrs. Michalakis was forgetful and her children, fearing that she might forget to turn the stove off, decided to put her in a nursing home. This was perfect timing for Uncle Harry, because he lost everything, and the apartment was there with no rent to pay.

CHAPTER TWENTY

Trouble with the Daughters-in-Law

The daughters-in-law were jealous of my grandmother. If it wasn't Aunt Ellen slamming the door in her face, then Aunt Helen wouldn't talk to her not even saying good morning because she would think that she gave her other daughter-in-law more than her.

My grandmother, Sofia, tried to give my mother some money, but she wouldn't take it. My mother and Uncle Louie didn't take any money from my grandmother even though my grandmother offered it a few times. She wanted to help her children very much.

Once my mother, my father, and I went to Peabody to visit my grandmother, and there was trouble. My mother fought with her brother Harry as he did not take care of his mother and let his wife mistreat his mother. My grandmother almost got a shock from all the crying and yelling that went on.

Aunt Helen was not sad that her sister-in-law was hurting her mother-in -law. I can remember when we arrived, my grandmother was sitting by the window, crying. In Greek she said, "Maria is that you?" "Yes, Ma it is." "Thank God," was my grandmother's reply. "I went upstairs to see your brother Harry, and Ellen slammed the door in my face." My grandmother told this to my mother.

Immediately my mother went upstairs. I could hear the yelling and screaming. My Aunt Ellen saying to my mother, "I don't want that bitch up here." Well, that is all my mother had to hear. "You're the bitch," my mother said. "She gave you so much, and you treat her like a piece of shit. You got what you wanted from her and now she's no good. You Harry, you stand by, while your wife treats your mother like shit and do nothing about it." "You bastard, you're unfit for anything, you deserve nothing." My mother came downstairs crying and mad. I saw this and it upset me very much. I started crying, turned to my father and said, "Dad, why don't you do something? You just stand there." I started yelling besides crying, because I couldn't bear to see my mother all upset.

My mother said, to her mother, "Look ma, don't bother with them." Things got quieter after a while. We stayed the night since my father did not need to be at work until Monday morning.

I knew what was going on, even though I was a teenager. Across the yard I went to see my cousins and Aunt Helen and Uncle Charlie. They tried to get me to say if I knew what was going on over there with Uncle Harry. I said, "I don't know, talk to my mother."

On Monday, we left to return to Boston and the West End. We had our own troubles as we had to move. In August of 1959, we moved to Clark Street in Malden. My mother went to the probation department, juvenile section and spoke to the probation officer. Mr. Samuels, the probation officer, came to Malden to see our house. "Very good" Mr. Samuels said. Well, two days later my brother Butchie came home. It was now I started calling him by his baptismal name of Nicky. He could not get over the sink, in the bathroom. We never had a sink in the bathroom to wash our hands. We had to wash in the sink in the kitchen. "Shower doors on the tub, wow Sonny this is great, what a difference," he said.

"New furniture, yes, look at the dining room. Only the living room is without any furniture, that will come eventually," I said. We were all together now, Nicky, my two younger brothers, Leon and Johnny and I. My mother was happy. I don't think my father cared one way or the other. He was working for someone at the Raleigh Restaurant in Kenmore Square in Boston.

It wasn't long that a deal was worked out between two lawyers whom my father knew, Mr. Sam Cohen and a Mr. David Stockpole, to buy a great restaurant in Sullivan Square on the Somerville and Charlestown line. Located on Maffa way, it was called The Broadway Diner. Here I would help him, and so would my mother. This diner had a huge basement and a walk-in refrigerator. During the summer my mother would take a chair and sit in the huge refrigerator to cool off. Again we had to go to Peabody.

My Uncle Harry, with my grandmother's help, bought a house in Merrimac, Massachusetts. My grandmother was going to live with them. My mother tried to talk to her, to stay where she was, but she wouldn't listen. "He is my son. He needs my help, and I am going with him." Her mind was made up. I even spoke to her. "Grandma," I said, "why are you doing this?" "He is my son, he also has a hearing problem, and I feel sorry for him."

"All the time my mother has come here to Peabody, because your daughter-in -law Aunt Ellen was giving you problems, and was after your money. No grandma," I said, "stay here, you are better off." To no avail. You could not change her mind. We left not realizing what lay before my grandmother. She had been better off. Time was not on her side. We had our own problems, after living on Eaton Street for ten years. We were moving. To me I was contemplating and rooting for this, as it would totally change our lives. While moving was not what I thought it would be, the excitement was there.

My mother had bought furniture, and had it put in Julia 's name, so my father could not have it sent back, and try to get the money for it. My mother, without my father's knowledge, paid for the furniture by cutting the checks from Dave's factory.

I continued going to school. I really didn't want to go to college, as I loved the movies from six years old. I wanted to do that, being an actor or a director. I wanted that life. My father saw to it that I would not go for it. I guess I started hating him from the time I was in the middle of an argument between my mother and my father. He mistreated her and I saw all this as I was growing up. So I had to make a choice to stay and try to protect her, or being selfish and go on to do what I wanted to do in my life. My father, as I was to find out, was very selfish and evil minded, but I never put this in my mind. I never thought of him as being selfish or evil-minded. I would find out later on.

CHAPTER TWENTY-ONE

My Grandmother's Beating

The telephone hung on the wall just off the kitchen. I heard it ring and I knew my mother would answer it, as she was closer to it than I was. Suddenly without warning I heard her scream. "Louie what is it?" she asked. "It's Ma, she is here with us. I went with Penny and picked her up." "Ellen hit her very bad," he said. "What?" my mother said.

"Those bastards, that daughter of a bitch, wait till I see her and get her. I'll knock her teeth out. Didn't Harry do anything to stop her from hitting Ma, or did he just stand there and let it happen?" Uncle Louie said, "Harry had called me to tell me that Ellen was hitting our mother." Louie went on to say that he rushed over there as fast as he could. My mother said, "Can you bring her here?" "Yes" he said, "I'll do that tomorrow after we see the doctor. She has had a very bad experience. She is shaken and trembling from the beating she got from Ellen." "Louie don't say any more, my blood pressure will be going up. I'll see you tomorrow," my mother said. The next day was Sunday, and Uncle Louie brought my grandmother to us.

Although we were very happy to have her living with us, we were very sad and angry at the sight of her arm where Ellen had hit her severely and made it black -and -blue.

All of her belongings came with her. My brother Nicky's face glowed. He was overjoyed, as he had lived with his grandmother for years when he had to leave the West End because of getting into trouble.

It was wonderful seeing my mother and my grandmother sitting, eating, and talking together.

I would get into a misunderstanding one day and I remember my grandmother saying that I was right and then saying something in Greek. At the time I really did not understand what the words meant. My grandmother was under the doctor's care. Who knows if she was taking her medicine when she was in Merrimac with Uncle Harry? We would soon find out. We were all home one night except my brother Nicky when she went into coma. She put her hand up, as she knew she would not see us again.

We called for an ambulance and they came right away. My Aunt Stella lived in the next city from us in Medford. My mother called her. "Stella, ma is dying." She didn't say anything but came right over with her daughters, Audrey and Sandra. My mother told her about Ellen and what happened in Merrimac. "I'll never talk to her for the rest of my life. What kind of a person would do such a thing hitting an old woman? Mary, I'll go to the hospital with you. Audrey and Sandra can stay here or go back home. We will have to call Louie, Charlie, and, of course Harry. I'll do that from the hospital. Okay, Mary, let's go," said Stella. We all left for the hospital. As this happened in the early evening hours, we would not return to our homes until after midnight. Before my aunts and uncles arrived from Dracut and Peabody my mother and Aunt Stella spoke to the doctor. He said, "If she pulls through she probably would be a vegetable since blood had seeped into the brain and she was hemorrhaging and there was nothing we could do for her." Before my Uncles Louie, Charlie, and Harry arrived at the hospital, my grandmother had passed away. This was such a blow to my mother as she was very close to her being the oldest daughter. My brother Nicky came home, and noticed that a lot of cars were parked on the street. This was very unusual for this time of night. When he came up the stairs and noticed all the relatives, he knew that something was wrong. The moment that I told him what had happened, he turned and punched the wall in the dining room and yelled out, "Why?" The Maistrellis funeral home was located on Elm Street, not far from Wallis Street where my grandmother lived originally. My mother was in charge with all the funeral arrangements.

"Mary, no more fights." That remark came across to my mother from Ellen. "Okay Ellen," my mother said. There my grandmother lay in her coffin now, and could not ask her daughter-in-law why she had hit her and made her right arm black-and-blue. I had not been to a wake and a funeral since I was ten years old. It was shocking as I never thought of people dying as I thought people would live forever and ever. I was so naïve that, I would be shaken again. The funeral parlor was packed with people, as my grandmother was well known. My grandfather had helped start this church, Saint Vasilios Greek Orthodox on Paleologos Street. The church would celebrate a special funeral Mass before interment at Harmony Grove Cemetery.

Actually going in the front gate on Walnut Street to Harmony Grove Cemetery on the Peabody side, my grandparent's headstones are the first two inside the gate on the left. My mother and my brother could not contain themselves. Now all I have is memories. So many. She saved me quite a few times when I had sprained my legs.

She knew how to make a cast, as she was a midwife in her town in Greece. My mother, my Aunt Stella, and Uncles Louis, Charlie, and Harry all wore black. My grandmother wore black from the time my grandfather died. She never wore anything else from that time. My mother could not stand wearing black and within the forty days she would stop wearing black. We went back to the church for the memorial dinner, which consisted of fish, and I remember listening to people speak of how they loved my grandmother.

My grandmother had left a will calling for the houses and the land to be sold, and the money to be divided among my mother, my Uncle Louie, and my Aunt Stella. This meant that Uncle Charlie, who had seven children, would have to move. Where would he go with seven children? No one would rent an apartment to him.

My mother was the first to say, that she did not want to see her brother with seven children being thrown out in the street. My Aunt Stella was the executor of the estate and she also did not want her brother Charlie thrown out in the street with nothing. It was decided that no one wanted any money and Charlie and his family would not be thrown out with no place to go. This left Uncle Louie. He, of course, said he did not want any money only to see his brother out in the street. My Uncle Harry and Aunt Ellen had gotten plenty from his mother. Aunt Stella tore the will up, and after coffee we all said our good-byes. I was nineteen years old going on twenty when all this took place.

CHAPTER TWENTY-TWO

Back to Reality, The Pain That Will Not Go Away

Suddenly, I was being shaken and someone was calling me. "What? "Who are you?" I said, half asleep. I looked up and it was a nurse, who answered. "You're at the Vincent Memorial Hospital, part of the Massachusetts General Hospital. Mr. Grigoropoulos you have been sleeping for about two hours or more. Your mother is being admitted and Doctor Richardson would like to talk to you in his office." I decided to go and wash up and that would wake me up a little more so I could talk to the doctor.

Now I realized that I had fallen asleep when my mother was brought in an ambulance as we came here early in the morning. In falling asleep I had thought of my mother's life until the moment I was awakened by the nurse, and realized that this was reality and not a dream. Now I was to meet with the doctor who knew her as a friend as well as a patient. I waited as the nurse announced me.

"Dr. Richardson will see you now." I went into his office not knowing what would lie ahead of me. "Sonny, can I call you by that name as your mother told me about you, and I am so happy to meet you. I met you mother through my wife quite a while ago and I feel that I know you as your mother talked about you so much. We'll be keeping your mother overnight to complete our tests, and I want to tell you things don't look good. I want you to sit down, because what I have to say is important. Sonny, your mother has cancer of the ovaries and we...." Just as he was going to continue, I looked up at him and yelled and screamed. I started to blurt and cry and went into deep crying and couldn't stop. Dr. Richardson came at me with tissues, as my tears were coming down my face so fast I couldn't stop them. Everything seemed blurry to me. I lost the sense of where I was for the moment. "Sonny, no words can express how I feel for you and your mother."

Why, oh why, was this happening? This can't be happening to me. Why couldn't I stop this? Was I so naïve about life? Did life mean anything? Inside of me I could almost hear myself being torn apart. I never expected this pain. I lifted my head up to see Dr. Richardson's face trying to console me with his eyes. He said, "Your mother will be discharged in two days after doing some more tests. She will be having X-ray treatments and this will slow down the cancer, but will not cure her. She will live for only another six months. I thought of an operation but I don't think it will help.

There are no words that I can say to bring you comfort." "Dr. Richardson, can't you take something from me so that she can live?" "I am not God, Sonny." "Should I thank you for giving me the worst day in my life? Please, Dr. Richardson I don't want her to know any of this. Okay?" I asked. "I understand," the doctor said. This pain I would carry all the days of my life. My mother would be discharged in a few days. I had to do a complete metamorphosis. One slight word might make it known that something more dreadful was wrong with her. Dr. Richardson would tell her that she was having X-ray treatments and the problem would be eradicated. I knew that if she was told that she had to have radium treatments then she would know that she had cancer. So when I went up to her room, I told her what the doctor said. Since she was having a few x-ray treatments she knew that she didn't have cancer. People with cancer usually had radiation treatments. Dr. Richardson would also assure her that she did not have that disease. "Sonny," my mother said, "I know the X-ray treatments are not a sign that I have cancer." In two days my mother was discharged from the hospital and came home. In a few days, she returned to work at Dave's factory just off Scollay Square.

A day later after work my mother was in Filene's Basement on Washington Street in Boston. My mother would always look for bargains, and Filenes's was the place to go. When the Davy Crockett craze was on in the country, you could say, and it was a fact, we were the best dressed kids on the street. I remember my brothers Leon and Johnny wearing the Davy Crockett tee shirts and shorts. My mother met Aunt Stella in Filenes' Basement "Hi Mary, how is everything?" "Okay, Stella, I've been to the doctor and I am having X-ray treatments to shrink a small cyst." "Okay," Stella said. "Keep in touch." They kissed each other and parted. It was extremely hard for me to carry on.

Every night secretly I prayed and cried. Then one day I read about some new experiment going on in Buffalo, New York at a hospital there. I called to the doctor in Buffalo, New York. He said, "Look Mr. Grigoropoulos, I am sorry I can't help you as this is in the experimental stage and we have months, and maybe years, to go before it is proven." I was crying so loudly and I only remember saying thank you and good-bye.

Time was passing. I was trying to take care of my mother at home and every time I would go into her bedroom I would try to hide my feelings. Then one day my mother caught me wiping my face and said to me "I don't want my son to cry." My mother then said, "Sonny, do I have cancer?" I turned to her and said, "No Ma, what made you say that?" "I thought that I did." "No, if you did, you would be getting radium treatments not X-ray treatments." I thought to myself this at least assured her that she did not have the disease.

I would leave her for a few minutes and go into my bedroom and cry and cry.

What a person. She helped get people jobs, and even fought with one of her girlfriends, Ann DiStasi, who had told her and Dave, their boss, "You let love interfere with business." It was no secret that Dave loved my mother. He had helped get the house that we live in. My mother had saved money through the Hebrew Free Loan Association without my father finding out. Dave had taken my mother on trips to Connecticut to see an old friend of my mother's, Sofia Tsatsakis, in

Brookfield. This girlfriend was the only one my grandmother allowed her to associate with when she was growing up in Peabody.

The phone rang, I answered it. "Sonny" the voice said, "it's Aunt Stella, can I come over, I haven't heard from your mother?" "Okay sure" I said. Ten minutes had hardly passed when the doorbell rang. I answered it. "Hi, Sonny." "Hi Aunt Stella, and kissed her on her cheek. "My mother is in the bedroom. I told her you were coming over." "Hi, Mary. How are you?" "I feel a little weak as I came back from the hospital from having an X-ray treatment." I left them alone for a minute. I was in another part of the house when Aunt Stella came to me. "Sonny, I want to take your mother to my house and look after her until she gets better. Is it all right?" I went into my mother's room and closed the door. "Ma, I don't want you to go." I said, as my eyes were like pools of mirrors that if you could hit them they would splash and break. Again the question came. "Sonny, do I have cancer?" "No, Ma," looking at her straight in the eye. "Look, Ma don't be ashamed of me, I came out of you. I am not ashamed when I have to wash you." "I know son," she said.

"It's just that, I know," interrupting her, "she's a woman too, your sister." "Yes, son," she said. "If that is what you want, okay, I am all for it." I got a suitcase down from the attic, and packed some clothes. We got her dressed and I hugged and kissed her and turned so she would not see the tears flooding my eyes, and put her in Aunt Stella's car. It was big and roomy. It was a Cadillac. My Aunt Stella liked Cadillacs of all the cars. I walked up the stairs and looked as the car sped off in the direction of Medford. I closed the door and cried and cried. Where is God? I thought to myself. I prayed so much in my bedroom, in church, and got no answer. For the next month, March, I would take the bus after work to Dave's factory as I had been doing. I had graduated high school two years before and what I wanted to do was to leave home. I just could not do it because of my father. He was mean to her and I could not think of myself so I put myself last. When it came to her, I did just that. It was March and nearing her birthday, March 17, Saint Patrick's Day.

CHAPTER TWENTY-THREE

My Mother's Last Days

I would take the bus from Malden Square to Medford Square, or I could choose to wait for the West Medford bus, which would take me to Winthrop and High Streets.

Here I walked about five minutes on Winthrop Street then turned onto Lawrence Road till I got to 372, a big white house. I rang the bell, the maid let me in. My mother was in my cousin Audrey's room. It was upstairs in the front.

Here my aunt had gotten a hospital bed for her. Then I saw Aunt Stella, who said, "Your mother ate good today." That wasn't going to last. She had visitors, first Ann DiStasi came by. They finally made up. After her visitors left, I stayed the night as I would every night and slept on a bed next to her. The next morning I would leave and return at night. The next day I saw Audrey, and I can remember her saying," She would be better if she died." When I heard this I turned and looked at her, with a hate in my eyes. I would want my mother alive at all costs. Who was she to say that to me? When I climbed the stairs, Aunt Stella was already in her room. "I am so sorry, Sonny." She was holding a needle; the doctor and visiting nurse had showed her how to administer the morphine for pain. Aunt Stella had called the family as the end was near. What a difference from the day before when she was talking with Ann Di Stasi and me. Dave had come as he did every night. I left the room just to get my composure. I was at the bottom of the stairs when Dave came down.

"She is out," he said, crying," I loved your mother, Sonny." "I know," I said, as I helped him to his car. We were both crying as I said good-bye to him. I went back into the house and upstairs to the room were my mother was. Everyone thought she was sleeping and they were downstairs scattered about the house, some in the kitchen and some in the living room. I entered the room; my mother's eyes were open and glassy. She could not speak. She tried saying something and mumbled something. I looked at her and just let go. "Ma, if you can understand me blink your eyes. Once for yes and twice for no, okay" I said. She blinked so I would know. "I promise you, Ma, that I will take care of Nicky, Leo, and Johnny." Leo was eleven years old and Johnny was ten years old and had not seen her in a week. Nicky had come and he was downstairs. After talking with my mother, I was completely out of it. All I remember is going downstairs, and going into the living room, and sitting on the sofa. I could hear someone going upstairs, but I did not look to see who it was. It was my brother Nicky who went upstairs and just as I got to the sofa to sit down, he came running down the stairs, saying, "Ma is gone."

I climbed the stairs again, entering the room where she lay. I put my hand on her forehead as her eyes were closed now. I kissed her forehead and realized that she died knowing peace and the promise I made to her, as a loving son made to one of the most wonderful of human beings that was ever put on this earth. Again, I broke down for now I would never see her again and I would know this pain all of my life, and I would remember the things she said to me and taught me.

CHAPTER TWENTY-FOUR

The Funeral & The Aftermath

The undertaker was called, Steven Maistrellis from Peabody. We had no insurance to speak of. I didn't know anything about these things. There was a lump- sum death payment that would help with the funeral expenses. The funeral and the cemetery where she would be laid to rest would be about thousand dollars and the casket, a steel one, would be cheaper than a wooden one, another thousand dollars The total for everything would be around two thousand dollars. We were all short of money. My mother had lent Aunt Penny three hundred dollars and now was the time I would need it to try to get it back to cover some of the expenses.

Aunt Penny said, "Sonny, don't worry I will get the money to help you. After all, your mother was good enough to give it to me when I needed it. "Thank you, Aunt Penny," I said. My father, of course, finally came. He wasn't even on my mind. So Steven Maistrellis came and took my mother's body. The wake would be on Thursday and Friday and burial on Saturday morning. The funeral parlor was on Elm Street in Peabody.

The funeral parlor hours would be from 2 p.m. to 4 p.m. and 7 p.m. till 9 p.m. both days. I cried and no one to console me. I felt betrayed by God. Why wouldn't God help my mother when she did many good things for so many people? My faith was shattered and I blamed God for this happening to a beautiful person inside and out. I don't remember how I got home. I only knew I would have to tell my younger brothers, as I did not want them to see her now, but to remember her as she was.

When I got home, they were in my room and I sat at the edge of the bed and hugged them and told them that Ma had passed away. They cried, and I knew that this was their first time finding out about death. I explained all this to them, and how in a few days we would be burying her. They would come to the funeral parlor and see their mother dead in a coffin. So I tried to prepare them for that. Just as I finished, the telephone rang. "Sonny, tell me your mother didn't die?" For a moment the voice caught me off guard. Then I knew who it was. I had not heard this voice since moving from the West End. It was Anna Comperchio; my mother had bought Christmas gifts for everyone in the family. I answered, "Yes, Anna, she passed away on her birthday Saint Patrick's Day" "Oh, Sonny what a person she was I can't believe this. How she fought for all of us against that bitch, Tina Schumann who was a mean and selfish person. I will try and come to the wake, God bless you all, and my prayers and thoughts are with you all."

Everyone came to the wake. It was so crowded that some could not get in the front door. Dave came. His wife was still in Florida, but sent her condolences. Dave's partner and his wife, Carmella, as well as their daughter, Virginia, who was their secretary at the factory came, Dave would not stay in the same room as my father. Louise (Lulu) Rizzotto sat in a chair near where I was standing, accepting the condolences from people. She called me over and said to me. "Sonny, your mother was a saint. When you feel depressed, go into her room and pray by her bedside. She will answer you." Just then my father made a remark. Looking at me he said, "You think it doesn't bother me." I looked at him as if to say, "Now that she is dead. It's too late now." I looked at him disgusted. I went into the other room. "How are you holding up, Sonny?" I looked up and it was Dave. "I am trying, Dave," I said. I kept thinking of what my father said. Look at what I am left with, a father who I don't like, and my brother Nicky who's just like him. How was I going to cope? My mother had died on her birthday. She had just turned forty-five years old. I was just shy of my twenty-first birthday on May 17. I would be of legal age then.

I was composed as possible the next morning for my mother's funeral, at Saint Vasilios Greek Orthodox Church on Paleologos Street in Peabody. It was a dreary day, no sun, not that I paid much attention to that. I was sort of in shock. I would never think that a day like this would happen to me. I would always pray, and God would help. How I prayed and prayed. She was too good. Why wasn't God more sympathetic, I thought?

He knew who she was. She had taught me so well. I do remember being helped from the car to the stairs of church. This church that my grandfather helped to build and who was president of the church. My thoughts drifted to another time, and I was numb.

But the moment I heard Father Nickolopoulos speak and say, "These boys, these poor boys." At that moment, I cried and cried. It was worse when everyone in church passed by the coffin saying good-bye to Mary. Father Nickolopoulos went on to say how she had done so much for people and would never tell anyone, only now it was known because people came to say good-bye. They had told their stories about her to the funeral director, Mr. Maistrellis, and to the parish priest, Father Nickolopoulos. "What a human being we are putting to rest. In God's name I wish her peace." I cried all the more. I don't remember who held me as my eyes were so glassy, I couldn't see the stairs. "Sonny, we love you," I heard a voice say. The funeral cars drove around Walnut Street, as this is where my mother grew up and then to Wallis Street where my grandmother had moved after my grandfather had died. We reached the gate of Harmony Grove Cemetery on Walnut Street. Superstitious people would say, aha the mother took the daughter. My grandmother had been dead only eleven months. My mother was laid to rest on a hill. We reached the top of the hill. Mr. Maistrellis and his assistants were giving flowers to everyone to put on her coffin as a gesture of saying good-bye and rest in peace.

I could hear Father Nickolopoulos saying a few words. I yelled, and said, "I want to go with her." Father Nickolopoulos said, "Look, no you can't." "Yes I can, I have nothing to live for." "No, you have something to live for.," someone said. I could not control myself. I could not remember who held me or how I got to the car. I was at the car looking at my mother's coffin as it was being lowered in the ground. Why did I not have the strength to do away with myself? I thought. Look whom I am left with. A father whom I despise. He killed her as surely as if he pulled a trigger of a gun or stabbed her. I could never hope to forgive him. Why wasn't it him, not her? He abused me sexually when I was small, and was jealous of me all through my adolescent years. He never said, son, I love you. The only time he took me to the movies, he abused me. If he was teaching me sex, he taught me all wrong. He could sit there and masturbate with another man or jerk off, as it was commonly known. He never hugged me or said I want to help you, son. It was too late for that. The son of a bitch. I could have spit on him. We were now returning to the church, going downstairs into the church hall. They're to have the memorial dinner in memory of my mother. It was a fish dinner that was the custom to have after a person had passed away. To me I did not care one way or another. My only hope to be what I wanted vanished. The jealousy of my father would prevail. Saying good-bye to many of my mother's friends was sad. I knew that I would see some of them again. Dave said, "Sonny, I'll see you at work." "Okay," I said. Yes, I returned to work in a few days and I was just trying to compose myself. I tried doing my work as best as I could.

CHAPTER TWENTY-FIVE

My Father's Jealousy

One night at supper, my father brought up the subject of the house and put it square to me by saying, "You don't care about us. They will throw us out. Your mother may have bought the house, but there is nothing here to prove it. This house is in Dave's name and his wife. They will throw us out of here." He kept this up most of the night.

"Okay, okay," I said. Well, the next day I went to Dave, and asked about the house. "Sonny," Dave said, "the house is not mine, it belongs to you boys. I'll turn it over to you as long as your name is on it too because I don't trust your father." "I know," I said.

My birthday was approaching May 17th. I would then be of legal age to have the house turned over to me. That evening I told my father that Dave would sign the house over to us as long as my name was on it. May the 17th arrived, and I was now of legal age. My father thought he was crafty, but I had the papers. Dave wasn't crafty, he was good. It was my father who was evil minded, because there were more sinister things to happen behind those eyes of his. I would have to go to the bank. The Malden Savings Bank was in the square. I would have to fill out a mortgage application. These things I knew nothing about. I filled it out and took one to my father to fill out. I returned them to Peter Patriquinn, the mortgage officer. "Thank you," He said. I would go to work at Dave's place, now moved to Kingston Street behind Jordan Marsh. Looking around I could see that Mary Bright, Carmella Mastrangelo, and Louise Rizzuto were the three stitchers left.

Gone were the happy days when we would talk and laugh, talking about different subjects. Each day was the same. I was numb and always down. I was depressed. I could not see my mother any more. This I tried to put in the back of my mind. My little bothers were only ten and eleven years of age. I had promised my mother to take care of them. I would keep my word. By now my aunts thought, maybe I would not be able to do it. My father was here, but then there was money to be had. There was money to be had. My Aunts Stella and Ellen both knew there was money. "We can take Leon and Johnny off your hands," they said. Yes, indeed they were ready. From Social Security you had survivors' benefits until the age of eighteen years of age. I had gone to the Social Security office in Malden. We would collect over three hundred dollars a month. Wow, what help I thought. It would help now so we would not lose our house. My aunts knew about the money before I did. I received a letter in the mail from Mr. Patriquinn. My application was approved for a mortgage. I was happy. I could not wait to tell Dave the next day. My father on the other hand only said, "good." Noting nothing of jubilation in his voice.

The next day I told Dave, he was happy. He and his wife, wonderful people. Two human beings that really cared about us. The next day I received another letter from Mr.
Patriquinn. The passing of papers would occur next week on Wednesday. That was okay with me. So on the eleventh of July, I became a homeowner with my father as joint tenants, which meant that if either of us died the property would revert to the other.

Not so long afterward Dave told me one day. "Sonny, I will have to lay you off."

Business was really slow. It was sad. Here I was leaving a place that I worked at after school and now after high school. I was to finish out the week. It was sad saying good-bye to Dave, Tony, and the rest of the workers. Dave, of course, was a wonderful human being. I would now be unemployed. I would collect unemployment benefits for five months.

CHAPTER TWENTY-SIX

The Lahey Clinic

I had started looking for work, but I could not find anything as there was a recession going on. Looking in the Boston Globe newspaper, one day I found that they were looking for record locators at the Lahey Clinic in Boston on Commonwealth Avenue. I could get there on the subway. I left the next morning and I arrived a little after nine o'clock. In charge of human services for hiring was a man named Robert Pringle. His black-rimmed glasses protruded from his face in an ugly fashion. He gave me an application, which I filled out. I returned it to him. He asked me a few questions. I guess I gave the right answers. I got the job subject to a physical examination to make sure that I had no diseases. The next day I came in for a physical examination. I passed it with flying colors. I was to start the next day, as they needed the record locators as soon as possible.

The clinic had three floors as well as the basement. The job consisted of locating patient records so blood work or other results could be put in their records. The clinic was associated with the New England Baptist Hospital and with the Deaconess Hospital.

There were many doctors whom I got to know as on a first -name basis. The woman doctors who were there were also grand people to know. Many of the hospital secretaries were great to work with.

One in particular was Bessie Touloumtzis. She did not know I was Greek. I had introduced myself but did not tell her my last name. I knew that she was because I saw her name on her desk. One morning while looking for a patient's record, I said, "Excuse me" in Greek, and she looked up at me from her desk. Then I said, " yiasou thespenis Touloumtzis." "How wonderful" she said. Then she said, "I am sure we will become good friends."

John F. Kennedy had been president for more than a year and a picture of him hung in Dr. Poppen's office. Actually it hung near his secretary's desk. Alice Gargan was Dr. Poppen and Dr. Fager's secretary. She also was related to the Kennedy family. She was one of the cousins. In fact, one of the Gargans accompanied the President's mother, Rose Kennedy wherever she went. It was around this time that Joseph Kennedy, Sr. had a stroke, which left him paralyzed and in a wheel chair. He would not live too long afterward. At least he got to see his son become president. There were the financial secretaries like Florence Haskett. She loved to paint. I soon acquired one of her still life of flowers, which I loved and still have. One day while going to Dr. Sedgwick's office, I was told that he had a patient in his office. Why it's the movie actor Claude Rains. He had been diagnosed with cancer and was having treatments for it. Not much later that he succumbed to the disease. He was living in Hanover, Massachusetts. One day going downstairs to Dr. Wise's office, I met Raymond Massey, who was playing a doctor on the television series Dr. Kildare which also starred Richard Chamberlain. I met Byron Economou, an electrician, and John, these fellows were Greek boys. John was in building maintenance. We would converse in Greek, especially in the lunchroom.

I kept writing to my aunts in Greece, especially my Aunt Marianthi. My Greek had improved very much as I had been writing to them over five years. I made sure that the spelling was correct, as the Hellenic language is very difficult, one of the hardest languages in the world. I increased my vocabulary very much. My conversation grew by leaps and bounds.

At about this time Boston was in the grip of a maniac known as the Boston Strangler. His first victim was near my old neighborhood of the West End. An elderly woman on West Cedar Street had been strangled. One night as I was working late, I noticed a man peeking in a bedroom window at the back of the Lahey Clinic. I opened the third floor window and yelled out, "What are you doing down there?" Immediately he looked up and saw me and ran off. Other people opened their windows when they heard me yelling. They had heard me yelling. I immediately said, "There is a prowler on the loose. Lock your windows." One looked up at me and said thank you very much. I said, "You're at risk because you are on the ground floor." "I know it," this person said. "Thanks again." Another day had come and gone.

I noticed Bessie Touloumtzis hands as I was looking for a patient's record on her desk. It seemed to me that she had arthritis. Such a beautiful woman. Pretty eyes. I was still pretty naïve back then, even though I was now twenty-three years of age. There were other people looking for records beside myself. One such person was a fellow from New Bedford named Alfred Kaczynski. He was Polish, and one day I noticed something strange about him. Someone had said, "I think he is weird." I wanted to find out if this was true. I never liked to judge what people would say about someone else. I became friendly with him, and finally one day after work I told him let's go and get an ice cream.

We did and there he opened up to me and said that his father thought nothing of him but his mother was wonderful. His father was very domineering and wanted nothing to do with him as he thought his son was a homosexual. I remained friends with him until I left the Lahey Clinic.

At home I would try and organize things, as we were five men with no woman in the house. The clothing bill was way out of sight. I did not have a washing machine so I had to put the dirty clothes in a huge laundry bag and take them to the laundromat. So I decided to buy a washing machine. This would cut the cleaning bill in half. My father put up a stink and went to the department store and told them that he wanted the money back and to come to take the washing machine back. He never contributed any money to the bills and let me struggle along. With five men in the house, the clothes were like we were in Brooks Brothers. My brother Nicky changed clothes twice a day. I was trying to lower our cleaning bill. It was running seventy dollars every week and no end in sight. I paid cash for the washing machine and by the time my father got through with Lechmere Sales I was making time payments. He took the money and I never saw it again.

It was now the fall of 1963 and November was milder than usual. Things were quiet I thought. I was still working at the Lahey Clinic and the Thanksgiving holiday was in a few days. My mother had been dead for three years. It was November 22,1963, a regular day. My lunch hour was from 12:30 P.M. to 1:P.M. Suddenly people coming into the clinic said that President Kennedy had been shot in Dallas. The hospital secretaries put the radio on. Each floor in the clinic had two or three radios to listen to what was happening in Dallas, Texas.

Suddenly, Walter Cronkite spoke and said that President Kennedy, traveling in an open motorcade, was shot in Dealy Plaza in Dallas, Texas. Shortly afterward he was pronounced dead at the hospital that he was brought to.

Young people in America like myself looked up to him and admired his humor at the weekly press conferences. I always watched him. It was a delight. He had humor, good looks, and knew how to speak well. Well, everyone went home a little early, as this was a huge catastrophe. When I got home and put the television on the reporters said that he died at the hospital and the country would go into mourning for a whole week. Lyndon Baines Johnson was sworn in as the next president aboard Air Force One, with that remarkable woman, who I admired so much, Jacqueline Bouvier Kennedy present. I cried as many people did. My father's words in Greek, "To skotosane to paidi" "They killed the lad."

I kept writing to my aunts, Marianthi and Suzanne in Piraeus Greece. My father's sisters Aunt Marianthi, Aunt Suzanne, and Aunt

Paraskevi all lived in Piraeus, Greece. The two brothers that were alive, Demetrios and Costantinos, lived in Constanza, Romania. I did write to them, but I had to be careful as the letters were censored and read by the government. My father felt sorry for Aunt Suzanne because the Nazis killed her husband, Daniel Markides. My father told me how he died as Suzanne had written to my father years earlier and told him. The family was destitute and hungry.

Daniel spoke fluent German, so there was no problem of communication. He went seeking help. He asked the German officers for food for his family. The Nazis took the butts of their rifles and whacked him. He returned home. He told his wife, Suzanne, "I am tired and I want to lie down." Suzanne did not know that he was bleeding inside. He lay down. There he died. When she went to lie down beside him, she found no movement and screamed and cried. She had two small girls to take care of.

My knowledge of the Greek language continued to increase as my aunts knew very good Greek and grammar. The Greek or rather the Hellenic language goes back about four thousand years, and has an immense vocabulary. There could be two to three words to one English word.

Meanwhile, I would send money to Aunt Suzanne because I felt sorry for her situation. No one really took care of her. At this time my father finally gave me one compliment. He said, "Of all of you four boys," looking at me, "Sonny is the Greek in the house." I think my father was buttering me up. Shortly thereafter he said to me, "Let's sell the house and move to the South End of Boston." I balked. "What?" I said, "Dad, I don't want to move there." My father and my brother Nicky were present when this conversation took place. "I don't want to do that." I said. My father said, "Oh, yes you will, I'll make you sign," he said in Greek. I fired back with, "I should die first, for me to sign to sell the house. Never." At that moment my brother shoved me down a flight of stairs to the front hall and I got up in pain as my legs both felt as if they went through a chamber with knives on each side pricking me to no end. They thought that I would lie there; they did not come down to see if I was all right or not. As long as my name was on the deed and the mortgage, he could do nothing to force me to sign outside of killing me. He could do nothing without my consent. I would never give in.

CHAPTER TWENTY-SEVEN

Aunt Suzanne

Time passed, and I finally investigated to see if I could bring his sister, Aunt Suzanne, to this country. I wrote to her, and she jumped at the chance. I had to fill out papers, to prove that she would not be a burden on society. I could prove all this as the house was in my name as well as my father's name. This proved to be a happy time for my father, as he had not seen her for forty-five years. That was a lifetime, I thought.

He also forgot about putting pressure on me to sign over the house, which I would never do. There were papers to fill out. She would have to go to the United States Embassy to get her visa, once I had sent her the ticket. Coming by ship was cheaper than by air at that time. The jets were starting to come into service. The fare was double what it was by ship. The ship, the Queen Fredericka was the ship that usually brought people to the United States, It was the fall of 1966. It would take ten days to cross the Atlantic Ocean and arrive in New York City. It was the tenth of October when she left and she would arrive on the twentieth. I had the ticket from the Philip Anastos Travel Service. I was happy. My father was happy. However, the friction with my father would never go away for deep in my heart I knew he was an evil man. I just put this in the back of my mind and was on my guard. I had made a promise to a dying woman, whom I loved more than my life. I felt I would try to get close to my father by doing this, helping to bring his sister here. At last I would get to know his side of the family. I had become disenchanted with my mother's side.

I had not bought a car until 1965 when I was twenty-five years old, and finally went and took the exam and the road test to get my license. My first car was a 1960 Chevrolet Impala, five years old. I was so happy, but having my first car wasn't to last.

When I went to bed I would hang my pants behind the door in my room. During the night, my brother Nicky took my license and the keys to my car. Back then you did not have your picture on the license. The next day as I was looking at my car from one of the bedroom windows, it looked odd. "No it can't be," I said, to myself. Something was not right. As I came to my car I noticed my front headlight was damaged on the passenger side. I don't remember hitting anything. Two days after that when I got home from work, I received a letter from the Registry of Motor Vehicles. I opened it right away. I was shocked as it said, that I had been involved in a car accident and my license was suspended. I was to cease operating the motor vehicle at once, and I had a court appearance. I sat down in the kitchen dumbfounded. I thought to myself, "Could I have been in an auto accident and forgot about it?" My court appearance was in two weeks. Now I can't drive. Oh boy, what next? The day arrived. I went to court in Malden. When I approached the court to say my piece, the judge spoke and said, "You are charged with speeding, running a red light, and hitting a parked car. How do you plead?" I responded, "Not guilty, Your Honor."

The case was continued to the following week at 9 A.M. Then the officer who pulled me over would testify. I was freed on my own personal recognizance. When I came home later that day and told my brother, he thought nothing of it. "It is your first time in front of a judge and you have no record. He will probably give you a suspended sentence, and put you on probation," he said. I looked at him in disgust. The following week came, and I returned to court. As they called the case, the judge asked me to stand. I saw an officer approach the bench and speak to the clerk. "Your Honor, my name is officer John Hayward, and I was on duty the day of this incident. This is not the man that I pulled over." I stared up to the ceiling and back, as I thought, "Oh my God, it was my brother Nicky that caused this accident." "Your Honor may I speak? I asked. "I believe I know who was involved in this accident, my brother, Your Honor."

The judge ordered the case continued, and asked me to have my brother come in voluntarily. I said, "Thank you, Your Honor," and left the courtroom. The case was continued until the following week. I suspected my brother in all of this since he did not have a car, and was envious of me for having one. That evening, I confronted him.

"Nicky, you took my keys and my license and drove my car. You know, they have suspended my license indefinitely. I may never drive again. Do you realize Aunt Suzanne is expected here in ten days? I won't be able to go to New York to pick her up. This Friday you and I have to go to court. "Why, oh, why, what the hell is the matter with you?" I sat down and cried. "Go and get a license yourself, instead of getting me into trouble." The following Friday, he came with me, and admitted everything. The judge could now give him what he deserved. In the end, he was put on probation as he came in voluntarily and that was in his favor. The judge gave him two years probation. He was lucky. I had to reapply for my license. I would go to a hearing at the Registry of Motor Vehicles to let them decide after hearing my case. They fully agreed and reinstated my license. My father did not say much to his son Nicky and did not side with me. The only thing on his mind was his sister is coming to America, and he would see one member of his family after forty-five years.

Aunt Marianthi had written to me of how she tried to help Aunt Suzanne and her daughters during the Second World War.

She kept the youngest daughter, Irene, with her, and the other was put in an orphanage all this during the Second World War after the Nazis beat their father.

Aunt Marianthi said this in her letter. "The send- off was sad and happy." Happy as she would be embarking on a new way of life. Sad in leaving her two daughters behind, even though they were both now married. The time was coming; the Queen Fredericka was due to dock on October 20, 1966. We would have to be up to drive to New York, which would take four hours. It was Thursday, October 18.

Nicky, as usual, was late coming home. He was dropped off by one of his friends. He was drunk, nice and drunk.

He could not put the key in the door. Ringing and banging the front door woke me up. "Nicky, what the hell, you're drunk you son of bitch." He was like deadweight, carrying him up the stairs. "I'm all right, leave me the hell alone," he said. "It's your fault I'm like this," he continued. "Go to hell you bastard," I said. I then went off to bed.

Somehow he managed to take his pants off, but also light a cigarette. During the night I awoke, smelling smoke. I was a light sleeper. Going down the hall, I approached my brother Nicky's room. I noticed the smoke was the thickest here.

When I reached his room the smoke was very thick. I had to put my hand over my mouth to try and stop coughing. My brother Nicky was in bed in a dead sleep. The cigarette had fallen and had lit the mattress on fire. It was burning slowly but it hadn't reached him yet. I yelled and called, and my brothers, Leon, and Johnny, came running down the hall toward me. My father too. Nothing else was on fire, fortunately.

We struggled to get him up as quickly as possible. He was dead weight. All of us grabbed a piece of the mattress that was still not burned. My brother Johnny had opened the back door. We reached the kitchen, and continued right on to the back porch and threw the burning mattress over the railing, and into the yard. Wow, oh boy what a close call. We all could have been dead the next morning. Nicky was still asleep on the couch where we put him

That evening when I came home, Nicky was home getting ready to go out. "Do you know what you did?" he stood in front of the bathroom mirror as I asked him this.

"We could all have been burned to death, as you fell asleep smoking a cigarette you ass," I said to him. "All you care about is yourself." The words were coming right out of my mouth as fast as he was combing his hair. "You're no good, I wish I never had you for a brother. I hope you croak, you bastard. I wash your clothes, iron your clothes, and try to keep this house clean."

You're selfish, and jealous." He finished dressing and I could hear him going down the stairs. "Good," I said, "stay out." His room was always a mess. Everything came out of the bureaus. Clothes piled high on one bureau. I would always clean his room as he was very messy and never put his clothes back in his bureau drawers or hang them up in the closet.

CHAPTER TWENTY-EIGHT

Meeting Aunt Suzanne

I had checked with the Philip Anastos Travel Agency, and found out that the ship, The Queen Fredericka was arriving on Saturday, instead of Friday. Saturday came. We left at 7:30 a.m. The ship was due in at 2:30 p.m, at pier 45 West, New York City. I was excited, as was my father. Leon and Johnny didn't come and went to stay with friends of theirs. One way or the other Nicky was glad because of our father. He was happy if our father was happy. I bought a map of New York City to know where to go.

The drive was long and we stopped to stretch our legs and get a snack and gas. We arrived at 1:00pm, but needed a pass to get onto the pier. You had to go to the Custom Building in New York City. There was no time for that. So we waited patiently.

Standing next to me was an elderly gentleman. I could see that someone he recognized was on the pier. He had a pass and I said, "It's wonderful you're able to meet and help your daughter arriving here." Someone said, "Shut up. That's his wife not his daughter." He was very old and she married him to come to this country. He must have been at least twenty-five years her senior. People were coming and going in hundreds and possibly thousands. More people than there were passengers. After two and half hours I could see a small woman with a black kerchief tied around her head. It looked like, it was, Aunt Suzanne. I ran as my father looked and I shouted yiasou Aunt Suzanna. I grabbed her, smothering her with hugs and kisses. As we approached my father was crying. I never saw him cry, not even for my mother. Here were a brother and sister who had not seen each other for forty-five years. He grabbed and kissed her and would not let go. I said, "Dad, people are waiting to get by." "Leave me," he said. I finally unshackled him from his sister's arms. We headed for the baggage area to claim her luggage and pass through customs. This would take us another forty-five minutes. She saw her luggage. She had three pieces and passed through customs with not much to declare.

As we headed to the parking lot, she told us of getting sick on the ship and luckily a nurse and a doctor were on board. She told us if it weren't for them she would have died.

They pulled her through. She could not get over our having a car. We all piled in and headed back to Boston. The stories she told my father. "George our mother had three more children." "What?" my father remarked. "Thirteen children. She always talked about you. You were fourteen years old when you left to join the French Foreign Legion." She related how they left Turkey with the population exchanges in 1922 going to Varna, Bulgaria, and then to Constanza, Romania, and finally some of them going to Piraeus, Greece. She told him his brothers, Kostica and Demetrios whose nickname was Mimi decided to stay in Romania. They got caught behind the Iron Curtain after the Second World War.

We stopped for a snack and to stretch our legs. It wasn't until 9:30 p.m. that we arrived in Malden. We were all tired from this trip. Aunt Suzanne could not get over the house. She never had anything like this. Running water, flushing toilets. I said, "Aunt Suzanne you can see everything in the morning." She said, "I know, I am tired too." I gave her my room and went and slept on the couch. The next day, she awoke early and luckily it was Sunday and no one had to go to work. "Great" I said. I made breakfast.

She liked Greek coffee. Fortunately, I had some. She liked it strong. She never dreamed things are so great. I said, "Aunty you have to work. Nothing comes into your hands easily." We now had a woman in our house after nearly four years since my mother passed away. It would not take long to get used to this again. For dinner she would cook. "I'll make you a leg of lamb," she said. I went out to Lesbos Agora in downtown Boston near the Greek section, of town. Here I bought the leg of lamb and a few other things that afternoon. Greek olives and garlic and bread. We all loved lamb and salad. I then went to the Stop and Shop and she could not get over the supermarket here.

They did not have one like this in Greece. The meal that she prepared was delicious and a rest for my father as he did not have to cook. She was amazed at the television set which broadcast in color. Back then not every program was in color.

Luckily Walt Disney had pushed color TV and more and more programs were in color, but not all.

That night when I went in to say good night to Aunt Suzanne she said, "Anastasi," my Greek name, "please take a picture of me in bed here so they can see it back in Greece." I said, "Sure Aunt Suzanne." So I took a picture of her in bed in my bedroom.

She wrote to her daughter, Valentina, and sent the picture along with it.

CHAPTER TWENTY-NINE

My Father's Illness

Sometime later, my father's feet started to swell up at his ankles. We thought it was maybe because of standing on his feet all day. The fault, that he had, was to stop at Max's barroom as he got off the bus coming from work every day. You could not miss this barroom, as you got off the bus, it stared in your face.

He drank beer and whiskey. I hated it. It brought back terrible memories of the arguments my mother and father had and I was in the middle of them, especially about his womanizing.

Dr. Saperstein made house calls and I called him right away. "George you must stop drinking." At that moment, I turned to my father and said, "If you don't care about me think of Nicky, Leon, and Johnny." "You know, don't put a guilt trip on me," he said. I then lashed out to him. "You know that you killed ma as surely as if you put a knife in her." He turned to me and said, "I don't know what's going to become of you, when I am gone." "You tell me that," I said. "I am sick of arguing with you." "Leave me alone, will you." Then I said, "You never really loved me. How could you be jealous of your own son? I hate you. You never bought me a pair of socks. You took me to the movies once in my life. I was seven years old at the time. 'What did you do? You jerked off with another guy. Here I am a seven-year-old kid looking at you at what you are doing. Is that the way you were to teach me about sex? Jerk off some guy then I'll know about sex. You were never a father to me. You never were. You never said I love you, son, or put your arms around me."

"You were jealous of me even when I was saving money. You went to ma, and said you leave him have money. What kind of a father is that?" I cried but the hurt was there, as he looked at me. I left and went out. I could not stand to look at him. He had Aunt Suzanne for company. She did not understand English, but knew something was wrong. He had his sister for company, and here again I may have made a mistake in bringing her here to America. I went out not only to get some air, but also to fill the prescriptions that Dr. Saperstein gave me for my father. I had the prescriptions filled, and returned to the house some time later. Everyone had gone to bed. The next day, I gave my father his medicine and he took them as the doctor had prescribed. I took Aunt Suzanne shopping. I bought her a pair of shoes and a winter coat. She had two watches that I gave her.

My father came home not too well. The swelling had increased. I called Dr. Saperstein and he came right over. He said, "I'll have to put him in the hospital, the swelling is worse. I told him he would have to raise his legs so the swelling would go down." Our problem of who was going through our bureau drawers had to take a backseat. At the hospital, Dr. Saperstein had some tests done on my father. The following day after work I went with my younger brother Johnny to the hospital and spoke to Dr. Saperstein. He said, "The tests done on your father came back and he has cirrhosis of the liver caused by excessive alcoholism. "He added, "The damage had been done." I thanked Dr. Saperstein. He said he would have to be transferred to the Lemuel Shattuck Hospital for prolonged illness. He said, "There may be a chance that, with care, he might pull through." Johnny and I went in to see him and told him that he was being transferred to the Lemuel Shattuck Hospital, in Jamaica Plain. I told him that I would try and get up there to the hospital at least five times a week or more. Aunt Stella called me, and asked me why my father wanted to see her. Again his evil mind was working against me. I didn't know it at that time. It had to do with the house. He was still trying to wrestle the house from me. He thought that I would throw my brothers out into the street. I would never do that because of the promise I gave to my mother.

Aunt Stella and Uncle Nick went to see my father before he was transferred to the Lemuel Shattuck. That night she called me. "Sonny, do you know why your father wanted to see me? It's because of the house," she said. "So what about the house?" I said. "So you won't deprive your brothers of their share in the house, if you sell it." I snapped back and said, "What an evil bastard he is. I'll tell you something, Aunt Stella, the night my mother died at your house, on Lawrence Road, I made her a promise, but I didn't tell anyone. Now I am telling you and you are the only one I am telling. We were able to talk through her eyes, as she couldn't speak because of her illness. I promised her that I would take care of my brothers no matter what. I would never want them split up. She understood me, and was able to die in peace knowing that I would keep my word as long as I lived. All, of his life he has had an evil mind. Before and after my mother died, he has tried many times to wrestle the house from me. Aunt Stella, thank you for going to see him." "Sonny, listen I know of what you are going through." "Really? Aunt Stella, no one knows unless you live through this. I made the papers and I brought his sister here, and still I am no good as a son. Aunt Stella, I am going to see him tonight and I'll call you. Sorry, I let everything come out. I'm disgusted." I hung up the telephone, and started to get ready to go and see my father. I had made supper for my brothers and Aunt Suzanne. I told them that I was going to see our father and would be home right after that.

CHAPTER THIRTY

My Father Dies

When I arrived, I went up to see him. I said, "Hi, Dad." He begged me, "Sonny, take me home. Please, don't let me die here." "Is that what you want, Dad?" I asked.

"Okay, I'll bring you home. Aunt Suzanne and I will take care of you at home. I will make the arrangements for the ambulance to bring you home." I said good night to him, and told him he would be home tomorrow. When I went home I told my brothers, Nicky, Leo, and Johnny that Dad wanted to come home, and I had made the arrangements for him to come tomorrow. I told Aunt Suzanne in Greek so she would be prepared for his arrival. The next morning, the ambulance arrived from the Lemuel Shattuck Hospital. I had his room ready. The paramedics brought him up in a stretcher and placed him on his bed. I thanked them, and they left.

When I returned to see that he was all right in bed, he put his hands up and clapped that he was home. For days I took care of him. Eventually, he could not go to the bathroom, and I got a bedpan for him. I would change his sheets twice a day, and wash him up. Aunt Suzanne did help me as much as she could but everything rested on my shoulders. I noticed his stomach was getting bigger, and I called Dr. Saperstein. The first thing he said was, "I'll have to put him back in the hospital. I can see that you have had a tough time. I'll make all the arrangements for the ambulance, Ernie. This is to much for all of you to handle." I went over to the bed and told my father, "Look, Dad, it's awfully hard. They will take care of you better at

Malden Hospital, and I'll be up to see you every day." The next day my youngest brother Johnny, and I went to Malden Hospital to see him. When I saw him, I said to Johnny, "Dad's asleep." I kept looking at him, as he lay there in bed at the hospital. I went over to wash him with Johnny on my right side. "Dad, Dad wake up," I said. There was no response. I felt his forehead. It was warm, his hands lukewarm. "Oh God, Johnny, I think Dad died." I called for the nurse to examine him. "Your father passed away," she said. I felt numb, but I could not cry for him, neither could I love him, like I loved my mother. He had not given us a good life.

There and then I said to myself if ever I got married and had children, they would never go through what I am going through. The hurt would always be there. No one or nothing could make it go away. You must live it to know what it is. I had to call Maistrellis, the undertaker, and start calling some of my relatives and my father's friends.

Where my mother is buried there was another grave that I bought, but it was a grave that was not next to my mother's. My father would be buried a grave over from my mother. The wake would be from 5 p.m. to 9 p.m. one day only, on Thursday and the funeral on Friday with burial at Harmony Grove Cemetery. Father Nickolopoulos would be officiating at the church services on Friday at Saint Vasilios Church on Paleologos Street.

At the wake I introduced Aunt Suzanne to many people that she did not know.

Flowers were sent from the family. I would not cry looking at my father in the casket. I could only reflect on the hurts that I remembered so well. As solemn as it was, the funeral only helped me remember my mother's funeral just five years earlier. After the burial, and the traditional fish dinner in memory of my father at the church hall, I thanked everyone for coming. It was such a dreaded day. I had the weekend to reflect on everything, and what I would do now.

CHAPTER THIRTY-ONE

My New Job

Something caught my eye in the Sunday paper. Jobs are waiting for you in the airline industry. I went to the Bay State Airline Academy and applied for the six-month course, which I would attend twice a week. The instructors were from the airline industry, and I learned quite a lot. In the meantime, I confronted My Aunt Suzanne about fishing in my brother's bureaus as well as mine. We all knew she was doing this. To get her out of the house, I took her to see my father's friends, Tasia and Sam Tzouvalekas in Ipswich, Massachusetts. I would take her to see Aunt Penny and Uncle Louie in Dracut, and then other visits to Aunt Stella and Uncle Nick on Lawrence Road in Medford. I would take her to visit my koumbara Sofia in Cambridge. In this way she wasn't home constantly.

Time had passed and now the six months were up. The airline school also guaranteed placement service. There were two jobs available, one at Trans World Airlines and one at United Airlines. There were eight of us that applied.

Unfortunately, I didn't get either one. Two days later the placement director, Tom Benson, called me at home in the evening to say that there were six openings at Eastern Airlines at Logan Airport. Mr. Benson told me they were part-time positions, but they could lead to full time. He told me to see Bruce Tilson at Eastern Airlines at Logan Airport. I called the Lahey Clinic to tell them that I would not be in the next day as I was not feeling well. I was so excited, I couldn't wait to take a shower and get my suit on.

I drove to Logan Airport, and parked in the terminal parking area. Then I walked to Eastern Airlines. There I was directed to Bruce Tilson's office. I walked down the long corridor past gates one through four and finally reached his door. I knocked and walked into his office. There sitting in his chair behind his desk I was greeted by a handsome man with blond hair and blue eyes. "Hi I'm Bruce Tilson he said. "Hi, I'm Ernest Gregory. I'm glad to meet you,"

He said, "Well, Bay State Academy called me and I told them that I had part-time openings. It is part time and different hours," he said. I said, "Great when do I start?"

"Okay how about this Thursday at 7 a.m. sharp?" he asked. "Okay, thank you very much, Mr. Tilson." "Ernest, call me Bruce." "Okay Bruce." I was so excited I did not want to trip over myself. I drove home back to Malden and told my brothers of my good news. They, Leo and Johnny, were happy for me. I turned to Aunt Suzanne and told her in Greek and she seemed happy for me. Nicky wasn't home yet. I told him later.

So he seemed happy for me. I could not wait for Thursday to start my new job. I called my old job and resigned.

In the meantime, I noticed my brothers Leon and Johnny packing their suitcases. I said, "What are you doing and where are you going?" "Sonny, we didn't want you to worry big brother," said Johnny. "We have signed up for the Air Force. You can't stop us." "Why didn't you at least tell me what you were doing?" I said, looking with disbelief. "You would have tried to stop us, Sonny," Leon said. "We leave tomorrow," Johnny said. "Dad is gone, and we wanted to do something, and now we can." Leon said.

"So instead of getting drafted with the Vietnam War going on, we did the better thing and enlisted for four years. Don't worry, Sonny," Leo said, "we will be fine." I just collapsed on to the kitchen chair. My eyes became glassy. "I've taken care of you all these years," I said. "We will be in Texas for a few weeks, then one of us is headed for Alaska, I believe it is me" Leo said. "I am going to Thailand, Sonny," Johnny said. "What?" I said. "Oh my God, Vietnam is next door," I said. "Why is this happening?" Good news, and bad news altogether.

Vietnam was not news. I was fourteen years old when I had read the French made a last stand at Dien Bein Phu in 1954 against the Viet Cong. The French had lost.

President Eisenhower sent in military advisors. Gradually, after that, military forces were added. Then when John F. Kennedy became president he inherited this problem, and the military buildup began on a much more rapid escalation. Now there were thousands in Vietnam. It was a full-fledged war, and undeclared when President Kennedy was assassinated, President Johnson made things worse by sending more troops over there to Vietnam. The next day was one of the worst days in my life, seeing my brothers leave. I don't remember how many times I cried as I said good-bye. "If there is a God, please protect them from harm." I said to myself as I hugged and kissed them. It was sad, very sad. A part of me was leaving with them. After they left, I took my aunt, and went to see Aunt Stella and Uncle Nick in Medford. There Aunt Stella talked with Aunt Suzanne and tried to get to know her better. We returned home that evening to Malden. It was Wednesday evening, and I was getting ready for my new job at Logan Airport the next day. I told Aunt Suzanne I would be working all day, as I would be training on the job.

On Thursday morning I reported at 7 a.m. I knew that to make full time I would never say no to anything that they would want me to do. I would never be absent even if I had a cold. I was introduced to Richard Grinnell, who would be with me for the next week and a half. He taught me to take the passenger's tickets and baggage, also to weight and balance the aircraft. Eastern Airlines had a lot of different aircraft; the Constellation, D C- 6, the Lockheed Electra, and the new jets coming on from McDonald-Douglas. The Lockheed Electra had a different configuration as the first-class section was in the rear of the plane, not in the front section, or in airplane talk, the first- class section was in aft and the coach section was forward.

Every time a passenger was seated in only the aft part of the cabin the weight changed for the captain to adjust his instruments for takeoffs and landings. Eastern Airlines had eight gates. Gates one and three were for the hourly shuttle to New York's LaGuardia Airport. This shuttle service ran from 7 a.m. until 10 p.m.

Gates seven and eight were for the Newark, New Jersey shuttle and started at 7:30 a.m. and went until 10:30 p.m. Eastern also had Boeing 707s and DC- 8s. These larger aircraft were for longer haul flights to San Juan, Puerto Rico, and Los Angeles, California via Atlanta, Georgia. I was learning from Richard Grinnell. He would take me on board the aircraft to teach me how to put the liquor on board. I was classified as a ramp agent. Two agents would always work a flight. One would work the weight and balance of the aircraft, and make sure it was mechanically fit for travel by talking to the maintenance supervisor, and then to see that the aircraft had been fueled, cleaned, and catered. Back then meals were served on flights of longer duration. The other agent would take the passengers tickets, and announce when to board the flight.

The Eastern shuttles to either LaGuardia and Newark were different. Passengers showed up before departure time and were guaranteed a seat no matter if there was just one passenger in a second plane. The first plane was usually a jet and the second a Constellation. There were no jetways then. You went from the terminal building then outside to the aircraft. If it rained the airline supplied umbrellas to the passengers, who would return them to a cart at the bottom of the stairs of the aircraft. I enjoyed this very much and I did my utmost to do a good job. I can remember saluting the captain when I worked the weight and balance of the aircraft. This was to indicate that all was set for him to taxi from the gate and proceed to the runway for takeoff. Back then when there were no jetways, aircraft would taxi out on their own power. Today they are towed away from the gate area by maintenance. There was never a dull day on this job.

One day Richard Grinnell and I were sitting on a Boeing 727 in first class waiting for a flight to come in, so we would work the flight out. Richard Grinnell turned to me and said, "Ernie, I swing both ways." I looked at him puzzled. I guess I was pretty naive, because the next thing he said was, "I enjoyed having sex with men and women. Ernie, I was married and I have a twelve-year-old son." I said, "Richard, try and be a father to your son." "Why? I didn't ask to come here in this life," he said. Then to my surprise he opened up to me. "Ernie I loved my wife very much, and I mean very much. I came home one day and found her in bed with another man." "Oh, Richard I am very sorry to hear that." "No, don't be sorry," he said. "Look," he said, "you're ripe for marriage." "Me, I am not even thinking of that. Let's just be friends." "I'm for that," he said. I liked him for his honesty, and we became good friends. I met my other fellow employees and I never said no to working at any time day or night.

At the airlines you worked at totally different hours and had different days off, I was entering my fifth month at Eastern Airlines and, of course, I wanted to become a full- time employee. I wanted to know if all my hard work had paid off. I thought, would I be made full time? One day, when my workday was almost finished, I heard my name over the public- address system. "Agent Gregory report to the supervisor's office." Bruce. whose voice I recognized over the public- address system, would always pronounce my name as if I were Russian. I laughed. I reached the supervisor's office and knocked on the door. "Come in," said the voice on the other side of the door. I opened the door to his office and walked in. He looked at me. He had accented my name again, as if he knew I was Russian. "Bruce I am not Russian." "No, but you look it" he said. "I do, thanks," we laughed "Ernie we are going to make you full time," he said.

Just as he said that, I let out a sigh of relief and yelled "wow" with a loud voice. "Bruce I have to get back to work. I am working with Richard Grinnell." "Okay, Ernie." He looked at me with those big blue eyes, his blond hair hanging over his forehead. I was so excited, I could hardly work. The joy of knowing that I could finally establish my roots since the tragedy of the last five years was overwhelming.

CHAPTER THIRTY-TWO

Full Time

I returned to gate seven, to work the flight to San Juan, Puerto Rico which we called the "Roach Coach." The reason for the name was that when this flight came back to the States, it had cockroaches on the plane. Of course, the plane had to be sprayed. So now when I returned to the gate the flight was already boarding. Richard turned to me, and said, "What' s the matter Ernie?" "Well I'll bust if I don't tell you." "Okay," Richard said, what?" "I am being made full time" "We will able to go on trips together," he said. I looked at him puzzled and said, "Okay." Now being made full time. I would now have regular days off, even though they weren't Saturday or Sunday. I was a morning person while others liked the afternoon shifts. I knew that I would not see Richard Grinnell, because I liked the morning shift and he liked the afternoon shift. I would now be working flights and meeting flights and have my own schedule each and every day.

I had to buy two black uniforms. Now I felt full time. I had to wear a hat. One day when I was getting ready to go home as my shift was over, I met Richard Grinnell coming into the locker room. We hadn't seen each other since I went mornings and he stayed on the afternoon shift. He exclaimed, "Ernie, wow, I see you got your uniform, swell. Say you look sexy with that hat on." "Okay don't over react. I have to catch the bus, we'll talk another time, all right Richard?" "Okay, Ernie, I'll see you later, and we can get together soon," Richard said. "So long," I said, and went out the door, and up the corridor to catch the bus to the subway.

One day while I was working the 11 a.m. shuttle to New York's LaGuardia Airport, I noticed across the way from Gate 3 from where I was, there was a blond headed fellow with one of his legs up on a chair. I kept looking at this fellow, who seemed familiar. I got it, after gazing three times at him, and he knew I was looking at him. "Are you going on the shuttle to New York," I said. "Do I still have some time before I decide to take this shuttle or the next one?" he said. Then I realized who he was.

It was Troy Donahue, the movie actor, I was staring at. I went over and introduced myself to him and told him of I had seen most his movies.

I didn't recognize him at first because he had a beard. He had ten minutes to decide to take the 11 a.m. shuttle or the next one. We spoke for about five minutes more, and I told him if he wanted to get on board he would have to do so now.

He decided to get on board. I said, "I hope to see you again and have a pleasant flight." I returned to the desk in the waiting room and made a final boarding call and looked up the corridor to see if there were any other passengers trying to take this shuttle.

There were none, and I went on board to give the weight and balance graph to the captain. I spoke briefly to the flight attendant, and at the same time I turned, and looked down into the cabin. There I saw Troy Donahue, and I waved to him without telling anyone who he was. He acknowledged, and waved back to me. I immediately went down the stairs of the aircraft, and retracted the stairs. The captain had already started the engines, and I had put my earplugs in my ears. I retreated farther back from the aircraft. I saluted the captain. This salute told him he was all clear to leave the gate.

The customer sales representative Ed Landis had a celebrity boarding the flight to Miami, Florida, which I was working. I had to preboard him from the VIP lounge; you could go from the lounge to the flight without being noticed. He was the singer Tom Jones.

Just prior to ten minutes before departure time I would call the paging center for a final boarding call for the flight. Eastern Airlines would overbook flights, as did other carriers. People made reservations and didn't cancel them so usually there were enough seats for the passengers who showed up. But this particular flight was overbooked. The last passenger who got on the flight was a Mr. Cheng. When, John the fellow who I was working the flight with, went out to the aircraft to close out the flight there were more passengers than there were seats.

When John returned to gate 4,he asked, "Who was the last passenger to board the flight?" I said, "It was a Mr. Cheng." "Okay we will have to pull the Chink." "What?" I said. "The Chink." Yes, the Chink, he said. John went on board the aircraft and asked Mr. Cheng to deplane. Mr. Cheng was furious and demanded to see a supervisor. He started talking in Chinese as I brought him inside the building to see my supervisor. Ed Conlon was the supervisor on duty. Mr. Cheng was told that he would be put on the next flight to Miami. He was still mad as hell. He threw his garment bag down and wanted to punch me out.

"Wow," I said. John was on the phone to the state police. "We have a live one that wants to punch the agent out." "We'll be right there," the voice on the other end said.

Mr. Cheng jumped up and down, waiting for me to get angry so he could have something to pin on me, and then he would be justified in taking a punch at me. I turned away from him and tried not to show any emotion. Just then two state troopers showed up. They grabbed him, handcuffed him, and led him to their car.

Towards the end of my shift, I thought it would be quiet. I was mistaken. I was working the next flight on my shift. I noticed the short, roly-poly comedienne, Totie Fields. "I've seen you on TV." I said. "Do I know you?" She said. "No, but" "No nothing, don't bother me." I said, "Excuse me, I need your boarding pass." "What are you looking for a date?" "No." "Well, what?" "Please I would like your boarding pass, there are other passengers." "Okay, okay, I'll see you again young man. My phone number is there in case you change your mind." Boy, if this wasn't a pickup, I don't know what it was? After the plane was cleared for takeoff, I looked up and saw a hand in the window. It was Totie Fields waving to me and throwing kisses. I laughed, and waved good-bye. Wow a pick up. I thought to myself.

The next flight was even more interesting than the last one. This was my last flight on my shift. I was meeting the inbound from New York's LaGuardia Airport. I got to know the crews of various flights. One girl that I knew from meeting her earlier was Alice Farwell; she was a flight attendant who worked this flight.

Alice Farwell was a pretty girl with a good shape and big boobs, wow. She was the last one off the plane. She greeted me, "Hi, Ernie, you are looking handsome tonight. Here, this is for you," she said. It was a paperback book by Grace Metalious, called Peyton Place. I noticed a bookmark inside on which was written, 'I am staying at the Park Plaza Hotel, please come up and see me." "She looked back at me. I was stunned, but what the heck, she was gorgeous. I felt what did she see in me? After my shift was over, I couldn't wait to get home, and shower and shave, and away I went.

When I got to the Park Plaza I asked the desk clerk for her room number. I figured I would surprise her. I took the elevator up to the fourth floor as the clerk told me her room number was 405. I knocked a few times. Just as I was about to leave, the door opened and there standing in the doorway was Alice. She had a bikini lounger on, and just then I noticed someone else. "Excuse me," I said, "I am sorry if I am interrupting something. Listen Alice, I won't bother you again." "Ernie, I didn't know you were coming tonight." "I can see I would have to wait around for my turn in bed."

"You know, you are nothing but a whore," I said. "Get out of here, before I."

"Before you what?" I said. I left disgusted to know that she didn't care whom she had in bed as long as she could get laid.

The next day I heard that a movie crew was coming to do some filming of the movie "The Thomas Crown Affair" with Steve McQueen. My supervisor told me to be prepared as I more than likely would be in the movie. They were going to film the 10:00 o'clock shuttle to LaGuardia, and I was the gate agent working that flight. I was so excited. Wow, I was the envy of my fellow employees.

I met Steve McQueen and it was a great thrill. I told him how I enjoyed Wanted Dead or Alive on TV. We got along great. The filming lasted for about thirty minutes, and it was over. I thanked him, and hoped that the movie would be a big hit. He thanked me, and left. The rest of the day was normal until I heard my name over the public address system. "Agent Gregory, contact the control center." I called the control center.

It was Joe Mozzarella. "Okay, Joe, what's up?" "Ernie, Rose Kennedy is on the inbound from New York and you are scheduled to meet the flight. Listen, Ernie her luggage is in the front bin and the rest of the passengers' luggage is in the rear. Instead of getting a porter for her, when you meet her, take her luggage of the plane, and take her and her luggage to a car that will be waiting for her outside the terminal."

"Okay Joe, I'll take good care of her." I said. I met the flight and put the stairs down, and stood at the bottom of the stairs as the passengers deplaned. All the passengers got off, and then the flight attendant signaled to me that Rose Kennedy was coming to the front of the aircraft to deplane. As she came the stairs toward me I offered my hand, and she thanked me. I told her that first I would get her luggage, and then we would go up to the waiting car. She told me she had closed the house in Palm Beach, Florida, and was coming to open the house in Hyannis Port on Cape Cod. I told her that I had worked with her cousin Alice Gargan at the Lahey Clinic in Boston. "Yes, she is Dr. Poppen's secretary. What is your name?" "Ernest Gregory," Mrs.

Kennedy. "I want to remember that, so when I see Alice Gargan and tell her I met you." We approached the front doors of the terminal. As I opened the doors, I could see the car, and the state troopers by the car, to make sure she left all right. I said, "Good -bye." She thanked me, and said, "I will mention you to Alice. If I take the shuttle again I will ask for you Ernest." With those kind words we parted. My shift was nearly over, and I was glad I was going home. It was long day.

CHAPTER THIRTY-THREE

Trouble with Aunt Suzanne

When I got home there was a letter from the immigration department. It had to do with Aunt Suzanne. I had gotten a six-month extension before and I was entitled for another one. I was happy about that. I knew eventually I would have to take her back to Greece. On my days off I would take her to see my Aunt Penny and Uncle Louie, and also to see Tasia and Sam Tzouvalekas in Ipswich, Massachusetts. Aunt Penny and I had become close since my mother had passed away. Of course Tasia and Sam Tzouvalekas were old friends of my fathers. The visit to Aunt Penny and Uncle Louie was always good. Aunt Penny had a barroom on Textile Avenue in Dracut, right next to her mother's house. Aunt Penny and Uncle Louie lived on Homestead Avenue in Dracut.

I always enjoyed going there. This visit was unusual. Aunt Penny took me aside to tell me some shocking news about myself. "Sonny, your Aunt Suzanne isn't exactly as good as she pretends to be." "What do you mean?" I asked.

"She says you are a queer, a fag." "I am what?" "She accuses you of immoral things." I was furious. I did not say anything. I kept my cool, but when we reached home, I confronted her and she denied it. "Listen Aunt Suzanne, I don't go with gays.

All I do is work and come home." Of course I could not tell her that I had a date with a flight attendant that went sour. That was my own business not hers.

The things got worse at home. One day my brother came and told me, "Either she goes or I go." She had gone through my brother's bureau looking for money as he would keep his wallet in his bureau and she had seen him put it there. Now I thought to myself.

Did I do a good thing bringing a stranger into our home, even though she was related to us? I spoke to her, "Aunt Suzanne, look, I bought you clothes, a winter coat, and you have two wrist watches. You are still not satisfied."

"Aunt Suzanne, in a few months I will be eligible to get tickets at a reduced rate, and take you back to Greece. I know you miss your daughters Valentina and Irene. She was happy as now she would see her daughters, and we would have peace form her snooping in our house.

One day I was passed by Joe Mozzarella in the control center "Ernie, there is a general up at the ticket counter. He's Greek, but he speaks some English. He is on your flight 187 to Washington D.C." "Okay I'll take care of him." I said. When he arrived at gate 6, I greeted him in Greek. "Oh," he said, "a Greek boy. Good-day to you."

"And to you" I said. "What's going on in Greece? You generals have toppled the government, you have strangled democracy and have a dictatorship over there." I said. "What are you talking about?" he said. His voice rose to the pinnacle of an opera star. He was mad. "Where do you live?" he asked. I said, "I dare you to come to my house to talk about this. You brought down the elected government. How can you say that it is good for Greece, you hypocrite, you liar?" I infuriated him. They could hear the shouting all the way up the concourse. People were all startled; my co-workers came down from the various areas where they were working. The ground hostess Alfreda Tosai said, "Ernie has a live one down at the gate for Washington, D.C.. He is like a madman.

My co-worker Michael Cleary was working the flight with me and had returned to the gate to tell me the flight was ready for boarding. I proceeded to take the general's ticket and wished him a good flight. I then noticed his name on the ticket. It was Efstathios Papamichael. Finally, through all the ranting and raving, he boarded the plane.

I had spoken to him in Greek and no one knew what I had said. He never lowered his voice during all of our conversation. I never saw the general again, and he never came to my house as I dared him to do. The rest of my shift that day passed without excitement.

The next day I was working the Newark, New Jersey shuttle and it was around 1:00 p.m. when a man and woman approached gate 8. I recognized him immediately. It was Robert Young and his wife. I spoke to him and told him "Father Knows Best" was one program that I had always watched. He said, "We were at the end of the series because the children were getting older and we were running out of ideas and story plots." I had watched his new show "Window on Main Street," but it didn't bare well. I wished him and his wife a pleasant flight as they boarded their flight. Toward the end of my shift I was asked to work overtime and I said yes as they were in a bind.

Someone had called in sick. I was working the 6:30 p.m. shuttle to Newark when I met the actor Cameron Mitchell. I remembered him in the film "Love Me or Leave Me" with Doris Day and James Cagney.

"I have acted in more films than that," he said. He was coming from Cape Cod where he had a home.

CHAPTER THIRTY-FOUR

My First Trip to Greece

Time passed and Christmas and New Year's came and went. It was now February and my duration of waiting was over. I had now passed six months, and was eligible to start to receive my benefits. This month brought me what I wanted. My first flight out of the country. February 18, 1968. How could I forget this date?

I told Aunt Suzanne to get ready. I helped Aunt Suzanne pack, and my brother Nicky was happy that I was taking her back to Greece. Since I supported my aunt I was able to buy her ticket at a very reduced rate. I paid only ninety dollars for a one-way ticket to Athens, Greece.

She did not like it here. The language was difficult. She knew only a few people that she had met through me, when I took her out in my car, on my days off. I brought her here, so my father would see one of his sisters after forty-five years. He saw her and now he was dead. There was no reason for her to stay any longer. She had some people, who were Greek, so she could converse in Greek, and make her more comfortable while she was here. I took her, and she met one of my mother's co-workers from Massachusetts Leather Products, Sophie Panos. She had met her husband through my mother and grandmother. I was Sophie's best man-years earlier. Sophie had one child named Mary and I was her godfather.

I made arrangements with some of my fellow workers and swapped days with them and I could now go my first trip out of the country. I had called Sophie to say good-bye and told her that I was leaving the next day with my aunt to take her back to Athens, Greece.

Well, the next day we headed for the airport right to Eastern Airlines flight 41 to New York's JFK Airport.

I was surprised to see Sophie and Mary my godchild and two of Sophie's friends, Mary Anastos and her daughter Betsy.

"Sophie, I never expected to see you here. What a surprise?" I said. I greeted them all, as did my Aunt Suzanne. I looked at Mary Anastos's daughter and said, "I am going to call you when I get back." Betsy said, "Yeah, yeah sure." She had the most beautiful eyes that I had ever seen. Cat's eyes. I kissed them all, as did my aunt, and they said in Greek, Kalo Taxidei, meaning have a good trip. I turned and gave my tickets to Richard Grinnell. In those days we had no such thing as security as they have now. Family and friends could come to the gate and see you off on your flight. "Well, Ernie, you're finally on your way, have a good trip, and enjoy yourself," Richard said. I gave my aunt's and my ticket to Richard, and we boarded the plane. It took us about 70 minutes to arrive at JFK airport as we had to wait for clearance to land.

We checked in at the Olympic Airways ticket counter and the ticket agent told us the gate we would have to go to. They would give us our seat assignment at the gate. On this particular flight since it was not summer season, Olympic's flight 812 would make two stops before arriving in Athens. The stops would be Paris, and then Rome. I sent a telegram to my cousin Valentina that we would arrive at 5:00 p.m. Athens time. I only hoped that our luggage would get transferred. Going to the gate back in 1968, there was no security like there is now. You had the freedom to come and go, which is not the case today. I bought Aunt Suzanne a cup of coffee and a snack. I bought myself a cup of tea.

Soon we went to the gate to get ready for boarding the flight. I remember looking out the window, and seeing the Boeing 707 and looking at the fuselage and it had written on it "City of Knossos." The agent made an announcement to come to the counter to receive your seat assignments

The gate agent made the announcement that the flight was ready for boarding. We boarded in customary fashion by the gate agent calling passengers with the rear seat numbers in coach. We had seats toward the middle of the aircraft. I recognized that my aunt was nervous about flying, as this was her first flight on an airplane. So I sat at the window. I can still remember that evening as if it was yesterday. The flight attendants in blue uniforms and white blouses. These are Greece's flag colors, blue and white. I got our carry-on baggage and stored it under my seat and under Aunt Suzanne's seat. She said, "einai orairo pedi mou. It is very nice" and I said, "Malista tis eipa Yes it is." I then said in Greek "Tha anaxorisi eis oligon diastima. The airplane will depart shortly."

This was my first flight out of the country. I was nervous and excited all rolled up into one. We finally got to relax. I told Aunt Suzanne that she should try to relax and put the armrests up. With her small size (she was only five feet 6 inches) she could lie down on the three seats easily. I told her we would probably have something to eat before that. En taxei the words for all right came out of her mouth. Of course, she wanted to smoke. Back then you could smoke on the airplane when the no smoking sign was turned off. I could see up the aisle that the flight attendants were putting their aprons on and it looked as if we were going to be served dinner. This was great, then Aunt Suzanne could take her nap and I could read my book. Eventually the flight attendants arrived at our seats. They asked us if we preferred chicken or beef. Aunt Suzanne preferred chicken, I preferred beef. "What the heck, it's probably better than nothing," I thought. We finished our meals. I had put the armrests up so now she could go to sleep as the flight attendants would shut the cabin lights and only the reading lights and emergency lights were left on. I said, "Theia eisai en taxei. "Aunt Suzanne are you all right?" She answered, "Yes I am." She was on one side of the aisle and I was on the other side. I took my shoes off as I was going to try to sleep. Our first stop would be Paris. It would take us six and a half hours to get there. I had just settled to rest my head on a pillow that I had taken from the overhead compartment, when I heard a faint cry from two rows in front of me. I got up from my makeshift bed and went to see who was upset. I walked up the aisle and there was this little old lady sitting there crying. In Greek I said to her, "What's the matter?" "My boy I am going home and I am alone. I visited my daughter and my son-in-law. I would like something to drink, okay." "All right" I said, and I turned around and walked back to where the lavatories were. There I saw three flight attendants asleep. In Greek I kept saying, "Excuse me," "Excuse me," to awaken them.

One of the young ladies opened her eyes. "What is it?" she said, in a soft voice. "Please there is a lady in seat thirty-three c who's asking for a glass of water." "Okay, okay" she said. "She is by herself." I said. "She is lonely and she wants a glass of water." She got up and went to the galley and immediately got her the water.

The lady thanked her. I spoke to her to reassure her that I was just two rows back. She thanked me several times more and said, "I don't know what I would have done without your help. My name is Eleni." "It's okay," I said "I am here." I returned to my seat, and as tired as I was, I got off to sleep. Later, awakened by air turbulence I raised my window shade to see the sun rise above the clouds. It was a beautiful sight. I thought of the elderly lady two rows up, and went to tell her what was going on. I wanted to keep my eye on the helpless soul. She was awake. I told her that they would be serving breakfast, and that we would be landing in Paris in about an hour. Then we would go on to Rome, and finally on to Athens.

As we had finished breakfast, the captain made an announcement over the loud- speaker telling us we would be landing at Paris's Orly Airport in about 40 minutes, and to fasten our seat belts. After a short layover, it would be about one and, a half hours before we reached Rome.

Looking out the window the weather looked good. We flew over the Alps. What a beautiful sight, and we turned south flying on to Rome. After about a thirty-minute layover in Rome, we were headed for our final destination to Athens.

I turned and looked at Aunt Suzanne to see if she was all right. As we approached the Athens airport, I said, "Aunty we are here, we will be landing soon." Aunt Suzanne was smiling as she was coming home, and would soon be with her daughters Valentina and Irene. She had not seen them for over two years. We circled Athens, and looking out the window I could see a wonderful sight. It was the Acropolis. The famous mount where the ruins of the Parthenon are. This is the "Masterpiece of Architecture" and just across from it are the Kariatides, or the Porch of the Maidens. I had read so much about them. I could not compose myself. I started crying I was so happy, genuinely happy to know that I would be able to see and touch these historic monuments. To see that man can make something so beautifully proportioned in architecture, and realize that the ancient Athenians lived under pure democracy. In the Agora they spoke freely, not fearing anyone or fearing being killed for their thoughts. We were coming down for a landing. I could not believe it. I was finally here. Olympic flight 812 had landed at Ellinikon Airport. I could see out the window that they were building a new airport, but we still came in at the old terminal.

Besides helping my aunt, I helped Eleni off the plane with her carry- on baggage. The local time was 5:00 p.m. and the weather was sunny with a temperature of around 20 Celsius. After clearing customs, suddenly I saw through the doors someone's hands waving over the people's heads. As soon as we came through the doors a woman ran up to Aunt Suzanne and grabbed and kissed her. George, her husband shook my hand and called me Taso as that is short for my name in Greek. He said, "Welcome to Greece." Valentina turned to me; her eyes full of tears, she kissed and hugged me. "I never thought that I would ever meet you," she said. She was so happy that she had met a cousin from America. As we walked toward a taxicab, I said, "Valli, why are you holding on to me so tight? You want to see if I am real?" "Ach, Taso," she said. The grip from her hand to my right arm became tighter and tighter. I turned to her husband and said, "George, I don't want you to feel jealous. We are first cousins and she hasn't seen other cousins, except the two from Aunt Paraskevi that live here in Piraeus. Valli, where are we headed?" To the cab driver she said, "We are going to a neighborhood in Piraeus called Drapetsona, 15 Kolokotrones Street." The cab driver said, "En taxei, malista." Meaning, "yes, all right." All this conversation of course was in Greek, as no one knew English. We would take the coastal road towards Piraeus from the airport. I could not see everything as evening fell on the city of Athens. Valentina told me, we were passing through the Tourkolimano then the Pasalimani. These two areas are very exclusive areas by the sea. We were passing the center of the port of Piraeus, Valentina said. The cab driver said, "Your first time in Greece." "Malista, proti fora." I answered, "Yes, first time in Greece?" Turning into Kolokotrones Street, we saw number fifteen, which was lit up.

It was still early as I adjusted my watch to the local time, which was 6:00 p.m. I took money from my wallet to pay the cab driver. "No Taso, I have it," George said. I insisted.

The drachma was thirty to the dollar, and the American dollar went a long way. The fare was sixty-five drachmas, and I gave him a tip besides. We got out and climbed the few steps to the front door. Upon entering the house there were numerous people I didn't know. Valli's sister, Irene, her husband, Stavros and their two sons, Daniel and Steven. The table in the dining room was long and spread with food for a king. I was urged to stay most of the night talking about our trip and how are things in America. They asked me about President Kennedy. I told them as much as I knew. The young people in America really looked up to him, I told them. I told them Bobby Kennedy was now running for president. President Johnson had befriended Greece when he stopped Turkey from invading the island of Cyprus in

1964. The majority of the island wanted union with Greece. Thus the friction between Greece and Turkey. The Greek government had been elected and headed by George Papandreou. When Nixon and Kissinger came into the White House, with the help of the C.I.A., the government was toppled and a dictatorship headed by Georgos Papadopoulos came to power and things changed and the movement to unite Cyprus collapsed. We had to be careful about talking freely as Greece was under a dictatorship. I said, "It's getting late." I thanked them all. I turned to Valli and said, "On second thought, I want to go and see Aunt Marianthi."

CHAPTER THIRTY-FIVE

Meeting Aunt Marianthi

It was Aunt Marianthi with whom I had corresponded for fifteen years. "Taso," Valli said, "I don't know if she is here. She is maybe with Uncle Vasili in Kefalonia."

Kefalonia is an island in the Ionian Sea off the coast of Greece on the western side toward Italy. Greece has two thousand islands, some are uninhabited, and most are very popular with tourists. Aunt Marianthi lived in Piraeus but in another part called Xatzikiriakeion.

I would have to take a cab there. "We will take you there," Valli and George said. I thanked them all and kissed Aunt Suzanne good-bye. I thought to myself as I left that Aunt Suzanne would talk more about my brothers and her relationship with her brother, my father. She would be good for that. She was always scheming. Who knows what she brought back with her smuggled in her clothes? Again I said good-bye. I walked out onto the street. Quiet, peace and quiet. Now to walk and get a cab to the neighborhood called Xatzikiriakeion. Valli and George hurried behind me. Soon we had walked to the main street. Soon I could see cars coming toward us. So as not to get run over we made sure that we stayed on the sidewalk. Valli was behind George and then me. Finally, a taxicab approached us and stopped as we made gestures with our hands. "I would like to go to Xatzikiriakeion," I told the driver, in Greek, and Valli and George came with me. I continued in Greek, "Do you know the neighborhood," I asked?

He answered, "Yes." I told him the address. "It is 48 Alexandrou Zaimis Street."

"Okay," he said. Valli then said, she was afraid that Uncle Vasili might be there.

"Well, that is the chance we will have to take," I remarked. Uncle Vasili was not liked by any of his wife's side of the family. He had caused a lot of trouble with my parents when he was in America during the war in the 1940s. The feeling was mutual as far as Valli and George were concerned. It was close to midnight now, and I did want to rest and sleep. I mentioned to Valli and George that I was sorry for inconveniencing them.

They said, "Don't worry about it." Soon we had approached the street where Aunt Marianthi lived. I told the cab driver to stop as I could see we were near number forty-eight. I paid him, thanked him, and we all got out of the cab.

Valli said, "Taso, we will wait here just in case Uncle Vasili is home." "Okay," I said. I walked up the few steps and rang the bell. Valli and George hid around the corner on Kairak Street. I rang the bell once more. A light went on, and I could see a figure coming through the portion of the door that had a smoked panel. The door opened slowly, and a figure of a woman gazed out on me. With that she gave out a loud scream. I said, "Aunt Marianthi," Not finishing what I started to say, she fainted and collapsed to the floor. I called for Valli and George to come quickly. George helped me to put her on the couch. I then looked to see were the kitchen was, and ran for a glass of water. Valli went and got a cold towel to put on her head. I happened to have an inhaler that I took with me no matter where I was. Inhaling the Vicks and drinking some water, she was coming out of it. Looking up at me, in Greek she said, "Anastasi is that you?" "Yes, aunty, it is I."

"My boy I can't believe it." "It's okay I'm here in the flesh." "My boy" she repeated. "Aunty, is Uncle Vasili here?" "No, he is in Kefalonia."

"Good" I said. I turned to Valli and George. "I am sorry for dragging you with me." I told them. "I am going to spend the night here with Aunt Marianthi, and go to my hotel in Athens tomorrow. I will be staying at the King's Palace just off Constitution Square. Is it all right Aunt Marianthi?" "Oh yes, Anastasi, I am so happy to have you stay." I said goodnight to Valli and George as did Aunt Marianthi, and they left. Aunt Marianthi was resting on her couch, and she looked up at me. "I can't believe that you're here," she exclaimed, tears in her eyes. "I know after fifteen years of writing to you, keeping in touch with so much that has happened to you and me. I never got to meet Aunt Paraskeve who went to live with her daughter in Corzensa, Italy. There she passed away, according to what you wrote to me." We talked for hours, and I asked her, "Why didn't you listen to my father and you would have been in America today and not here with your crazy husband my uncle?" "It is my fault I should have done so, but you can't go back my boy." She kept saying, "Taso, I still can't believe it. My boy, how wonderful to see you, and to touch you." Aunt Marianthi said. I said, "Uncle Vasili has been mean to you all these years. He is a tyrant. How could you stand him?" "I know," she said, I've gotten immune to him." I replied, "You would have had a much better life in America. Imagine no gambler for a husband, for which Uncle Vasili is famous."

My mother told me stories that when he and my father were partners, he would gamble very heavily. Luckily my father stopped him from losing his shirt, as we say in America. "You are not only my aunt, but you would have been my godmother, as the fellow who was my father's best man, Nicholas Theodore, would have been your husband. He was a good man." "Taso, it wasn't meant to be." "Don't say that, Aunt Marianthi." "Taso, I have to call him because if he finds out from someone that you are here, and he wasn't told by me, he will make it very difficult for me." "Okay, aunty, call him." "You know, Taso, he hasn't seen you since you were four years old." "Aunt Marianthi, we have to get some sleep, and we can talk some more in the morning."

In the morning, I could hear Aunt Marianthi opening the shutters as I turned to see what was waking me up. People were passing by in the street and I could hear her say that, her nephew from America had arrived. "Really," one woman said, "oh how wonderful. Is this the first time he has come to visit you?" "Yes it is." "I would like to come over to meet him and my daughter would too." "Aunt Marianthi," I said, "Please, I have to get dressed first before someone comes to meet me." "I quickly said, "Aunt Marianthi would you let me change my clothes," as I had my pajamas on and wanted to freshen up. "Taso these are only my neighbors," she said. "Aunt Marianthi you know them, I'm sure that they are very good people, but I need to get dressed before anyone comes in here." She was so excited from yesterday evening, that she kept looking at me to make sure it wasn't her imagination. A knock on the door brought this old lady into my aunt's parlor.

"Good morning, my boy. Oh, how wonderful it is to meet you. Your name is Anastasi, well my boy, my daughter's name is Anastasia. I forgot to introduce myself.

My name is Georgia and, of course, this is my daughter Anastasia." It wasn't long before the whole parlor was filled with neighbors, coming to meet me and possibly seeing if one of their daughters was right for me to take as my bride. I tried to excuse myself. Aunt Marianthi understood I was very uncomfortable. So my aunt asked everyone to come back later. I asked Aunt Marianthi, "Why are you crying?"

"Sometimes I can't stand it with your uncle but to see you here after writing to you for over fifteen years it brings me such great joy in my heart." "Listen, I am glad that all the neighbors are gone. I want to get dressed, and go to Athens as I have paid for my hotel there." I told her that I had my Polaroid camera with me and that after I got dressed I would take our picture together. "You will see it in a minute, I told her.

She could not believe it to see the picture in a minute." I freshened up and got dressed. Aunt Marianthi was in the kitchen. I set the camera and put myself in the picture and assured her that she would see herself in a minute. Just then the doorbell rang, and in came two nieces from Uncle Vasili's side of the family. I invited them to be in the picture. They couldn't believe that it would be seen in a minute. "Amazing," they said.

After saying my good-byes, I turned to Aunt Marianthi and said, "I am leaving for Athens, aunty, I have a hotel already paid for. I am staying at the Kings Palace Hotel in Constitution Square. It is next to the tomb of the Unknown Soldier." "Okay, my boy," she said. I called a taxicab from her telephone. I kissed her good-bye, and said I would be in touch within a day or so. I had a complete itinerary starting the next day. I had arranged for Chat Tours that would take me to places that I had only read about. I arrived at the hotel and checked in. The desk clerk asked me, "We were holding your room since yesterday, sir?" "Yes I know I was visiting relatives in Piraeus. Thank you." I went to my room, and went to bed.

CHAPTER THIRTY-SIX

Delphi

The next morning, I came down stairs and had breakfast. I then asked the desk clerk where the Chat Tours office was. He said that the office was around the corner. I knew that I had to be there early. I went around the corner from the hotel on Constitution Square to the Chat Tours office. A woman who introduced herself greeted me. "My name is Eleni, I will be your tour guide." "It is nice to meet you. You speak English and I speak Greek. My name is Anastasi." I boarded the bus for Delphi, which is about 100 miles north of Athens. Our first stop would be Daphni, which is just outside of Athens, where they were having a wine- tasting festival. I did try a variety of wines. Some were excellent. We passed by a monastery named Cassianes. We were on our way. I loved the winding roads through the hills. Our next stop was a Byzantine church; the name of it was Ossios Loukas, and it had beautiful icons.

Eleni, our guide, spoke fluent English. Everyone was a tourist and the one advantage was I spoke fluent Greek. Eleni enjoyed our conversation as we spoke in Greek and she asked me many things about America. She had to be careful as Greece was ruled by a dictatorship under Papadopoulos and freedom and was not like it was in America.

Eleni and I would talk freely away from any officials trying to spy on us. We passed the town of Arachova where the famous flokata rugs are made. At midday we finally arrived at Delphi. The place is beautiful. The oracle was situated on the side of the mountain. What a spectacular view. I could see that they had restored an ancient temple.

Fortunately, with my Polaroid camera I was able to take a picture with myself leaning up against one of the columns.

From this small temple we climbed to where the Oracle of Delphi was. Ruins prevail here, but a few columns are still standing. Here the priests gave out their predictions as to what would happen to various city-states. Greece, or Hellas, being a very mountainous country each city-state was independent of one another. Traveling from one city-state to another was difficult because of the mountains.

Democracy flourished and it was true democracy, representative not as it is in the United States. Eleni was very helpful and informative. I mentioned that I knew of a famous statue here, it was the "Charioteer." Climbing down the side of the mountain, I encountered a battalion of Greek soldiers. I greeted them with the familiar, "yiassas" in Greek. They stopped and greeted me and asked me where I was from. I said, "From America" They said, "Where in America?" I said, "Boston Massachusetts."

"We are glad to have met you," they said. I said good-bye to them, and had finally come to the door of the museum. It was cool as it was February 1968. Greece was not as cold as Boston would get, but cold enough. I walked through the entrance of the museum.

There were two rooms. Whatever they found here in the excavations of the Oracle of Delphi was here in the museum in the first room. The next room was the best of all. Here on a pedestal stood the famous statue of the Charioteer of Delphi. It was so great to see this. The Grecian Style hair on his head. A face that gave you a sort of a smile. Then there were those eyes, so lifelike I thought he would speak in Ancient Greek. How the ancients were able to place whole eyeballs into the head and give it life, amazed me. I stood staring at it. I walked around it for a good fifteen minutes.

Wonderful, beautiful, I still was so amazed that they had the knowledge to do something of this size. The partial left arm of the charioteer and of course the chariot was missing. I was so happy to see this in person.

Time had come to leave the museum. It was time to go for lunch as the bus was waiting for us on the road below. Climbing down the stairs, I noticed a small ruin in the distance in the valley below. This was called the Tholos; it was used for purification purposes before entering the sacred Oracle of Delphi. This may be only a guess from the archeologists. The exact use of this building may never be known. Everyone reached the bus. All on board. Eleni came on the P.A. system, and asked if everyone enjoyed the trip so far? Everyone said, "Yes." "The hotel Amalia is just ahead for lunch," she said.

The hotel is built on the side of the mountain; very scenic no matter which way you looked. Our lunch was egg lemon soup called avgolemono, with salad, and mousaka, which is beef and eggplant, with a white sauce. Very delicious. We were now ready for our return to Athens. It would be night when we would reach the center of Athens and Syntagma Square. Actually, it was 8:00 p.m. when I got off the bus. I thanked Eleni for everything, and I would see her again for our trip to Ancient Corinth and Mycenae, this time going to the south of Greece. I reached my hotel and as I came in the front door, the desk clerk saw me and turned to my room number. "There were a number of messages for you." He said. My cousin Valentina had called, as well as Aunt Marianthi.

I wanted to shower, and relax a little before I talked to them. After taking my shower and lying down for about a half an hour, I got up and telephoned Aunt Marianthi.

She said, "Uncle Vasili will come from Kefalonia in two days, so please come for supper." "All right Aunt Marianthi, I'll be there. Goodnight." Valentina was a little more difficult to get in touch with. She didn't have a phone. I had to call Kyria Kitsa, a neighbor of hers. It was good that Kyria Kitsa was home, and she went next door to get her to come to the telephone. I told her that I was going to see Aunt Marianthi, and that afterward we could get together.

"Okay" she said. "We could go to one of the tavernas in the old part of Athens called the Plaka district, and enjoy bouzouki music." The Plaka district was the old part of Athens just below the Acropolis. It has small winding streets, lots of tavernas with bouzouki music, and plenty of antiques. The next day I was free from traveling, and visited more cousins by taking the train to Stasis Victorias and arriving at Academias street. Here I went to visit relatives that had come to Greece from Romania.

Eugenie and Niko were first cousins on my father's side. They had managed to flee Romania before the Communists took over the country.

On entering number 15 I noticed a name that I had on a 45 recording. The name was Danae.

Danae knew the great songwriter known as "Attik" who had a place in Athens, called the Mantra. Oh how tempting it was to ring her bell. I went along to meet my cousins from Braila, Romania. I reached their door and they opened it and immediately his wife greeted me. "Anastasi, how wonderful Aunt Marianthi told us about you and how you surprised her the other night." "Yes," I said, "I knew it was late, but I wanted to see her as soon as possible. It was unbelievable. I have been writing to her for over fifteen years.

I met cousins Eugenie and Niko. Niko said, "You know we had to leave Romania because of the Communists, and we had thought of applying to come to America. I blame myself for not applying to coming to America where opportunity was greater than here. We were sorry to hear of your father's death." I spent a few hours with them, and learned about what they went through before coming to Greece. I wished them well, said my good-byes, and left. I took the train back to Plateia Syntagmatos (Constitution Square) I was crossing the square at 4:00 p.m. and the changing of the guard was taking place at the Tomb of the Unknown Soldier. What a sight to see, their dress, their height, how magnificent in their colorful dress uniforms. The precision that they had, so even, and symmetrical.

I entered the hotel, and the desk clerk told me I had messages from Valentina. I called and I spoke to her, and we agreed to meet in the square in about a half hour. I wanted to go to the Acropolis, and go up to see the Parthenon, and the Karyatides, the Porch of the Maidens. I sat down at an open-air restaurant, and did what the locals did. I sipped lemonade and watched people walking back and forth. It wasn't long afterward that Valentina and George arrived. I had enjoyed people watching. It had started to get dark, and the beautiful blue sky against the Parthenon and the Acropolis gave it a copper color that could not be matched anywhere in the world. When I saw this I said to George, 'The ruins are below, not above." He knew what I meant. All the while Valentina was listening to me. Athens has two more high spots; one is called Licavitos, and the other is Philopappou. On the top of Mount Licavitos is a chapel of Saint George. Licavitos looked almost as beautiful as the Acropolis. So we went ahead, and started to walk toward Licavitos. We reached the bottom of Licavitos. There is a cable car that takes you to the top. As I paid for the trip to the top, two people rushed past us to try to make it on the next car going up to the top. We decided not to take this car, as it was too crowded. In about ten minutes we were on our way. The view unsurpassed, you had the Acropolis on one side with the Porch of the Maidens, the Karyatides, holding up that porch for almost three thousand years. We would make a visit there in two days. Again, I was taken with the view.

I said, to be able to see these things, to touch them to know they are real is such a fantastic miracle. I, a boy from the West End of Boston, who had lived in a tenement five floors up from the street. I was worse than a little kid. Tomorrow I would be going to Epidauros and Corinth. George congratulated me on my grammar in Greek.

"Excellent, Taso." This was a big compliment. We descended Mt. Licavitos and went to Plateia Syntagmatos toward my hotel. Here we went to a nearby shop and had loucoumades and I told Valli and George that I would be gone all day to Corinth and Epidauros and would not be back until the evening. We talked about going to the Acropolis as we watched people dodging traffic in the square. I turned to the waiter and asked him for the check as it was late and I knew I had to be up early. I said my good-byes to both Valli and George, and that I would call them upon my return to Athens. I would see them tomorrow night.

I returned to my hotel. The desk clerk said I had a message from my aunt. I was to call her. It was late. I wondered, should I? Yes, I thought to myself, because I would not see her. "Who is it?" the voice on the other end of the phone said. "It is I your nephew Anastasi. I have gone around to Athens to the Plaka district and I will leave tomorrow for Corinth, Mycenae, and Epidauros." I told her that I had planned all this before leaving America. I wanted to see the sights that I only saw in history books. "I will call you tomorrow night when I get back to the hotel." "Okay, my boy. I'll be waiting to hear from you. I wish you well. Have a good time, and good night." "Good night Aunt Marianthi." I said, and went to bed.

I could hardly sleep that night with my excitement reaching great heights. I had set my clock for 6:30 a.m.to be able to have breakfast, and then go around the corner to the office of Chat Tours to board the bus for Corinth.

CHAPTER THIRTY-SEVEN

Ancient Corinth & Mycenae

I was sound asleep when the alarm clock went off. Oh, how I wanted to turn over. Nothing doing get up sleepy head, I said to myself. Come on, get yourself into the shower, you have a long day ahead of you, with lots to see. The cold water from the shower woke me up. I was glad because I didn't want to miss anything. I dressed comfortably and took a jacket with me. I took the stairs down instead of the elevator, and went past the desk in the lobby, and greeted the clerk. "Good morning," I said. He responded, "Good morning to you, sir." The clerk after greeting me asked me if I wanted breakfast. "Yes," I said. "I am going on a trip to Corinth and Mycenae." "Good, have a good time. The dining room is open, Mr. Grigoropoulos." I looked at the menu and knew a continental breakfast would not sustain me. Luckily there was what I wanted: an American breakfast of eggs, toast, potatoes, and American coffee or tea. The waiter approached, and asked me in English. "What would you like for breakfast?" I responded, an American breakfast.

I looked at my watch it was now 7:05 a.m. I knew the bus only would be around the corner on University Street. The Chat Tours bus would leave at precisely 8:00 a.m. for Corinth, Mycenae, and Epidaurus. I was so excited; I was eating fast, gulping the food down. Within minutes I had consumed two eggs, my potatoes, toast, and my tea.

I had gotten used to the drachmas, when I converted the American money to the drachmas, the oldest currency in Europe. I got up from the table where I was sitting, and asked the waiter for my check. He gave me the bill and I in turn gave him what I owed him plus the tip. Outside, Constitution Square would not awaken until afternoon and evening when the nightlife would begin. I turned and looked up University Street, where a few blocks down was the Chat Tour Bus. When I arrived at the bus, the driver was standing outside with our guide, Eleni. As I approached the tour bus, the driver asked my name. "My name is Ernest Grigoropoulos." "Yes, Mr. Grigoropoulos I have you on the list. Glad to have you with us." I thanked him, and turned and spoke to Eleni for a moment. The day, although cool, would be comfortable. It was the first week in March. It would be around fifty-five degrees. It was warm to me after winter in Boston with fifteen and twenty degree temperatures. The driver Evstratios or Strati for short and our guide Eleni Kaloyiannidis boarded the bus.

"All right" she said, "I am happy to see that we have a nice day. Today we will be traveling to the southern part of the country. We will be touring several places. The first thing we will be doing is crossing over the Corinth Canal, and then on to Ancient Corinth. Ancient Corinth was where the Apostle Paul spoke to the Corinthians. Then we go on to Epidauros to see the outdoor theatre and on to Mycenae."

"We have a full day of sightseeing ahead of us and a lot of things to see on this tour of southern Greece, so sit back and relax and enjoy it. Welcome to Greece," she said. As we left Athens, and approached the port of Piraeus, looking back out of my window I could see the three hills. The Dora Stratou Theater is located on a hill called Philopappou. Here is where the national dances are held in native costumes.

Mt. Lycavitos where the chapel of Saint George is and the Acropolis with the Parthenon. Driving south the countryside was picturesque with winding roads until we came to the Isthmus of Corinth. Here was a steel- frame bridge that separated the Peloponnesus from the rest of Greece. We stopped at Loutraki where people from all over Greece came to drink the therapeutic waters.

They say drinking this water is good and beneficial for a variety of ailments. The bus did make a short stop and we were able to purchase a bottle of water. The mineral springs were impeccably clean. You could eat off the ground it was so clean. Our first stop, Ancient Corinth, was an hour and a half from Athens. We were shown where the Apostle Paul preached to the Corinthians.

Walking around here an elderly lady came in my direction. "Good day to you Mrs.," I said. "Who are you?" she asked. I said, "A stranger" This conversation was in Greek. The woman introduced herself. "My name is Paraskeve," "And my name is Anastasi," I said. She came towards me, "Is this your first time in Greece?" "Yes," I said.

"Anastasi, Paraskeve said, I can tell that you are one of a kind. It got to you, to see these places, and what you feel in your heart." I spoke to her in Greek telling her it was a momentous experience in my life. I had always wanted to come to Greece, and I did not regret it one iota. The next stop was Epidauros, with its ancient amphitheater where classical plays are still performed. The acoustics are phenomenal. A captain from Eastern Airlines and his wife, who were on the tour, asked me if I would ask Eleni to say something in a natural voice. We were many rows up from the center of the theater. Eleni was on the stage. I went down to the stage and asked Eleni in Greek, "Will you say something to us?" The other tourists were all in different areas of the theater. Suddenly all was quiet as Eleni recited a part of a play that she remembered. We were all amazed at the distinct sound of her voice. She spoke in a natural tone and behold, you could hear every word distinctly. What acoustics, another Greek word.

I told Eleni, "I am humble and grateful to be here in my life." She spoke to me in Greek, "You're not like most tourists that I meet. You breathe life, and it is worthwhile to be able to meet a person of your stature. Your enthusiasm is not phony" "No, Eleni, I am a very sincere person." I said looking at her straight in the eye. "More than people or anyone can understand." We walked over to the museum. When we went into the museum, there were artifacts of a soldier's armaments. Nearby was a glass-covered casket of a Greek warrior. Dust had come. Not much remained after 2,500 or so years. I was reminded of the Bible. "From dust thou art and to dust thou shall return."

We boarded the bus for Mycenae. Ancient Mycenae was the beginning of the story of Helen of Troy and Paris who swept her away to Troy. The true story of Helen who was the wife of King Agamemnon and who fell in love with Paris, who came as an emissary representing his city of Troy. They escaped to Troy. This united the Greeks and a thousand ships were launched to battle the city of Troy on the coast of Asia Minor.

Also the story of Sophocles' Antigone took place here. Antigone defied the tyrannical King Creon on burying her brother during an insurrection that pitted brother against brother. The countryside was beautiful, winding road with olive trees scattered everywhere. We approached Mycenae, and the bus stopped, and Eleni said, "We now need our walking shoes as we are going up to the ruins from here." We approached these impressive ruins, the Lions Gate, ancient tombs.

Many of the findings unearthed here are in the Athens museum, including a gold mask and cups. Eleni reminded us that we were to have lunch. The restaurant was quaint and it would be near Epidauros. The lunch consisted of lentil soup and souvlaki with a desert baklava. Today the Armenians, and the Arabs know of these dishes because the Turks, those barbarians, who conquered Greece spread those dishes to all the lands they conquered and it became the Ottoman Empire.

It was already dark as we returned to Athens. My watch said 8:00 p.m. when reached my hotel. This was another full day, yet there would be time to explore the Plaka district with its the nightlife below the Acropolis. The Acropolis looked beautiful lit up at night. I had said good-bye to Eleni, as I would be leaving Greece in a few days. She held my hand tightly, but I did not want to respond to that. I said, in Greek, "Good luck and it was my pleasure to have known you." At the hotel I asked the desk clerk if there were any messages. He said, "Yes, of course." In his hand there were at least a half a dozen. First from Aunt Marianthi, then Valentina, and friends that I met on the plane from Rome to Athens. They lived at the Pasalimani in Piraeus. A beautiful picturesque harbor with yachts of the well-to–do -Greeks, and yes, of course, a yacht owned by Onassis. The other quaint harbor is the Turkolimano where other yachts anchor.

My first call was to Aunt Marianthi. She reminded me that Uncle Vasili was coming from Kefallonia tomorrow. I said, "I'll be there at 7:30 p.m. for dinner. So long." Next I called Valentina and George. "Taso you have been invited to a wedding." "What? Whose wedding?" I said. "My neighbor Kyria Kitsa wants you to come. It's her son.

He will have a reception at an open taverna in Piraeus. There will be a live orchestra and the bouzoukia." Okay, when is it?" I said. "It is on Saturday," she said.

"Saturday is perfect. I will be leaving on Sunday to return to Boston." Visiting family and friends would be the order of the day. "Listen, Valli, I would like to spend the day with you, and George around Athens. You know, visiting the Acropolis, the Parthenon, The Kariatides, the Porch of the Maidens, as well as the Dora Stratou Theater. Uncle Vasili is coming from Kefallonia tomorrow." "Taso I don't like him, he is a mean and a conniving person. I would be very careful of him." "Listen, Valli, I am not a kid. I can take care of myself. I'll see you and George tomorrow." "Taso, I'll be at your hotel at nine thirty in the morning. We can talk more then."

Valentina arrived at the hotel without George. He would join us later. She and I walked near the Zappeion, the park near the parliament building and the Tomb of the Unknown Soldier. We then walked toward the Plaka, to see the old buildings of Athens.

At night this area comes alive with the bouzoukia music in the tavernas.

We came upon a church named Kapnikarea, a small Byzantine style church, built during the Middle Ages and before the barbarous Turks took over Greece.

Sometimes cars could fit in the small streets and sometimes not. Looking up I could see the Acropolis and part of the Parthenon. We planned for a visit there on Thursday. It was a magnificent sight. We stopped and Valentina told me that the other hill is where the Dora Stratou Theater is. Here the folk dancing of various parts of the country and the islands is performed in native costumes.

Greece has about 2,000 islands, some uninhabited. Each island is completely different from the others. To name a few, the islands in the Ionian Sea, Zakinthos, Ithaca, the island of Odysseus, Kerkera or Corfu, near the Albanian frontier. In the Aegean Sea, is the island of Milos, where the statue of Aphrodite of Milos was found. It's better known in the Latin way, the statue of Venus de Milo. This statue and the Victory of Samothace are both in the Louvre Museum in Paris. These two statues were stolen from Greece. My cousin Valentina told me that her favorite island was the island of Kos near the Turkish coast. It was here that the Father of Medicine, Hippocrates, was born.

Time passed quickly. I asked Valentina where George her husband would meet us. She said, "He will meet us at your Hotel, the King's Palace Hotel in Constitution Square at about four thirty." In the next few days I wanted to see as much as I could as Kyria Kitsa's son's wedding was on Saturday. I did not want to miss it as it was my one chance to see a Greek wedding in Greece, and be part of it as an invited guest.

We got back to the Tomb of the Unknown Soldier and soon we saw George near my hotel. "Why don't we go to Piraeus?" Valli said. "You will be near Aunt Marianthi's house. I don't envy you meeting Uncle Vasili. I never liked him. He is a mean selfish man. I would be very careful of him. He is an evil man. We are all in agreement no one likes him," she said. I told her, "I remember my father telling me how he tried to get my mother in bed before my father caught him, and threw him out of the house."

Aunt Marianthi never knew this. I wasn't going to tell Valli and George, but since we were talking about Uncle Vasili I told them.

Valli's mother Aunt Suzanne was telling all her neighbors and friends of her time in America. Valli said, "Why didn't she stay?" I responded, "It was difficult for her, not knowing the language and living with four nephews wasn't very easy. We had our ways." Each of us had our own ways. I was the Greek in the house. My brothers Nicky, Leo, and Johnny couldn't give a hoot about Greek ways or the language. I told Valentina that my brothers would move out of the house if her mother came back to live with us.

I changed the subject. I told them, look, let's take the subway down to Piraeus.

We could eat something at a restaurant there. Sure enough there was a fine restaurant named Tsakalians. Two Armenian brothers owned it. I could see the wine barrels up on the shelf. Valentina and George had their meal. I settled for a xoriatiki salata (a country salad). I loved it with the Greek olive oil, nothing like it in the world. I kept looking at my watch. Valli noticed me.

"I know Taso just be on your guard. He is a crafty man, that is the way he thinks.

Many times we have heard of things he has done. He knows a lot of people even in the government. He likes cigars so he can give them away as gifts to important people for favors," she said. "I'll watch my step," I told her. We finished our meal, and headed for the buses. One would take Valli and George to Amfiali where they lived. The other bus would take me to Xatsikeriakeion, another neighborhood of Piraeus. I bid them goodnight and had told them I would see them tomorrow. I boarded my bus and left for Aunt Marianthi's house and my meeting with Uncle Vasili.

CHAPTER THIRTY-EIGHT

Dinner at Aunt Marianthi's House

I knew the street and the bus stop was a few feet from her house 48 Alexandrou Zaimi Street. I asked the bus driver to call the stop. He turned to me and said, "You are not from here. I can tell by the way you are dressed. Americanos" I said, "Yes" in Greek. "You speak very good Greek," he said. "I am self-taught," I said. "Bravo," he said. Just then he said, "Your stop. Good luck, my boy." I returned his good wishes.

The bus stop was just above my Aunt Marianthi's door. I stepped up to the door and rang the bell. Not even a few seconds passed when Aunt Marianthi answered the door and greeted me. Uncle Vasili was waiting, and I greeted him with, "How are you Uncle Vasili?" He said "fine." Aunt Marianthi had prepared a wonderful supper: Mousaka, salad, and roasted potatoes. For desert she had made galaktobourico. During my conversation with Uncle Vasili he said, "Your aunt could not have children, so I thought of adopting a child." His back was facing Aunt Marianthi who was in the kitchen getting ready to serve the meal. I said, "Yes, that was a good idea." I could see Aunt Marianthi's hand waving back and forth indicating "no." I continued, "Yes, a good idea, but when you and she were younger, not now, when you're in your senior years. This would be no good for both of you."

Then he said, "Why don't you stay here and get married to a Greek girl and inherit my property." I looked at him in amazement. My eyes wide open. Here was a man whom I hadn't seen since I was five years old, and he was conniving to see how he could get me to agree to anything he said. I fired back.

"Uncle Vasili, I came to visit Greece and my relatives, not to get married." That ended the conversation, and I wanted to leave as we had finished eating. Aunt Marianthi said, "Please don't leave. "Okay, I won't. I'll stay a little longer."

Again I heard his voice. "Anastasi, would you please sponsor me to come to the United States so I can collect my pension. I stayed and worked for five years in America during the war." I said I'd see if I could. I looked up and saw an icon of the Virgin Mary. "Would you give me that icon that is up on the shelf?" "Here take it, and don't forget me," he said. Again, I said I'd see what I could do. I said my goodbyes to them. I hugged my aunt and kissed her and thanked her for the wonderful meal that she prepared.

I turned and shook hands with Uncle Vasili. I left taking a cab to Athens and my hotel. I had an exciting day. I knew that Valentina and George would want to know how everything went. The next day was Thursday with only a few days left before my departure on Sunday for Boston. I would visit the Acropolis and actually see and touch things that I only saw in pictures. Wow. I would not believe it until I could climb the steps to see the masterpiece of architecture.

The next morning, I met Valli and George at my hotel and we started to walk to the Acropolis. I told them what happened at Aunt Marianthi's house. They laughed and told me, you see he wants something and that is for you to sponsor him to go to the United States. When I told them he wanted me to stay and get married here and inherit his property of course they laughed. I told them forget him, as he was a selfish and self-centered man all his life.

CHAPTER THIRTY-NINE

The Acropolis

We finally reached the entrance of the Acropolis. We climbed the steps, they were new. They had been replaced exactly as the old ones. Greece had marble all right. This was Pentelic marble. The Propilea, the gates as you entered the grounds and then come upon the Parthenon so majestic in scope and in size. I felt so small.

Secretly, I was to do something that was punishable by imprisonment. I took two pieces of marble when no one was around. I managed to put the two pieces in my camera bag. I had purchased all the accessories for the Polaroid. One of the accessories put you in the picture. So I set it up that the three of us would be in the picture. I had done this with Aunt Marianthi, and Uncle Vasili. They marveled that they could see the picture in sixty seconds. Greece had nothing like this.

I took pictures walking inside the Parthenon as well as sitting on the steps. I then went over to Erectheum and took pictures of the Kariatides, the Porch of the Maidens. At that time only one was a copy as the others were the originals. Lord Elgin had replaced only one as he took that one and the top of the Frieze of the Parthenon. They have been in the British Museum and Greece has asked for their return. Valentina and George followed me around. I walked over to a small temple of Athena Nike. This particular temple is of the Ionic style. The Turks, who controlled Greece, had dismantled this little temple. Luckily when Greece fought for its freedom and won against the Turks with the help of England, France, and Russia, they found the temple and it was restored to its original place on the Acropolis. We went down into the small museum behind the Parthenon. The film The Boy on a Dolphin with Sophia Loren and Alan Ladd was filmed here in 1955.

Melina Mercouri, the movie actress, became minister of culture under the Papandreou government and requested the Elgin Marbles be returned to Greece. At that time the Conservatives were in power in England. The Labour Party, the opposition party said if they were returned to power they would return the Elgin Marbles to Greece where they belong. So far, that hasn't happened. I met people from Indiana, and they were astonished by my knowledge. They said they didn't need a guide as they had me. I laughed; it is just that when you read all you can of these places, and come to see and touch these things it is a marvel in itself.

Valli and George had a surprise for me. They knew I liked a Greek songstress by the name of Sofia Vembo. Was she still singing? Yes, she was still singing. Near Omonia Square was a theater named Theatron Vembo. Sofia Vembo had bought the theater years before. George said, "She is giving a performance there." The Kalouta Sisters had hired the theater and between their performances Sofia Vembo came out and sang a few songs. It was for the older people to remember and for the young to learn, which is what she called it. During the Second World War, she was instrumental in giving courage and entertaining the troops.

When the Greek forces repulsed Mussolini, Mussolini cried for help from the Nazis. Hitler's army crushed Greece, and was looking for Sofia Vembo who had given morale support to the troops. She escaped to Crete and then crossed over to Egypt.

Singing on the radio and sending encouragement to the Greek people. She was now an institution, no one else like her. I was excited because I wanted to meet her in person. The doorman said at the intermission you can go backstage to see her. Another highlight of my visit to Greece was meeting her. At the intermission I went backstage, and I was ecstatic. I introduced myself, and said I was from America. I went right up to her and kissed her.

She was excited herself. I asked her why. She said, "Because a young man kissed me." I wished she would come back to the United States. She asked, "Why? Do they want me?" I said, "Yes." "What you are doing here at your theater is perfect." She gave me her telephone number and called me Taso. She signed my program, which I still have. It was a wonderful time and I would never forget these moments. The time was flying by, and by Thursday evening I was getting tired. Two days left. Tomorrow we would go to Salamis, an island just outside of Piraeus. Here a big battle took place against the Persians, four hundred years before the birth of Christ. We finally reached my hotel and I bid them good night, and I would meet them tomorrow. I went in and the desk clerk said I had a message from Aunt Marianthi to call her. I waited until the next morning to call her. In the morning after my breakfast I called her. "Hello Aunt Marianthi, how are you?"

I told her that I was invited to a wedding and I would not be able to come. She told me she was going to Kefallonia and she wanted me to go with her. I told her that on Sunday I would be leaving for America. "I am sorry," I continued, "that I would not able to see you, until next time." I would be back in a few months I told her.

I got dressed and met Valentina in Piraeus at the subway terminal near a loukoumades shop. Loukoumades are small round balls of dough sprinkled with nuts and honey poured on them.

You are served a half a dozen with a glass of water and honey that you put on with a spoon. Once you put the honey on them, you put the spoon in the glass of water and stir it and then drink the water. It makes the water sweet. I met Valli and George and treated them to loukoumades. We were soon off to Salamis and a visit to a Byzantine Church with old icons. So old you could not make them out. After kissing the icon, George said, "Well I didn't see anything in the icon."

"I sometimes think this is the work of the devil. How can anyone know if it is an icon of Mary or a saint or the devil?" I said. He looked at me shocked, "Well, it's the truth," I said. "Anyway, I am not impressed with this. Let's keep moving." They showed me where the battle had taken place. I remembered Themistocles. It was a nice looking island. You could see the mainland of Greece. It reminded me of Martha's Vineyard off Cape Code. I told Valli and George we are lucky in Massachusetts, because we have two islands. People go to both of these islands in the summer.

I told Valli that Aunt Marianthi had called. "She wanted me to go to Kefallonia." Valli said, "Luckily, you know Greek for they are trying to get you married to some girl unknown to you on the island. Be on your guard." I told her that I don't have the time to go to Kefallonia. I don't want to miss Kyria Kitsa's son wedding on Saturday at the Pasalimani in Piraeus. "Good" Valli said. "They will probably try something again before you leave," Valli said. "Let's forget them," she said. "Okay" I said. "Let's go to Castella, another picturesque part of Piraeus. We can get a beautiful view of Piraeus from there." Castella was indeed beautiful and the view magnificent.

We finished our walk through Castella. I said, "Goodnight" and took the subway back to Athens to my hotel. I took a shower, and just then I had a knock on the door. "Mr. Grigoropoulos, I am sorry to disturb you, but I wanted to tell you in person rather than calling you on the hotel telephone. It's your Uncle Vasili. He has had an attack." "What?" I said. "Your aunt needs your help." "Thank you" I replied. I got dressed and hailed a taxicab "I am going to Alexandrou Zaimis Street," I told him. "The number of the house is forty-eight." "I know where that is. My mother-in-law lives on that street." Driving in Athens was no picnic. They are bad drivers as is the case in Boston or New York City. It would take us about twenty minutes to get there. I thought I could relax while not driving. I feared for my life as he sped away fast. The question that was on my mind was will I make it? This could be it. I could see Castella in the distance and the Pasalimani.

We were getting close. "We will be there in ten minutes," the driver said. The screeching of the brakes gave me a jolt. The taxicab driver said, "My boy, we are here." I said, "Thank God. How much do I owe you?" He told me 140 drachmas. "Here, take 180 drachmas." I walked up the few steps and rang the bell. Opening the door Aunt Marianthi was crying. "Taso, I had to call for an ambulance and he was taken to the hospital. They are going to call me. They will have a cardiac machine on him."

Uncle Vasili did not have a heart attack. This was done to try to keep me from returning to America. I did not know this at the time. They really wanted me to go to the island of Kefallonia and meet a girl and possibly get involved with her. Then they would say you have to marry her or she might kill herself, now that her virginity was taken from her. My mind was working. Why didn't we go to the hospital?

Something wasn't right here. "Listen Aunt Marianthi, I am going back to the hotel." "No, no, my boy, you have to help me." This was getting out of hand. "Good-night" I said. "There are no taxis," she said. "I'll find one." It was so quiet you could hear a pin drop. No one was out, it was after eleven p.m. I walked briskly to the corner of my aunt's street. There, to my delight, was a taxicab, and it so happened it was the same taxi driver who I had before. I called out to him. He pulled right in front of me. He said to me as I got into the cab. "You know, when I brought you here I knew you were coming here on an emergency as you acted very strangely. So I decided to stick around." "You are a godsend. My aunt, I believe, wanted to take me to the island of Kefallonia to try to marry me off. "Oh my, get in," he said. "I want to get to my hotel," I said. "Okay right away. Athens and Constitution Square here we come." It was past midnight when I reached the hotel. Now for a good night's sleep.

Saturday was a casual day as I awoke at 8: a.m. I had taken my shower the night before. All I had to do is get dressed for the wedding. I went to the lobby, and the moment I headed for the restaurant I could hear people saying, "Look at him. He is well dressed." They stopped and starred at me. My thought was should I take a cab or the subway. I decided on a taxicab because of the looks I was getting from passersbys. I had bought a card for the couple whose wedding I was invited to and I put fifty dollars in it. In Greece at that time it was a lot of money. I wrote my good wishes for them, signed my name and sealed the card.

The taxicab headed for Piraeus and straight for the entrance of the subway. It was here that I would meet Valli and George. I composed myself, looking at my watch several times. I spotted Valli and George coming towards me. "Good Morning" I said. "Valli, what a night I had last night. I was getting ready for bed when a knock came on the door. It was the bellhop who said there was an emergency, and that I should go to my Aunt Marianthi's house in Piraeus. You know, Valli, I put my shoes on and ran down the stairs and came out on the square. I was lucky, as I was able to hail a taxicab.

"When I got there, Aunt Marianthi said, that Uncle Vasili had an attack and he was rushed to the hospital. It seemed very strange." "I told you, Taso, you have to be on your guard with them. Can you imagine the trick they picked to try to get you to the island, and you would have a great disaster for in getting married, you would be trapped with a wife you don't want? A very tricky situation," Valli said; "The girl would become a disgrace, and she would end up maybe committing suicide. It would be all over for you, poor man," said Valli. "It was a close call for me" I said. "Let's forget them."

CHAPTER FORTY

The Wedding at Pasalimani & My Farewell

"I can hear the music. I want to enjoy my first wedding in Greece." The Tsamikos wow it is danced very different. In the United States the Greeks there don't know how to do this dance. I remembered the dance and how I learned it when I was just fourteen years of age. The music is addictive, and you want to get up and dance. We had come to the Pasalimani where the wedding reception was held. Kyria Kitsa and her family had arranged for the wedding reception at a restaurant called Frosos. There were a lot of people there. It looked like the whole neighborhood of Amfiali had come to this wedding. Dancing the syrto, the kalamatiano, and the balos, I enjoyed it so much. I did not want to sit down. All of a sudden the groom raised his glass. He called my name, and said, "To you when you get married." Valli, and George laughed, "It almost happened." "You're telling me." I said. The wedding lasted until the evening hours. I had such a good time. They were going to one of the islands for their honeymoon. Someone had mentioned Rhodes. How wonderful. The time had come to say goodnight. I kissed the bride and hugged the groom. Achilles was his name and her name was Angeliki. They thanked me for coming, and I thanked them and his mother for inviting me. They wished me a good trip to America. His mother, and friends who I had met said, "We wish you well," and Valli and George, and I wished them well. We took a taxicab back to the subway entrance in Piraeus.

I told the driver to wait, as I wanted to say good-by to Valli and George. I told her to kiss her mother for me, and tell her I would write. I kissed Valentina, and shook hands with George as I said good-bye to them. "God be with you," I said. The taxicab sped off towards Athens, and my hotel. When I got to the hotel, I paid the cab driver and went up to my room. I called Aunt Marianthi, and said good-bye to her. She replied, "So long, Taso." With that I hung up the phone, and started, to pack my clothes. I laid my clothes out that I was going to wear, for my trip back to Boston. I had my passport, and my ticket. I called down to the front desk, and had the desk clerk give me a 10:00 am wake up call. I got off to sleep about midnight.

Ten a.m. right on the dot, the phone rang. I awoke, and went straight to the shower, then got dressed and went downstairs to have my breakfast. I finished in just about an hour and decided to go for a walk around the block before returning to my hotel to bring my baggage down and turn my key in to the hotel clerk. I walked up onto Stadium Street and looked at the University of Athens then around Constitution Square before returning to my hotel. I dashed up to my room and took my baggage down to the entrance to the hotel. I gave my key to the desk clerk and settled my bill. He called me a cab. We were off to the airport. The flight back to the United States was uneventful, and my first trip to Greece was full of wonderful memories.

CHAPTER FORTY-ONE

Grabbed from Behind

Now to retrieve my baggage, go through customs, and take the shuttle bus over to Eastern Airlines's terminal, and connect to my flight to Boston. I picked up my bags and proceeded to go through customs. My overcoat was heavy, as I had taken the pieces of marble that adorned the Parthenon on the Acropolis in Athens. I had managed to take two, when no one was looking, and had put them in my overcoat. I had put my overcoat on coming into the terminal. I followed the signs to the baggage -claim area. I had taken my baggage off the belt. Now, I would have to go through customs. My overcoat looked heavy. I came to customs. Just then I felt myself lifted off the ground.

Two men had come from behind me, and lifted me off the floor. I totally was unprepared for this. One of them said. "Do you mind coming with us?" What could I say? They already had me. I knew what this was for. When I was finally put back on the floor, we were in a small room. "Would you mind emptying your pockets?" I proceeded to do just that. I started with my overcoat. The eyes of both of them were glued on me for fear they might miss something. I had not emptied all of my pockets, when I asked them, "Do you want a couple of rocks?" They were surprised. "Take them and get the hell out of here," one of them said. We all started laughing. I knew exactly what they were looking for. They probably thought, if I were trying to smuggle anything right in front of their eyes this would be the perfect way to do it. I was not what they wanted. I had been startled, but I knew I was quite in control. After getting my baggage back from customs I went to where Eastern Airlines was for my connection to Boston.

JFK airport already had jetways and was using an alphabet system to direct you to the airline terminals. It would be years before Logan airport in Boston would be up to par.

My small carry on I kept with me. I had my Polaroid camera with me. I kept close watch on them as all my pictures were with my camera and I did not want to lose them. My memories would not be in vain. They were exciting, to be cherished all my life.

The gate agent who would meet the flight was Richard Grinnell "Ernie welcome back. How was your trip?" "Great, Richard," I said, "thanks for asking. As much as I loved my trip to Greece, it was good to be home again," I said.

CHAPTER FORTY-TWO

Back Home

The day I returned to work I had the pleasure of meeting the actor Yul Brynner. He was in the V.I.P. lounge, which Eastern Airlines had for famous and important people. He was booked on a flight to Miami. The Customer Service Representative Ed Landis brought him to the gate to be preboarded. The moment that I met him I started to speak to him in Bulgarian. He looked up at me and answered me. He was astonished and spoke with me at length. The other agent working with me, Michael Casey and the C.S.R. Ed Landis were both starring at both of us. "Wow look at Ernie as he has made an impression on Mr. Brynner." I told Mr. Brynner that I had seen all his movies and enjoyed them very much. He told me that he would like to see me again as I made a great impression on him, and we had much more to talk about. I thanked him very much. I wished him a pleasant flight. I then made an announcement for boarding flight 211 to Miami Florida. Michael Casey said, "I think Ernie you have made a friend in Yul Brynner." I will always think of him as the King of Siam in the movie the "The King and I" with Deborah Kerr.

A few days past again I was to have some excitement. Two passengers going to New York had Turkish passports and I said, "You should be ashamed for what you did to a million and half of Armenians in between 1915 and 1922, plus you did the same to the Greeks. You are barbarians." "No, no" one said. "We are Armenian, we were born in Turkey, please see our names," the other passenger said. I looked. One was named Mr. Johannes Garabedian and the other was

James Adamian. Armenians. "I am glad of that." I said. They boarded their flight and left for New York City.

One day one of the supervisors, Frank Cardello, asked a bunch of us if we would like to visit the new terminal of Eastern Airlines that was being built right next to the old one. The building wouldn't be ready until the fall of 1969, which was still about eight months away. I certainly volunteered to see the new terminal.

You drove up one ramp and drove down the other. So parking was convenient, as you parked in the building, and took the elevator down to the lobby area and you went to the gate where your flight was and boarded the airplane. We had to descend down one of the ramps that wasn't yet lit. We did this by holding onto each other.

We finally made it to the lobby area. It was so huge with ceilings that you would never touch. On one side, would be gates 1 thru 6. This side would be for reservation flights, and it would also have the Ionosphere Lounge for first class -passengers. Here the Customer Service Representative would assist first -class passengers with flight changes, connections, and preboarding. On other side were gates 7 thru 12. Here were the shuttle flights to New York's LaGuardia Airport, and to Newark, New Jersey. The very new things, that I had not seen in Boston, which Kennedy Airport had, were jetways. Passengers now would not be subject to the weather. They would go right to the aircraft from the building, without going outside. This was a big plus. No more umbrellas for inclement weather.

Luckily, the stairs were finished on one side, and we were able to go down to the street level. As I was coming out of the building, and walking toward the outer sidewalk, I turned and gazed up at this monstrosity. The sign Eastern had already been placed between the huge columns. It looked great. I was excited, as I knew Eastern was growing. In those days, Boston was the end city. All flights originated, and terminated here.

One-day Joe Cicarelli paged me to tell me that I would have some important passengers on the 372 flight to Washington, D.C., and that I would have to preboard them. When Eddie Landis brought the two women, I could not take my eyes off of them.

They were Joan Kennedy, and the late President's wife Jackie Onassis. When I got to the gate, I could not believe my eyes. There were two women of great stature. Joan who was so beautiful, her long blonde hair down to almost her shoulders. I just could not help myself. I could not take my eyes off her. President Kennedy's wife, Jacqueline, was so attractive. It had been five years since her husband President Kennedy was shot.

I walked to the plane to make sure it had been cleaned, catered, and fueled. I spoke to the captain and the flight attendants. I informed them of preboarding the Kennedy women. All was ready for boarding. I walked back to the gate area. John Mallory was working the flight with me. I made an announcement to the passengers over the loudspeaker system in the gate area. I told them we would be boarding in just a few minutes and to have their tickets ready as we would be taking their tickets at the gate. I turned and went over to the two Mrs. Kennedys. I said, "I can preboard you now." I spoke to Jackie, and asked her if she had learned any Greek since being married to Onassis. She laughed, and said, "Yes." I then spoke to her in Greek to see how much she knew. She answered me by saying, "Thank you" in Greek for assisting them to board the airplane. I told Jackie that I would see her again, and we could speak in Greek, and she said, "I look forward to the next time." I wished them well, and a pleasant flight to Washington, D.C.

Now it was time to work the 10:30 a.m. shuttle to Newark New Jersey, and then meet the inbound from LaGuardia. After that to have lunch and return to work a Miami flight at 3:30 p.m. At 5:00 p.m. I would work a flight to Washington, D.C., and then Raleigh-Durham, N.C. On this particular flight 476, I had to be very careful working the weights of the flight. The aircraft was a Lockheed Electra. On this plane first -class was in the rear of the aircraft and coach was in the front. One to four passengers, or five to eight, the weight and the balance of the aircraft would change somewhat, so I had to make sure that I had plenty of baggage shifted in the bins below or else there would be a problem. It turned out all right even though I sweated this one out.

I started planning my next trip. However, it would not be Europe or Greece, but to Anchorage, Alaska. My brothers Leon and John both enlisted in the air force. The war in Vietnam was raging in southeast Asia. They would be in different places, and I felt very hurt as I was committed to having them close as they were a part of my life and only I knew that I promised my mother on her deathbed that I would keep us together, and that I would always be there for them. I did not have to worry about my brother Nicky as much, as he was home. The day that they left for the air force I was in shock and surprised but I remember telling them, "I don't care where in the world you'll be. I'll be there." So now I had to get myself ready for an exciting trip to Alaska.

So naturally I would take advantage of that. First, I had to make all the arrangements, with some of my fellow employees. I would swap about six days. I had paid back all the days I owed from my trip to Greece. I had to look on the schedule to see who was off, and speak with them to see that I would be able to do it. It was going to work. I would surprise my brother Leon, who now was stationed at Elmendorf Air Force Base at Anchorage, Alaska. I was excited. I would see Alaska for the first time. In the meantime, I had two days off. On most jobs people would be off on Saturday and Sunday. In the airline industry that was not the case. You had to be very flexible, working different shifts, and have different days off. My days off were very different as I worked the vacation relief shift. I worked mornings, and afternoons. Sometimes I would work midnight to 7 a.m. in the morning. On this shift I would meet inbound flights. These flights came in from the west coast via Atlanta. I would restock the ticket counter with baggage tags etc.

I enjoyed it very much as no day would ever be boring in my career with Eastern Airlines. So every week I had different days off.

Sometimes I would have four days off in a row and then work nine days straight. On my days off I drove north on Route 93 to see my Aunt Penny and Uncle Louie. I became very close to them after my mother had passed away. They were a well-needed lift. I can remember my father driving us there, my brothers and I. They lived in Dracut. I enjoyed my visits to Dracut. I would go there, and they would come to Malden. When my father passed away I continued going to see them.

My other relatives were estranged from me, as we had a terrible falling out. My other relatives wanted to split us up, as there was money to be had. Social Security gave us survivors' benefits for my brothers until they reached eighteen years of age. Each of my brothers were entitled to over a hundred dollars apiece. I was fortunate that I became of legal age. Now they could not do anything to plot against my brothers or me. Money was all they cared about, not the welfare of my brothers or myself. They knew nothing of the promise I gave my mother on her deathbed. She died peacefully knowing, I would be there taking care of them.

On some of my days off I would try to relax, but not knowing when the phone would ring and I might be asked to work. This particular time it so happened that I was home and the phone did ring, and it was my job. "Ernie can you come into work tomorrow morning at 7:00 a.m. I said, "Yes." I never said, "No."

While working the 7:30 a.m. shuttle to Newark, New Jersey, I was surprised to see two passengers. One I recognized the other I did not. It was Frank Fontaine, from the Jackie Gleason Show, which appeared on television in the fifties and early sixties. The other person was a newscaster named Frank Reynolds from ABC.

When you are a gate agent, you work in conjunction with another agent. One would do the check in of the passengers at the gate, and the other agent would make sure the aircraft was cleaned, catered, and ready for boarding. This agent also made sure that maintenance had seen the logbook to make sure the plane was in excellent shape mechanically. Freddie Starrett the maintenance supervisor was in contact with me, and I with him. We also let the control center know what was going on, as they were up to date on all the flights coming into and departing from Eastern Airlines. I would know before the control center if the plane had problems.

Usually a hydraulic leak or a bulb in the emergency row grounded the plane until these things were repaired. These planes were kept up to par. This is before the airline industry was deregulated. Back then The Civil Aeronautics Board, whose members were politically appointed, had the say as to which routes the airlines could fly. Eastern Airlines had the only nonstop service to Atlanta, Georgia from Boston. When an airline had a route such as this it was profitable.

My time for traveling again was drawing near. I also started dating my future wife, Betsy.

CHAPTER FORTY-THREE

My Trip to Alaska

I was getting ready for Alaska to surprise my brother, Leon. Both Leon and Johnny went to training camp in Texas. My brother Leon was sent to Alaska. My brother Johnny went to Thailand. The war was in nearby Vietnam, and I was worried. I had received my pass from Eastern Airlines, and my free ticket from Pan American Airways. My swaps with four other agents were all set. I was leaving on Saturday.

My baggage was checked through to Anchorage. Arriving in Anchorage, I found the city very clean as compared to Boston. After checking in at the hotel, I rented a car and went off to Elmendorf Air Force Base to find my brother. I went to the main gate and, of course, security had to call to see if a person by the name of Leon Grigoropoulos was on base. Security said, "Boy, you have the alphabet for a name." "Yes, I know," I answered. I had shortened my name to Gregory at Eastern Airlines because it was difficult to pronounce, and I could be easily identified.

Security told me to proceed to the main building, which was straight ahead of me. I went into the main building and spoke to the sergeant at the desk. I asked him about my brother Leon and spelled out the last name ever so slowly. "Boy you have the alphabet don't you?" "Yes," I said, "that's what security said at the gate, when I applied to see him." "Okay," he said, "your brother is a mechanic. He keeps us moving." "I'll have someone go with you to where he is working. Does he know you're coming?" "No," I said. The sergeant said, "What, a surprise?" I said, "Yes. It's been a year and then some since we've seen each other." He drove me up to the parts department, and I got out, as did the sergeant, and he said, "Follow me." We passed through two doors to a garage. I could see two trucks with mechanics working on them.

Suddenly from the other side came a well-built man. My brother Leon had a great build. He saw me and gave a yell. "Sonny," he said, "how? Why?" He stumbled for words. We grabbed each other, and I hugged him and I did not want to let go. "I told you no matter where in the world you would be, I would come to see you." As I was talking to him I could not hold back the tears. My eyes became so teary that I could not see him for a moment. "I'll wait till you get off work detail." "Sonny, I'm going to ask the commanding officer if it's all right, if I can leave early." The sergeant who was there watching us said, "Hold on, I'll check with my superior, I'm sure it will be all right. Captain Burnham, sir, I have a PFC here, Leon Grigoropoulos, his brother is here from Massachusetts. Will it be all right to dismiss him early?" I could see the response on the sergeant's face.

"Thank you, sir," my brother said. I turned and said, "Thank you, sergeant. You have been very kind." "My pleasure, you're welcome."

"Sonny I just can't believe it, it is so wonderful." "It's been a while, Leo. Are you in touch with Johnny?" I asked. "Sonny, all I know is that he is in Thailand." Leo took me into Anchorage and showed me the sights. I could not get over the totem poles. I finally got to see the Midnight Sun, which I had heard about. Back at the hotel I tried to fall asleep, but the sun was blazing at 2:00 a.m. The next day my brother was able to get a two-day pass and he took me to a small town called Seward. I remembered the name as it was named after Secretary of State William Seward as he arranged for the purchase of Alaska from the Russians in 1867, and it became known as Seward's Folly.

On the way I saw a huge black bear and salmon coming upstream. The black bear would not be concerned with me, as I would not give him any trouble. We stopped and watched the salmon coming back to spawn, fighting the current of the river coming upstream. I knew there was something bothering my brother from the way he acted.

He wanted to get something off his chest. "Leo, you can't hide anything. I know there is something you want to tell me as you have been uneasy since we left Anchorage." "Sonny, it is very important. I met a girl in Seward and I got married." I was shocked and I knew it was from loneliness, that this had happened. He is such a good-hearted human being. He would give the shirt of off his back to anyone who needed his help.

He was taking me to Seward to meet his wife and her parents. Leo told me she had two children, two boys. If this wasn't enough, they were both from different men.

Now I felt he ruined his life. I should have come sooner. Oh my, she was like a whore. I thought to myself why, Leo? You're a single young man and you had to get mixed up with this girl. "You were lonely, right?" "Sonny, she had a beautiful pair of legs." "Leo, you're a young man. You should know to have patience to wait. I feel I have failed as a brother bringing you up since ma died, and we had to try to stay together." "Sonny, I married her." I interrupted him before he could finish his sentence. "I know," I said. "Look, Sonny, we're almost there." "Okay, I'll pretend I don't know anything." "She comes to Anchorage on the weekends as I try to get off on the weekends to be with her. Her mother owns a barroom here in Seward. Her mother lives upstairs from the barroom. This is not her real father, but her stepfather."

We were coming into Seward, and I could see the harbor and that the town was small. There was something about the tranquility of a place like this. We drove up to the two-story building. The bottom was a barroom. The barroom was named Ma's Heaven. The second floor was where they lived. I could hear music, and voices as we approached the door to enter Ma's Heaven. There were a few men sitting at the bar. Farther along there were tables and chairs and booths. At a table beyond, I could see two people sitting together. An older woman and a younger woman. My brother introduced me, "Sonny, this is Ginger and her mother Eloise."

Ginger's stepfather was tending bar. Leo introduced me, his name was John. I felt somehow that I had betrayed my brother. Maybe I wasn't strong enough. He had married a girl with two children, and they did not have the same father. Two different men, oh boy. My brother knew I felt uncomfortable. We stayed the rest of the day, then drove back to Anchorage. "Sonny, what do you think?" "Well Leo, I can't say much. I just wished you hadn't jumped into this. Okay you're married, I'll try to accept this. Please don't ask me anymore, this is painful. I blame myself. I know it was lonely for you five thousand miles from home. You really had no one to talk to. Remember, Leo, I always have wanted the best for you, Johnny, and Nicky. Sometimes you probably don't understand that."

I was glad to be back in Anchorage, and ready for bed. It was eleven o'clock when I dozed off to sleep. I stayed a few more days visiting with Leo. I hugged and kissed him, and told him to keep in touch as I would. I returned home to Bosto

CHAPTER FORTY-FOUR

The New Building

Moving day into the new Terminal was on a Sunday. Oh my God, of all days, Sunday. Fridays and Sundays were the busiest days of the week. With the shuttle service to LaGuardia and Newark being very busy those two days, it would be a fiasco I thought.

I heard that ramp service had only one half hour of training on operating the jet- ways. I thought this was not enough time. If only we could move on a quiet day such as a Tuesday or a Wednesday. Oh, what dingbat chose Sunday?

It didn't take long for disaster to strike. The ramp service supervisor, Frank Marchesi said," This is a monumental catastrophe." Ten airplanes were damaged because ramp service did not have enough training on the operation of the jetways. Two jetways had to be shut down. People were taken down stairs only to go outside and go up the stairs into the airplane. This happened in reverse with flights coming in.

I could hear the murmurs of the passengers saying, "What kind of an airline is this, that they can't train their personnel to operate their equipment?" During this fiasco other airlines had heard of our troubles, and called, and said, "do you want us to send you some aspirin?" Wow, what a migraine.

It was one of my worst days at work. I wanted to crawl into the first hole I could find. One passenger, a woman approached me and lashed out at me. "Well, I never was so distraught going up and down stairs when you had jetways to go directly into the building. I will never fly Eastern Airlines again. You should go out of business."

All I could do is apologize for this situation, and promise better service in the future. The pain of moving from the old terminal to the new terminal had taken a drastic toll on all of us. I had gotten calls from Delta, Northwest, and United saying, "Would you like me to bring over some aspirin or excedrin? You guys must have a terrific migraine by now."

The next day I worked inside at the paging center. This was a cubbyhole next to the control center located downstairs away from people. I had my privacy. I started paging people who were looking to meet their party or were leaving messages. The time did pass. Al Sanders, one of my co-workers asked, "Was that you in the paging center?"

"Yes, Al, I am working in the paging center today. Why? What's up?" "Well when I heard you I wanted to jump through the microphone, and grab you." "What?

Why Al, I didn't mean to cause you to go to extremes." "No Ernie, it's your voice. It is so pleasant, that I just wanted to grab you." "Al, take it easy, I'll try to be a little rougher in my tone, okay?" I thought to myself is this for real? Al had feelings for me, but I did not understand at first. I turned to him and said, "Thanks, but no thanks.

It had been five months since my Alaska trip. I was now eligible for a free ticket to go to Thailand and around the world to see my brother Johnny, who was stationed at an air base there. Pan American Airlines had an agreement with Eastern Airlines. This agreement gave each Eastern employee a free ticket every year to anywhere Pan American Airlines went. This was my chance to fly around the world.

This time I spent time carefully planning my trip to the Far East. I would stop in Fairbanks, Alaska, then on to Japan, Hong Kong and then on to Thailand. My next stop would be India and a train ride to Agra to see the Taj Mahal. From India I would go on to Beirut, Lebanon, and back to Boston via London.

The next day Jacqueline Onassis appeared to board the one o'clock shuttle to LaGuardia. I greeted Mrs. Onassis with a smile, and asked her to wait to see if I could preboard her. I went down the jetway and spoke to the flight attendant and the captain. They said it was all right.

Mrs. Onassis remembered me, and we started talking in Greek as we walked down the jetway. I told her what she had done for the White House would never be equaled, as she was the best first lady this country ever had. Mrs. Onassis turned to me, and said, "That was wonderful of you to say that." "I mean it, I said, and took her hand and held it for a few moments. She told me that Greek was one of the hardest languages to learn. I agreed with her, as it was one of the oldest languages in the world.

She asked me if I worked the shuttles all the time. I told her some of the time. She said that she felt quite comfortable with me, and I reminded her that I took care of her and Joan Kennedy a few years earlier in the old terminal. She said, "I enjoyed talking to you and hope to see you again." We ended our conversation in Greek and I wished her a good trip.

My next flight had a celebrity too, Roberta Peters, the opera star. A big day for famous people. As five o'clock approached more passengers arrived for the 5 p.m. shuttle to LaGuardia. I roped off the area so no one would cut through the line to get ahead of the other passengers. No sooner had I done that, when a dark haired woman wearing a mink coat came up to me. "Can I cut through here?" she said. I said, "No, you can't." It was Ethel Merman, the singer and actress. I recognized her because of the movie, "There's No Business Like Show Business." She was mad, but I could not let her through the line, as it wasn't fair to the hundred plus people who were standing in line waiting to board the 5 pm shuttle to New York. I would not do that, and have a riot on my hands. My shift had ended and I wanted to get home and pack, as I would be leaving the next day.

CHAPTER FORTY-FIVE

My Trip Around the World

I would be gone for almost two weeks. My itinerary was long. I went home and packed and made sure the house was secure and told my neighbors to be on the lookout as I would be away. When one of us was away we would watch each other's houses to make sure all was all right. The next day I took a cab to the airport to Eastern Airlines.

Flight 71 to John F. Kennedy Airport was leaving on time, at 9:30 am in the morning. The flight was on time, departing out of gate six. My fellow workers who were working the flight, William Mooney and William Bateman, gave me a great sendoff. I thanked them for it.

"Good luck." they said. "See you when you return. Have a safe and enjoyable trip." Off I went and boarded the Boeing 707 to New York's Kennedy airport. It took about an hour. I had plenty of time to make my connection with Pan Am flight 2 to Fairbanks Alaska. It would take about five hours with the time changes. September was a great month to fly, as it wasn't that hot. We arrived at John F. Kennedy airport. I waited for the courtesy bus that took me around to the different terminals. I had 2 and half hours to kill but I was happy that I wasn't late running for a plane to catch, like I usually do.

The bus stopped, and the driver made an announcement that this was Pan American's terminal. I took my baggage and went out the door near the bus driver so as to thank him. "You're welcome, have a good flight." "Thanks," I responded. A skycap approached me. He asked me, "Do you need help with your baggage?" "Sure," came my response. "Yes right up to the ticket counter please."

"Okay sir." He turned and asked, "Where are you off to?" "I am going around the world." "Around the world, oh my, what a trip." "Yes Fairbanks, Tokyo, Hong Kong, Thailand, New Delhi, Beirut, and London and then finally home."

"Wow," he said, "that is some journey." "I know I'm excited and the main reason is my brother is in the Air force in Thailand and with the Vietnam War going on and I want to see him. I have two brothers in the Air force. One in Anchorage, Alaska, and I have seen him recently." "That's wonderful," he said. "I love them very much, and helped raised them." We approached the ticket counter and I tipped him and again he said, "I wish you well sir, take care." "Thank you," I said. I checked my baggage, and the ticket agent told me the flight wasn't full and it looked very good for me to make the flight.

"Wonderful," I said. The ticket agent checked my bags, and although I wasn't stopping in Fairbanks, we would be there for an hour and half, before going on to Tokyo, Japan. I walked to gate nine where my flight would depart from. I had one whole hour and a half. It was six o'clock, and I thought the best thing to do was make sure I had my boarding pass handy when I boarded the flight and my passport. I bought the New York Times and read for quite a while. Of course the paper was full of the war. That I couldn't escape even if I had wanted to. The time passed, I sat across from the gate area and I saw that there were not many passengers. I would fly into the freezer meaning the cold weather, and then towards the warm weather I thought. New York City to Fairbanks, Alaska, weather permitting would take about five hours, and five thousand miles I thought. I heard the announcement that the flight was ready for boarding. The captain came on the loudspeaker system on the aircraft to welcome us aboard, and to say that the flight would be on time. I looked out the window, and could see ramp service pulling the baggage loader away from the aircraft. The flight attendants came around to make sure we had our seats belts fastened. The gate agent closed the door, and we were ready to be towed out from the gate area. We taxied out towards the runway for takeoff. I was saying good-by to the continental United States for about two weeks and wondering what new adventures lay before me. I got myself comfortable. The plane was not full and I had the two other seats to myself. I had brought my stocking slippers that I had gotten from Alitalia Airlines when I flew to Athens, Greece via a connection from Rome, Italy. I simply placed my camera under one seat in front of me, and my carry on under the other seat in front of me. I took the armrests and raised them also. I could not lie down yet as we weren't airborne enough for the captain to turn off the seat belt sign. Then we would probably be up about 40,000 feet over New York State heading for Canada and Alaska. I didn't have long to wait. The sign was turned off, and I took the pillow and blanket that the flight attendant gave me. The cabin lights were turned off. The only lights left on were the exit signs in the emergency rows and the no smoking sign, plus the passenger's overhead reading lights. I had put my stocking slippers on over my stockings. I was pretty comfortable as you could be, and off to sleep I went. I was tired, as I did not have enough sleep the night before, as I had worked overtime and I had to pack for my trip around the world. I was sleeping pretty soundly when air turbulence woke me up. I stared at my watch and I did sleep three hours that is how tired I was. If it wasn't for the air turbulence, I might have slept another hour very easily. I believed it would be another two hours before we reached Fairbanks, Alaska.

CHAPTER FORTY-SIX

Fairbanks, Tokyo, & Hong Kong

Approaching Fairbanks I got my first sight of snow. My first thought was, I hope I don't get stranded here as it was coming down heavy. The landing went very well considering the weather was not good. We were told we would be here for about twenty-five minutes. I placed an occupied sign on my seat, and got off the plane to see a little of Fairbanks. I went out of the terminal and walked up the only street Fairbanks had. I wanted to explore this outpost as it reminded me of a town of the old west. If I wanted an old west-mining town this was it.

This town had a saloon with the swinging doors like in the movie westerns. It was real, not a mirage. It was 25 degrees out. We had left New York at 74 degrees. I kept looking at my watch, to make sure, that I would return on time for the departure from Fairbanks. I got myself back to the terminal, and saw that passengers had not boarded the aircraft. The snow had begun to accumulate on the wings, and I knew that their ramp service had to glycol the wings for us to be able to take off. In the terminal we were told that we would be boarding momentarily. We started walking towards the plane and up the stairs. In my thoughts I was glad to be leaving, as I knew if we did not get out, we could be here for days. This is snow country and once you're in one of these blizzards you might as well say that you are stuck here. Once on board, I went to my seat and put the occupied card that I had on my seat in the seat jacket in front of me. I was kind of worried. Just then the captain came on to tell us to have our seat belts on, and once off the ground we would fly above this blizzard. The anti-skid had to be working and no hydraulic problems. I noticed that we had taken off, and then the captain said, "we were doing fine, and in just a few minutes we would be above this." I was nervous as we climbed above this, and was glad to see the sun, and blue sky as we headed out over the Pacific Ocean. We were headed for warmer temperatures as we flew towards Japan. I finally could sit back and relax knowing that I would not be stuck in Fairbanks, with a blizzard on us. I now could take my shoes off and put my stocking slippers on. As we flew I did not realize we were passing the International Date Line. I now lost track of time. I fell asleep and awoke to the flight attendant shaking me so as to give me a meal.

I didn't think of food, as I was groggy. "Sir, I have your tray of food. Aren't you hungry?" she said. "Oh yes, I am sorry, I am still half asleep. Thank you." I took the tray from her and turned and looked out the window. I could now see the ocean below us as we continued flying south. The captain came on to tell us it would be about six hours flying time to Japan. I ate my food, and left the tray for the flight attendant to take when she came around to collect them. I got up to stretch my legs and walk around as the seat belt sign was turned off.

The time passed and the captain came on to tell us we would be landing very soon in Tokyo. I quickly took my stocking slippers off and put them in my carry on bag with a small plastic bag. I hurried to get myself ready for landing, making sure I had taken and put all my things in my carry on bag. Tokyo for me was like New York City.

We landed, and I knew that Tokyo was expensive, and I had to check into my hotel as I was only here for two days and then on to Hong Kong. We had to walk to the terminal building. A big sign said, in English, "Welcome to Tokyo." I followed the signs in English to claim my baggage and then to get to my hotel. I did just that, and outside the taxicabs were waiting. I took a taxi to the hotel where I would stay for two nights before going on to Hong Kong. The next morning,

I was going to have a look around Tokyo. The clerk at the desk told me if I want to see just Tokyo, then I could see something of the city by walking around near the hotel or taking a taxicab around. I was told that the women catered to the men and, of course, I wanted to see geisha girls. The clerk said, "How long is your stay in Tokyo?" I replied, "I am leaving tomorrow." I would say that my stay in Tokyo was okay, but it was way too expensive. That night I saw a geisha show, the women were beautiful. I got back to my hotel at 2 a.m. and realized that I had some light packing to do as my flight on Pan American Airways was departing at 5 p.m. I wanted to see were Pentax cameras being made but I did not have the time.

I had the desk clerk call me a taxicab at 2 p.m. and I went to the airport. I knew Hong Kong would be very inexpensive. After a two-and-a-half hour flight, we landed at Hong Kong's Kai Tek Airport. Kai Tek had only one runway for aircraft landing and taking off from Hong Kong. Every piece of land was valuable as there were far too many people for a very small area. Hong Kong Island, Kowloon, and the New Territories made up all of Hong Kong. The population was growing. People were coming down from China in sampans every day to escape the harshness of life there. We got the clearance to land, and it went smoothly. At the time that I went to Hong Kong they did not have jet ways. We deplaned and boarded buses to the terminal area. Once through customs with my luggage I boarded the bus, as did other passengers from the same flight. On the way to my hotel, the Mandalay Hotel on Hong Kong Island, we drove into Hong Kong on the Kowloon side and I noticed many bars and dives. All the hookers, I mean girls, started waving at the bus as we went by. No let up here for sex, as this was one of the places the G.I.s came for "R and R," rest and relaxation, from the war that was going on in Vietnam.

The hotel lobby was gorgeous with fountains and plants all around. Money was spent here all right. I checked in, and went up to my room. The room was beautiful and had a jacuzzi which I made use of every day I was there. This was the tallest building on the island with twenty-five floors. As I unpacked, I looked out my window, and there to my surprise I could see a family living on the roof of a building. They had a sofa, chairs, a table, and a refrigerator I was amazed. What would they do if it rains? I guess you would put out the umbrellas. There was still time to go on a tour. The nightlife would come later. Since it was still daylight my first tour would be to tour Hong Kong Island.

I was a movie buff, and I had seen two movies filmed here on location. The first movie was, "Love Is a Many Splendored Thing," with William Holden, and Jennifer Jones, and the other was "The World of Suzie Wong," with William Holden, and Nancy Kwan.

Hong Kong Island was the classy side compared to Kowloon. I would tour Kowloon later as it was only twenty-five cents to get to Kowloon. The Hong Kong tour would last about an hour. On the tour a large house was pointed out where Jennifer Jones, the movie actress in the film "Love Is a Many Splendored Thing," was supposed to have lived. In reality, a rich Chinese businessman owned the house. The road narrowed and driving wasn't easy, making turns on a winding road.

We soon slowed to a crawl, and the tour guide pointed out William Holden's house. Holden liked Hong Kong, and he bought a house here. We visited Repulse Bay with the Chinese sampans nearby. I had to start to get accustomed to the odors, and I do mean odors.

Nightlife was beckoning and I did want some excitement. I went to a bar not far from the hotel. It wasn't too long when a woman approached me. She spoke English quite well. "You want to buy me a drink," she said. I said, "Sure." We talked for a few minutes. She told me her place where she lived was not far from here. I loved her bustline, as Chinese girls do not have big busts. The two knockers she had really got me. I loved it. It was an amazing experience. I didn't have to worry about AIDS back then, and since it was legal to be a prostitute they had to be registered with the authorities. What a thrill it was for me. I loved it. Why should I feel guilty? I was single. I slept a little as she did. I awoke and noticed she was still sleeping. I left her money and left. I took a cab back to my hotel and showered and went to bed. Tomorrow I would visit the New Territories near the Red Chinese border. These territories would revert back to China, but before that hi-rises would take up most of the land to try and alleviate the problem of overcrowding. Everywhere that the bus took us apartments were being built.

When we finally reached the border between Hong Kong and Red China, I could see the Red Chinese guards beyond the checkpoint. There really were no barriers, only signs and the guards. If China wanted to take control of Hong Kong now, China could do so. There would be no stopping them. I believe the reason for China not invading and taking control of Hong Kong was the hard currency China got from the British crown colony.

When I returned after a whole day of touring I was tired and went off to bed to have a good night sleep. The next day was my last day in Hong Kong. There was one tour left and that was the harbor tour. We went down to the pier and took a ferry across to Kowloon. In Kowloon, I boarded a Chinese junk for a tour around the harbor. On board I met a passenger by the name of Andrew Lattimore. In our conversation he told me he was a minister from the Church of the Seventh-Day Adventists. He had been traveling throughout much of Asia. He had been to Korea, Japan, and southeast Asia, and Thailand too. He mentioned India. "Don't go to India," he said. He told me that in Calcutta people are starving and dying in the streets. I interrupted him. "There is one thing that I want to see in India and that is the Taj Mahal. I do not want to see misery, and I will not go to Calcutta or Bombay." While going around the harbor, I got the whiff of one of the worst odors in my life. I had to hold my nose. I can still recall it and it was disgusting. I saw sampans where people actually lived, and went to the bathroom right there. No wonder there was quite a stench. They had built typhoon barriers to help against the storms.

Looking over the side of the Chinese junk you could see the dirty water and some of the waste. Alongside the junk came two young boys. They swam right up to the side of the junk and started yelling so we could hear them. Although I could not understand them, I knew what they wanted. They started beckoning and begging for money. I had about four Hong Kong dollars.

The pastor said, "If you throw them your money, they will never leave your side." I did not listen to him and threw the money in. I did not throw them in altogether, so they could get them all. How could they dive in that filth? It looked like they both made out fine. I turned to Pastor Lattimore and said, "You see in a small way I try to help. I can't stand the stench of the harbor, I'll be glad when this tour is over. These people living like this, eating, sleeping, and excreting in the water, they will never get rid of the stench, most of these people never set foot on land. I can see why they are building new apartments in the New Territories to try to alleviate the problem."

The tour finally ended and, boy, I don't think there was one person as glad as I was. I returned to the hotel and took a nap for an hour or so and decided to go shopping.

It was a beautiful day. The temperature was eighty degrees. I walked along the street, it seemed to be raining. Funny, I didn't see any clouds. I looked up and, behold, the drops were coming down not from clouds in the sky, but clothes hung over poles from one balcony to another. This was the drip-drying of clothes. Just then a middle-aged man came up to me in the street. He was beckoning me to buy his Seiko watch. I nodded and shook my head to show him that I wasn't interested. I was warned that people would come up to me in the street out of nowhere and try to sell you something. If it isn't a watch, maybe clothes or shoes, almost anything. I passed one shop, and right in front of the shop was a bed all made up and ready for its occupant. It was my last night in Hong Kong, so I spent it taking a ride on the tram to Victoria Peak, and looking across to Kowloon from Hong Kong Island.

Thousands and thousands of lights. What a sight. It had been an experience. I did purchase silk pajamas and a Scottish cashmere sweater. The pajamas five dollars and the sweater for ten dollars. Bargains impossible to believe, but true nevertheless. I also bought a cross-carved out of solid ivory. This was only twenty dollars. Imagine ivory for that price. I returned to my hotel to retire for the night. I had a full day. I wasn't about to go out looking for excitement.

The next day I left for Thailand. I thought of my brother who I was going to visit in Thailand. I did not know at the time if my brother was flying or working on the ground, maintaining the aircraft. It was late afternoon when I arrived in Bangkok, Thailand. My hotel for the next few days would be The Asia Hotel. I asked the desk clerk for information on going to Utapao. "Yes, there is bus service," he said. "When do you wish to travel there?" I replied, "I would like to go tomorrow."

Rather than discovering Bangkok at night as I had imagined, sex here would be easy to have, and it was but I remembered tomorrow, and I did not want some hooker chasing me for some money. A night like that would have been a disaster. Here prostitutes were legal and made their living off the servicemen who came to Bangkok on R+R (rest and relaxation) coming from Vietnam. The next morning, I went down to the lobby, and the desk clerk called a taxicab for me. I asked the taxicab driver if he knew English. He said he did. I then asked him to take me to the bus station. "I want to go to Utapao." "I'll take you," he said. His English was good. "How much?" I asked. He answered "Twenty-five dollars." "No, too much money, take me to the bus station." "Okay fifteen dollars," came from his mouth. I said, "That is a very good price." We were off just as soon as I could get my baggage into the trunk. I realized that I was heading to somewhere that I knew nothing about. My life was now in the hands of this short, dark- haired taxi driver. Just as we left the city limits, oh my God, it happened with a jolt as he opened the engine right up. We were going one hundred plus miles. If this is it, I said to myself, let me die fast so I won't feel a thing. It was hot over hundred degrees, as we headed south. With no air-conditioning, I opened the windows on either side to circulate the hot air. Now I had to contend with not only the hot air but also the odor that entered the taxicab. It was the smell of manure, oh boy. The land was flat no mountains and that lovely air. I saw another sight that I did not see anywhere else. Here were houses on stilts; no foundation whatsoever and they all had TV antennas.

They loved their television. There wasn't a house without an antenna. Utapao was ninety miles from Bangkok. I knew the ride would be a little over two hours, but not with this driver. He was determined to get me there in one hour. Thank God there was no traffic on the road.

What an accident I would have made. The scenery kept going by me like a flash card. Now you see it, now you don't.

CHAPTER FORTY-SEVEN

Meeting My Brother

We were approaching Utapao. Just ahead of us was the base and we came to the gate. I told the sentry that I was American, and I had come to see my brother giving the sentry his name. He said, "Drive up to that building there, and go inside and see the sergeant at the desk." When we drove up to the building, I told the driver to stay there and, of course, I did not pay him. I did not want him to take off on me, so he had to stay as long as I wanted him to. I went in and spoke to the sergeant by greeting him and identifying myself. I said I wanted to see my brother. I knew that my brother would be shocked, as I never wrote him to tell him I was coming.

I waited for him for about twenty minutes but not without anticipation. Then out of nowhere came this huge yell, "Sonny" and two eyes so shiny that they looked like glasses shining on the window behind me. As for myself, I could not stop my eyes from fogging up with my own tears. "Here I am, Johnny, I told you that I would be here."

"Do you have something in your eyes?" "No, it's my tears getting in the way you crazy fool. How have you been?" "Okay, Sonny." "Now that you're here I feel better." I said to him, "I know that you can't tell me too much about what is going on here. I know that they bomb Vietnam from here, and I don't need to know any more."

He acknowledged this with his gestures and his eyes. "Go and take off for a while," the sergeant said, "I'll tell them that your brother came to see you." I was seeing Johnny for the first time in three years. I had been against them signing up and going in the service because of the war in Vietnam. I was afraid of both of them going to Vietnam. Leo of course ended up in Alaska, at Elmendorf Air Force base, in Anchorage.

Johnny was stationed here in Thailand right next door to Vietnam. In my heart I was so happy to see and hug him. He would never know how I felt in my soul. "I don't care if I sleep in the barracks with the men," I said. "Look even if I stayed just one day, just seeing you standing there before me, wow, it's just so unbelievable." "Sonny, you won't be able to stay more than a day." "Okay, I'll have to put the driver up for the night as well as I am not paying him until I return to Bangkok." So that is exactly what happened. I didn't care; to me it was like a month staying for a day. I knew there was a lot going on there at the base and they did not want many people nosing around.

The next day I said good-bye, even though I hated to part. We both got emotional. "Why don't you wipe your face? I said. "The perspiration gets in the way; it's so hot here," he said. Now it was time for me to return to Bangkok and take Pan Am to New Delhi, India I told my brother, that I would write when I got home. "Sonny," he said, "I know you will, but if you forget, I'll know you are busy." "No, no, Johnny, I'll write to be sure." I grabbed him, and hugged him and I didn't want to let him go. "Sonny, you have to let me go." "No, I can't," I blurted out with tears streaming down my face, and my frantic cries for him. It made other servicemen turn and stare. "I love you, Johnny I miss you already," as I turned and opened the door to the taxicab that would return me to Bangkok. "Sonny, I love you too. Don't worry, I'll be all right," he exclaimed.

The taxi drove off and I waved to him, looking out the window. We returned to Bangkok at a hundred miles an hour amid the smells of the lowlands. After an exhausting two-hour drive, I arrived back in the capital and back to my hotel. I set my alarm clock for 10:00 a.m. so I could to the airport early. I knew that I had lost weight since I left the States. I hardly ate the food in the Orient, it would make me sick.

Hong Kong had been the worst, but thanks to the British, I was able to get a decent breakfast. In Bangkok they ate so many different foods. I could have been eating snake and not know it. I went down to the lobby to check out, and leave for the airport.

There in the lobby was the cab driver waiting for me. What a surprise! "I wait for you in the taxi, okay?" he said. "Okay" I said. The clerk had told him that I was leaving, and he decided to come to take me to the airport. Within twenty minutes I arrived at the airport. I said goodbye to the taxicab driver and brought my luggage to the Pan Am ticket counter. I received my boarding pass and proceeded to the gate for my flight to New Delhi. In a short time I boarded my flight for New Delhi, India. I was saddened as we lifted off, thinking of my brother Johnny.

We would be flying over Burma, and on into New Delhi. I had my reservations at the Hilton Delhi. I went through customs, and I saw a taxicab, and I asked him to take me to the Hilton Delhi Hotel. In his very heavy accent in English he said. "I will take you." "Thank you." I replied. Off we went to the hotel. No sooner had I checked in and told the hotel clerk I wanted to go to Agra. "There is a train that will take you to Agra, but it is not what you might expect," he told me. He told me it was a long ride. "It is a hundred miles south from here. "He was preparing me for what ended up being a cattle car. My choice was to go. I did not have a little man here that would bargain with me to take me to Agra for little money. My choice to go or not to go. Naturally, I said to myself full speed ahead. I did not come halfway around the world to miss this great opportunity of seeing something that I read about in books. Now I would be able to touch this magnificent and beautiful marble structure. I wasn't there yet. The next morning, I awoke early enough to see the sunlight coming through the blinds in my room. I showered and got dressed and went down downstairs. Luckily they had what I wanted to eat for breakfast.

It was an American Breakfast, which I enjoyed very much. I ate twice as much as I normally did, not knowing what I was in for as far as food was concerned. I told the clerk on duty that I wanted to go to Agra to see the Taj Mahal. "Well, I will tell you the train ride is nothing like the trains you have in the United States," he said. "Would you please get me a taxi?" I said. I got into the taxicab, and told the driver I want to go Agra to see the Taj Mahal. The driver said, "Yes, I will take you to the train station." I expected maybe he would volunteer to drive me to Agra so I would not have to endure the train ride. No such luck. A train ride it was. Good luck I said to myself.

I arrived at the train station expecting the worst, and after purchasing my ticket, I got on a cattle car. The natives spoke very little English. One dark- haired man approached me. "Excuse me sir," he said. "I would like to assist you." I replied, "Thank you, I am fine." He kept one eye on me and one eye on my luggage. "Are you traveling far from New Delhi?" He asked. "I am going to Agra." "Ah, it must be the Taj Mahal that calls you." He kept rambling on, "You must stay overnight at my house and be comfortable, sir." "I am going to stay at the hotel nearby, thank you." Again he was most persistent and I tried to ignore him. "Do you understand English, sir?" I asked.

He saw that I was traveling alone, and that I was American and he knew that he had a good catch here to maybe rob me at night if I spent the night at his house. This, of course, I would never do. I was now concerned more than ever as I was traveling alone in a strange country. He kept annoying me all the way to Agra. He kept eyeing me and, of course, I wasn't about to let him get away with anything. When I arrived in Agra, I had to push my way off the train. I asked at the station if the hotel was nearby. "Yes" the agent said, "a short walk from here." Meantime this man who had his eye on me disappeared. This was disturbing to me. Oh well, I do hope I don't see him again. I checked in at the hotel for the night. I kept a watchful eye, as I believed this man was watching me, and I wasn't going to let my guard down. I asked the clerk at the hotel how far the Taj Mahal was from here. He said, "Sir, the mosque is very near just walk out from here and take a right and walk for about ten minutes and you will come right to it."

The next morning, I followed the clerk's directions and beheld the Taj Mahal.

CHAPTER FORTY-EIGHT

The Taj Mahal

The Taj Mahal stood before me in all its magnificence. It was a sight to see and I could touch it with my hands to make sure I was not dreaming. No matter how many words I could write about it, they would not be enough to describe its splendor.

Here was the embodiment of a love story of the ages, Mumtaz Mahal and her Prince Charming. A mosque built because of the love of one woman.

I quickly did my sightseeing as I did not want to be late for my train ride back to New Delhi, and, of course, I was watching out for anyone who was suspicious. I saw the two tombs with their beautiful white marble-lace.

I quickly walked back to the hotel, checked out, and took a taxi-cab to the train station for my ride back to New Delhi. I dreaded the train ride, as it was again one hundred uncomfortable miles. As the train pulled out of Agra, I knew that I would never close my eyes on the ride to New Delhi. A man who sat across the aisle from me eyed me. He did nothing but stare at me.

He got up from his seat and came over to talk to me. "Pardon me, I wish to inquire if you are an American?" "Yes I am." "Are you going to New York, sir?" He asked. "No I am not going to New York." I said. "We know you work for an airline as we have inquired about you." "Why should you inquire about me? I am traveling visiting my relatives, and I do not wish to be bothered, thank you." Our conversation ended there. I could not wait for the train to arrive back in New Delhi.

Many things crossed my mind. Could this man try to stop me from leaving India? I didn't need this. I arrived in New Delhi in the middle of the afternoon. My flight was at 7:00p.m. I went directly to the airport.

The hours did pass, and I boarded the aircraft and sat by the window. Here I could see that the luggage was being put on the plane. Just as I thought I could relax, I looked out the window and noticed a trickle of liquid coming from underneath the plane.

It got larger and larger, and soon it was like a lake. My God, it wasn't water. It was jet fuel. The flight attendant came quickly up the aisle. "Sir you will have to get off, hurry please no time for anything." I could see many people operating water trucks. Many people were all over the plane. We would have to go inside to wait to see if they could clean this all up. One match and we would all be in paradise.

We got off the plane and headed for an area that was for passengers only, to wait this out. I joined other astonished passengers, some crying and others with the worried look showing in their faces. I could see some airline employees under the plane. I could see what looked like a maintenance crew working on stopping the fuel leak. They did, and I could see a man coming toward the waiting room to tell us what was happening.

The agent said that everything was fine and we would be boarding soon. There were shouts of joy and relief.

No one would dare light a cigarette for fear of sending us into an inferno from which we would never escape. Another employee of Pan Am said they had the necessary part, and it would take forty-five minutes to replace the part. After an hour we were told to board the plane. After getting seated and settled the captain came on the loudspeaker and announced that we would be on our way shortly and he thanked us for our patience. I noticed that ramp service was loading baggage and that was a good sign. We got the clearance to take off from New Delhi. We took off, and I looked out the window and there below was New Delhi. Circling, we headed east toward Afghanistan and

Iran, then to Beirut. We arrived in Beirut at a time when the country was pretty quiet. That is not the case today. I stayed at the Hilton, as it was the only hotel that I knew. I did go to a club that tourists frequented. It was called the Club Arabia. I saw belly dancers and it reminded me of home where the local Greek-owned nightclubs had belly dancers. I had food, which was a little familiar to me. They did have baklava, an original Greek dessert that was brought to the Arab world when the Turks conquered Greece about 500 years ago and stole the Hellenic cuisine, which had been around for a few thousand years.

The Turks knew nothing of cooking good food. The only thing they knew was of killing people and stealing their land as they had done to the Greeks and the Armenians who had been in Asia Minor for thousands of years before the Turks came there. At the Club Arabia, the Arabic music was inviting and I was familiar with it. I remembered back in Boston the Club Morocco and the belly dancer Morocco who danced across the floor.

I sat at a table not far from the musicians. A waiter came over to me and in a very heavy accent asked me, "What do you wish, sir?" I answered him that I would like raki, which is similar to Ouzo, the Greek liqueur. "Yes we have raki. What do you mean on the rocks?" "I mean with ice please." The music made me think of the many Greek dances that I had gone to back home. There were two belly dancers. While the first one performed, I drank my drink slowly. I wanted to see the second dancer. The two belly dancers were not beautiful girls. One was a little hefty and the other was too skinny. I didn't dare put any money in their bras or on the lower part of their body for fear of antagonizing someone. I did not know the customs there. I enjoyed the music very much. I had forgotten the time. I glanced at my watch and looked up and the waiter appeared. "Do you wish another drink, sir?" he asked. "No, thank you," was my answer. I had nursed my one drink for a while. What do I owe you? Here is six dollars," I said before he could answer.

Leaving the Club Arabia, it was warm and a beautiful night. I saw my driver there and I got into his cab. "Did you have a good time?" he asked. "I did, thank you. I would like to return to the hotel. Upon my arrival, I gave him another tip. He asked me, "When do leave Beirut?" "Tomorrow," I said. "I will take you to the airport." "I will be ready at 4:00 p.m. My flight is at 7:00 p.m."

I was tired with time changes traveling through the Middle East. Tomorrow I would be on my way to London, which would be my final city, before crossing the ocean. I would have flown 25,000 miles around the world. My flight was in the early evening and I wanted to be at the airport early. I hung around the hotel and decided to walk around outside but not too far from the hotel. I walked two streets away from the hotel, but no farther. I returned and had lunch. I was ready to leave for the airport. My taxi driver came to the hotel. Off I went to the airport. So for three hours I walked around the airport. I saw the sun go down. It was now getting to the point that I proceeded to the gate for the flight.

CHAPTER FORTY-NINE

Returning to Boston

I was on the flight to London, and then home to Boston. I would not stop over in London, although the flight would stop to deplane passengers to London and to board passengers going to the United States. I was too tired to get off the plane when I arrived in London.

Sometime in the future I would like to see London. Now was not the time. All I wanted to do now was to get home, back to the States. Someone had brought a wet towel and saturated my face. This brought a response from me. "It's cold who, what?" My eyes opened to find a pillow behind my head and a blanket. I pushed the call button and the flight attendant came down the aisle. "I just wanted to say how thankful I am that you took care of me during my long nap." "You are very welcome," she said. " I have traveled many miles and stopped at different places, like Alaska, Japan, Hong Kong, Thailand and India just to name a few." "My you have traveled sir," the flight attendant said. "Again I thank you for what you have done for me." Just then over the loudspeaker system came the announcement to fasten our seat belts to prepare for landing. I looked out the window.

We were flying along the coast of Maine. We would be landing in about twenty minutes. I kept looking out the window. Local time was 6:30 p.m. As I looked out the window I could see more and more land, and finally the skyline of Boston. Boy, did that look good to me. I missed home, I have wonderful memories but there is no place like home.

We circled to get in position to land. The touch down was great. I went to the baggage claim area. I had sent a telegram to my girlfriend Betsy telling her my flight number and arrival time. Going through customs and the customs officer learning that I worked for Eastern Airlines at Logan Airport, sped me through.

I came out of customs to hear someone calling out, "Sonny. Sonny." I turned to see my girlfriend Betsy. I immediately kissed her and held her tight. "Wow" she said, "I missed you." "I missed you too." I said. "Sonny, you look tired," she said. "I am," I told her "I bought you an evening bag in Hong Kong. It is all beaded. How are your mother and father?" I asked. "Fine," Betsy said. "I am going to take you to home," she continued. I told her that I would talk to her later on. I had gone through so many time changes and I was exhausted. She drove me home to Malden and I said good night. I knew I would sleep like a log as long as the phone didn't ring.

I knew tomorrow would be a very busy day, but I had it off. My first thing after getting a good night's sleep was doing the laundry, and getting ready for the next day at the airport.

I managed to get my suits dry-cleaned that I needed for work, and my shoes shined. Upon returning to work my fellow workers welcomed me back, and asked me a lot of questions. It wasn't long till spring and I started to pay back the days I owed to my fellow workers. Summer passed quickly and soon fall was upon us and winter not far behind. Now it would start to be very busy once again. The busiest travel time of the year was approaching once again. Thanksgiving.

This particular day I was working the 4:00p.m. shuttle to New York with Bill and he came up the jetway to tell me the flight was ready for boarding. I started collecting the boarding passes for the flight when I looked up, and saw Margaret Hamilton coming towards me. I stopped and greeted her and said to her that you will never be able to forget one role that you played. "I know, the Wicked Witch of the West from The Wizard of Oz," she said. I am so sick of that," she continued. She went on to tell me that she was visiting her son who was attending Harvard University in Cambridge. She thanked me for my good wishes and Bill and I closed out the flight.

I would have a second confrontation with Ethel Merman, as she would insist on going past many passengers to get on the shuttle to New York. I had to call security and a heated conversation ensued. In the end she was allowed to board the flight.

I can remember one busy day when Raymond Burr approached me as I was walking from the shuttle side to reservations side. "Can you tell me where American Airlines is?" I recognized him immediately, no guessing here. "Yes" I said, " it is the next terminal over." "You may walk or take a bus or taxi to get there. I am glad to meet you." No response, even when I said, "I enjoyed Perry Mason." His reaction was very cold, not a word, not even a thank you.

My encounter with Telly Savalas's brother George was very cordial and warm. I enjoyed talking with him. Kojak was a very popular program. I recognized him instantly.

Yiasou came right out of my mouth when I spoke to him in the front of the ticket counter. He was heading in the direction of the shuttle to New York. He returned the greeting by asking for my name and complimenting me on my knowledge of the Greek language. "You know the language well," he said. I continued the conversation in Greek and so did he. With the warmest of handshakes, we parted, not without telling him how much I enjoyed Kojak again.

CHAPTER FIFTY

My Trip to Israel

In spring of 1970, El Al the Israeli airline was offering a trip six nights seven days to Israel for one hundred and forty-nine dollars. It had just started non-stop service to Tel-Aviv from New York via the Kennedy International Airport I had never been on the Israeli airline and I was excited. Israel wow I thought to myself. I had no problem asking my fellow workers to swap days. I okayed it with my supervisor juicy Brucey as we used to call him. From his blue eyes I could see his grin. "So you're off again. You found a home here, Ernie." I laughed and said, "of course" "Great, Ernie, enjoy yourself and have a good trip." I had secured all my days off. Again I would be going to New York and Kennedy International Airport. I said good-by to my girlfriend Betsy, and told her that I would see her in about 10 days.

I would be traveling on the safest airline in the skies. El Al was at a terminal by itself. We were subjected to searches twice before being allowed on the aircraft. The cargo was even screened. Nothing would be left that wasn't searched or screened. I saw Israeli soldiers around the plane.

When we finally reached Tel-Aviv after ten hours, the passengers all clapped and thanked the captain for a safe flight from New York. We arrived in the afternoon around 5 p.m. to warm breezes and the sunshine. Tel-Aviv has a modern airport. A man approached the passengers asking who the airline employees were. He said, "All airline employees please come with me." Outside the terminal building there was a bus waiting for all of us. We all got on the bus. When it seemed all were on board a man went around counting heads. After coming forward to the front of the bus and turning he said, "we are missing one passenger, ah here she comes." As she got on the bus she blurted out, "I am sorry I kept you waiting." She found herself a seat. This man then introduced himself.

"My name is Myron Gallia. Please don't call me Moron, I am with the Israeli Office of Tourism. We will have an official from the government at a supper this evening at the Dan Hotel. I would like to introduce Hananya; he will be our bus driver for the next eight days. I will be your guide to tour Israel and explain our heritage and culture. We will try to cover much of the country and explain the why of this and that.

"Israel is a young nation only twenty-two years old. Israel was born out of hardship and toil for Jewish people everywhere to remember the homeland that we once had and realize the belonging to a place that was there long before there was a United States of America. Well, we're off to the hotel to get you settled, and freshened up for the events that are to follow."

We arrived at the Dan Hotel, a very modern hotel on the shores of the Mediterranean Sea.

We would only spend the night before leaving for Jerusalem and checking in at the King David Hotel. At dinner a gentleman came forward and introduced himself. "My name is Oscar Raditz from the Israeli Government Tourist Office." He went on to say that he was glad that we had come to Israel to see the country first hand. We each introduced ourselves and told of how we each decided to make a trip to Israel. I had met Ann and Jack Belkin at dinner when we all introduced ourselves. In our introduction we told of what airline we worked for. It so happened Ann worked for Eastern Airlines in Miami Florida. I said I would see them in the morning.

After the meal, our guide, Myron, told us to be ready for a 9:00 a.m. departure for Jerusalem. I knew that I would have to be awakened by 7:00 a.m. I stopped by the front desk and asked the desk clerk for a 7:00 a.m. wake up call. I was very excited, and I went to bed.

I awoke with the ring of the phone in my room and then the alarm went off. I jumped up grabbed the phone and told the desk clerk thank you very much. I had my bags all ready to go, and I finished getting dressed when there was a knock on the door.

The voice on the other side of the door said, "Ernie are you up yet?" I recognized Ann Belkin's voice. I answered her by opening the door and I said, "I am ready to go down to have my breakfast." "Great" she said. "Jack is all ready. All I have to do is just knock on the door to our room to let him know that I knocked on your door and you're ready." The door to Ann's room opened and Jack came out. "Hey Ernie how did you sleep?" "Jack, I was all wound up too excited." They both started laughing as we took the elevator down to the lobby, and then walked to the dining room. I knew that everything would be dairy and I was glad of it, as I wanted to eat a good breakfast. We sat and had a great breakfast. As we finished our breakfast, Hananya the bus driver and Myron Gallia came into the dining room and greeted everyone. He told everyone to be outside by the bus by 8:45 a.m. for our trip to Jerusalem.

CHAPTER FIFTY-ONE

Jerusalem & Bethlehem

The ride was over an hour, and as we approached Jerusalem, I had to pinch myself to see if I was really here. We arrived at the King David Hotel, checked in, and were told to meet in the lobby for afternoon sightseeing. Our first stop would be the Wailing Wall.

Here is the only part of the ruins of the Temple of Solomon that remains. Rabbis and many people stop and pray here. Many leave written prayers in the cracks of the walls. We climbed up to the temple mount and beheld two mosques. The first was the Mosque of Omar or the Dome of the Rock. This mosque was built around the 8th century and built over a huge rock. It is important for two reasons. First it is the place where Abraham was to sacrifice his son Isaac to God, and second, according to the Moslems, the prophet Mohammed ascended to heaven on his horse. The second mosque is the Al Aksa.

We next went to the Jaffa Gate. We could look down at the excavations and saw the original gate as it was in Christ's time. We proceeded in through this gate. You could not drive with a car or a bus into the Old City of Jerusalem. Only the camels, horses, or donkeys were allowed. We saw the pool where Christ gave a blind man his sight. In the fourteenth century, a map was discovered that supposedly showed the way Christ carried his cross. There were markings on the buildings showing that this was the Way of the Cross. We kept following this way and passed under an arch where Pontius Pilate said, "Behold the Man" to the crowd before the Crucifixion. We kept walking and came to a doorway with a sign over it, which read the church of the Holy Sepulcher. This church, however, was built around the twelfth century during the Crusades. The Moslems destroyed the original one here when they had captured Jerusalem around the sixth century. In 1964, a historic meeting took place here between the Patriarch Athenagoras of Constantinople and Pope Paul V1 to try and heal a thousand years of bickering and name-calling. The split occurred in 1054 as the Roman Catholic pope had claimed supremacy and the Eastern Orthodox Churches would not go along with the idea.

Scaffolding was in place, and I had learned that the Greek government was paying for the restoration of the church. An amazing thing happened during the restoration.

Ruins of the third century church that Helen, the Emperor Constantine's mother, had built were found. She had commissioned three churches to be built. This one in Jerusalem, the Church of the Nativity in Bethlehem, and the Church of the Annunciation in Nazareth. The Church of the Holy Sepulcher is shared by many religions, including the Greek Orthodox, the Armenian Apostolic and the Roman Catholic churches.

Many years ago, with the fighting of the various Christian sects, the key was given to a Moslem family who opens the church and locks it at night. When the Moslems captured Jerusalem back in the sixth century they laughed and would say, "You, who are supposed to have the true faith, fight among yourselves. This is why the key was given to a Moslem family to try to bring some peace to this situation."

Upon entering the church is the stone of Unction where Jesus' body was prepared for burial. I climbed up to Golgotha, the spot where he was nailed to the cross between two thieves. There are many cantilia or holy lights plus holy icons. I cried here as God let me see these wonderful sights. I could see where the rock split during an earthquake. I climbed down from Golgotha, and went nearby to the tomb of Joseph of Arimathea, where Jesus was buried after he was crucified. I entered the tomb where they placed his body. Each Pascha, Orthodox Easter, a miracle happens here and that is the fire that comes from the tomb and candles are lit. This happens at the Orthodox Pascha, which coincides with the Hebrew Passover. It is quite a miracle. I spoke to a priest there as he guarded the tomb of Christ. Speaking in Greek, I asked him about the night before the Resurrection at Pascha and the miracle of the fire that happens here. He told me the tomb is sealed as all the candles are blown out and when the patriarch enters the tomb there is no candle lit and he comes out with his candle lit. I had separated from the others that I was traveling with. Myron called out to me and I hurried back and found the rest of the group that I had come with. I bade farewell to a young priest I met who came from Greece to serve here as he told me, "I love God and where he was here, this is where I want to be," he said. He wished me a good trip returning to the United States. I thanked him, and said I would return.

Our next stop would be the Garden of Gethsemane. The Church of all Nations is here. This church was built over the rock where Christ prayed the night Judas Iscariot betrayed him for thirty pieces of silver. The olive trees are very old. Some think they date to the time of Jesus. An iron fence prevented us from touching the trees. Nearby is a Russian Orthodox Church of Mary Magdalene built in 1888 by Tsar Alexander the third. We would proceed to the ruins of Caiphas's house. He was the high priest of the Jews. It was here that Peter denied Jesus three times before a rooster crowed. I met a Franciscan monk here whom I spoke with and he gave me a cross made out of olive wood. Of course we did not see eye to eye on many things. I told him that you do not need a pope. Although we disagreed, we parted in peace. Next we went upstairs and came into a barren room.

The Moslems had written Arabic writing on the walls. This room was very important. Passover was celebrated here by Jesus with his disciples. The breaking of bread and the drinking of wine and a new covenant. It was here that Judas Iscariot betrayed him.

From there we went on to the Mount of Olives near the Garden of Gethsemane. Looking toward Jerusalem I could see a gate closed called The Golden Gate. This is the gate that Christ came through to enter Jerusalem at the beginning of Passover, a day Christians call Palm Sunday. Nearby is the Kidron Valley, where it is believed the resurrection of the dead will begin when the Messiah comes. Gehenna south of the city was a place where children were sacrificed to the god Moloch, and was later used to burn corpses of criminals and animals.

We also saw St. Stephen's Gate where St. Stephen, the first Christian martyr, was ordered stoned by Saul, who would later believe that Jesus was the foretold Messiah. What a majestic view of this Holy City.

We went on to Bethlehem, very close to Jerusalem. Probably about four miles separate Jerusalem from Bethlehem to its south. We arrived in Manger Square and getting off the bus I turned to see a huge church, The Church of the Nativity, different in architecture with a small entrance. This remarkable church holds a miraculous story.

When the Moslems conquered Bethlehem, the entrance to the church was much larger than it is now. People could go in on their horses, so the crusaders lowered the entrance when they wrested control of the holy places from the Saracens. When the Moslems entered the church to destroy it, they were shocked to see on the wall a tapestry of The Three Wise Men. The Wise Men appeared to be Arabs; all wore turbans plus one of them was darker than the other two. They refrained from damaging the church, leaving it as it is today. We lowered our heads and entered the church.

Myron, the tour guide, called me over. "Ernie, I want you to meet the priest." "Yes Myron" "Father Gerasimos, I would like you to meet this fellow." Recognizing his black robes, I turned to him and spoke to him in Greek. "Good day Father Gerasimos," I said. He told me the church had always been in Greek Orthodox hands between the time when the land was conquered until the present. The Greek Orthodox Church fought with other denominations. The Armenian Orthodox is permitted limited access. The Catholic church of Saint Catherine is next door and they are permitted access only to the grotto below but cannot hold services in the basilica.

Father Gerasimos took me to the altar, which is very old as are the icons and holy lights. We proceeded to go to the side of the altar where there are steps leading down to the grotto below. The original entrance is now all closed up. Here on the floor is a star with a Latin inscription on it saying, "Here of the Virgin Mary, Jesus Christ Was Born."

The original crèche was stolen and taken to Rome. I got the goose bumps as he showed me the original entrance. He also told me to look at Shepherd's Field as it was then and is now. I gave him some Israeli money and thanked him for all the information he gave me. Myron came over to me. "Ernie, how did you like it?" I answered him, "This was very interesting believe me, thank you Myron." We were off to Nazareth, which we had to make before nightfall. We had plenty of time. We would pass Rachel's Tomb and the Tombs of the Patriarchs. On the way to Nazareth was the valley where Samson slew the lion by breaking his jaw. We went to Cana, where Jesus performed his first miracle turning water into wine. We passed another town where the harlot Mary Magdalene came from called Magdala.

CHAPTER FIFTY-TWO
Haifa & Nazareth

We would make one stop before going on to Nazareth, the port city of Haifa. It is the headquarters of the Bahai World Culture Centre. We were told how they came to Israel after being persecuted in Iran. The centre building was impressive, sitting atop a hill.

Haifa was a very busy seaport with many ships in the harbor. As we continued on we suddenly became engulfed in a downpour. Then one beautiful thing happened, a magnificent rainbow spread over the fields, and I remembered the Great Flood, and the promise that God would never destroy the world again by water, and God placed the rainbow in the sky as a reminder that He would remember and keep His promise forever.

Next we came to where the Sermon on the Mount was held. Here a church was built and inside on the walls of the church are written the beatitudes. This is one of the most beautiful areas that I have ever seen.

As the sun was getting ready to set, we approached Nazareth. We stopped at a sign that read Nazareth in English, Arabic, and Hebrew. Myron told us that the majority of the population were Christian Arabs. Here in Nazareth we visited three places. The most important were the ruins of the house of the Virgin Mary where the Archangel Gabriel came to hail her, and tell her the Messiah would be born to her. The Church of the Annunciation is built over the ruins of the house of the Virgin Mary. We then visited another church where Mary drew water from the well, and then visited a carpenter's shop such as was in the Messiah's time. Myron told us we had almost two hours of free time and to return to where the bus was parked then. I returned to the Church of the Annunciation and the grotto below to look at where Mary lived, knowing that she would bear the Messiah. This was really very exciting from Bethlehem in Palestine to Nazareth in Galilee. We made our way to Capernaum. Here was a restaurant and we stopped for lunch.

We next toured the ruins of the synagogue where Christ spoke to the congregation and announced that he was the long-awaited Messiah. Nearby were the ruins of Peter's house, one of the first disciples to be called by the Messiah to follow him.

We crossed the Sea of Galilee. Here miracles happened with the Messiah walking on the water, and of the apostles catching a lot of fish in their nets. We were heading north to spend the night at a kibbutz named Ayelet Hatashar. We would spend the night here. This kibbutz is very near the Lebanese border. That night after our evening meal we enjoyed the play "Hair" in Hebrew. Bedding down for the night the coolness of the evening breeze reminded me that it wasn't as humid as it gets back in Boston. I had a good night's sleep.

In the morning, breakfast was kosher, which I got used to from the very start of the trip to Israel. Dairy was not mixed with meat products, and absolutely no pork was allowed whatsoever. The reason being the pig was a hoofed animal and it was created by God to devour the garbage, and so the Hebrew people were told by God not to eat unclean animals. We toured the kibbutz after breakfast. It was very interesting as everyone contributed and shared in the agriculture of planting food, and in the government of the kibbutz. In the early afternoon we said good-bye to our hosts at the kibbutz.

CHAPTER FIFTY-THREE

The Golan Heights

We now went farther north to the Golan Heights. The Golan Heights were captured during the 1967 war with the Arabs. The Israelis captured East Jerusalem, the Golan Heights, and the whole West Bank right up to the Jordan River. Israel now had all the land that God had given to them when they came out of bondage, led by Moses from Egypt. This area should never be bargained for as God originally gave it to them.

Many of the Arab sects, The Druze, live in the Golan Heights area. I could see why Israel captured it from Syria. It was very strategic. Here before Israel captured this area, the Arabs could take potshots at the farmers below working their land. We were more fortunate than most tourists for we went to El Quneitra, which was a Syrian town captured by the Israelis, and we had Israeli soldiers for protection. I spoke to a few of the soldiers. The soldiers were amazed at my knowledge of the trouble between the Arabs and the Israel. One of the soldiers said to me you should be our foreign minister with all your knowledge. I thanked them, and wished them well as their lives were on the line as war could start at any time. We now left for Tel-Aviv. Myron, our guide spoke to me, and said, "Ernie, I did not realize how much you know of what is going on here." "This is the truth Myron, anyone who says other things is a liar, and a deceiver." "You will come back to Israel," Myron said.

There were places where I wanted to stay longer. My visit to Israel was very exciting, as I had seen places that I read about, and a chance to meet people of different backgrounds. Our last night would again be at the Dan Hotel. After we checked in at the hotel, I decided to take a walk along the shore and then to Jaffa. This city is next to Tel-Aviv. Jaffa is much older than Tel-Aviv. There were interesting houses and shops all done in the architecture of this old city. The city of Jaffa reminded you a little of Jerusalem, and Tel-Aviv was more like New York City. The evening breeze was very pleasant and I enjoyed just walking and looking at the skyline.

The Israelis have done so much since the creation of Israel in 1948, just twenty-two years later when I visited, and it is a flourishing democracy in the Middle East surrounded by one-man rule dictatorships. I always hope that God will watch over this country. I had a pleasant walk, but I really looked forward to getting back to the States. I felt that I had been away for years. I returned to the Dan Hotel, and saw Ann and Jack Belkin.They insisted that I have a drink with them. I did, and thanked them and said, goodnight. I called the front desk and asked the clerk to call me at 7:30 a.m. I took my shower and went to bed.

In the morning I made sure that I packed and had my suitcases ready to take to the lobby. I had bought a few things, a few books from Israel, which was very interesting for my return trip to Israel. The other things were a charm for my fiancée's bracelet, which I started to do with one of my trips to Greece. In Hong Kong, I had bought her a beaded handbag, which she still owns. In Greece, I bought her a charm for her bracelet. There could be no mistake of where it came from, it is the Parthenon. The charm from Israel was the Star of David.

The next day I awoke and had my breakfast and went walking around Tel-Aviv.

When I got to one of the main streets, there seemed to be some confusion, as I saw emergency equipment around and the police. I was told that a car had crashed with three people in it. It had hit a tree and the people were being taken away in an ambulance. The three occupants in the car were hurt pretty badly. On transporting them to the ambulance the police discovered they were Arabs with strapped bombs to their bodies, and were on their way to blow up a place where there were a lot of people and cause a great deal of damage. The site they were looking for was a busy restaurant on the main boulevard. I believe this was a miracle that no one was hurt, except the occupants of the car. Wow, I was right near it. Of course the Arabs were mad that Israel protects itself and won the war against them. I was sure the incident would be broadcast around the world. I did feel very fortunate to avoid what could have been a major catastrophe. I turned, and started walking back to my hotel. I went to my room, to bring my luggage to the lobby.

Getting off the elevator I found Myron Gallia in the lobby, with the rest of the group. I came up to Myron and said. "I just came from walking around the boulevard and came upon a car crash with police and the ambulance." I know," said Myron. "I have a two-way radio and I know what goes on." "You are very lucky, there was no explosion."

The rest of the party heard our conversation, and looked startled. Myron told us we would be going a different way to Lod Airport.

CHAPTER FIFTY-FOUR

Returning to Boston Massachusetts

We boarded the bus, and we were off to Lod Airport for our flight back to the United States. It was a little past noontime when we arrived at the airport. We had prepared a gift for Myron and Hananya. We were sure that they could use money, who couldn't? We all chipped in and gave them an envelope of money. They were so grateful and we in return were happy to have such wonderful people taking us all around the country. We said good-bye to them.

Before we boarded, we were subjected to a body search and after that passing through a metal detector. We kept our baggage unlocked so they could search our baggage. I felt very comfortable with El Al's personnel doing this. I felt safe. We would have one stopover before arriving in New York, and that would be in Zurich, Switzerland.

We boarded our flight and got into our seats and we were ready for takeoff. The flight to Zurich, Switzerland was fine.

In Zurich we went through another body search and again boarded the plane for our flight to New York.

From Zurich, on to New York and then Boston. When we landed in Boston, I made a dash for the public telephone and called my fiancée Betsy. Twenty-five minutes and she was at the airport. We drove home to Malden and I told her about my trip. When I arrived home I told her that I had an extra day for resting from my trip. I would call her tomorrow. She understood and I kissed her good night and went in to go to bed.

The next day I went and got my suits cleaned and pressed and was ready for my return to work.

My first day back at work and we had weather delays and some flights canceling due to mechanical problems.

Time went by and a new season was upon us. Soon we would be entering the busiest travel season. During this time Eastern Airlines started a new policy the other airlines were watching closely. This was named the Conditional Reservation. This was implemented to see if the problem of no shows could finally be addressed. This was recurring problem with all the airlines. People would call the airline make a reservation and never show up for the flight.

This conditional reservation would prove to be a boom for Eastern as it might solve this continuing problem. This is how it worked. When a person called Eastern, and wanted to book a flight, and was told that the flight was booked, the reservationist offered the person a conditional reservation. The passenger showed up for the flight to see if he or she could get on. If the person could not get on the flight, he or she was given a refund, minus the taxes and put on the next available flight free. This was a very good plan as long as the passenger wasn't concerned about when he or she would get to their destination.

With the busiest traveling season approaching this would be a perfect time to implement this policy and thus fill the airplane up and at the same time to solve the policy of no shows.

When I came to work the Wednesday before Thanksgiving, the terminal was full of people. People had spent the night, with some sleeping on the floor using their luggage for their pillows.

I had been asked to work the ticket counter, as the lines were out the front doors. Looking at the computer after I signed in, it showed all the flights full.

My first passenger had no reservations, and came to me with a story that he had to get to Miami, Florida as his father was dying from cancer, and I went through all the flights going to Miami, Florida and they were all booked. I believed his story, and told him to hang on, as I would do all I could to get him on a flight tonight. I asked his name and he said, "My name is John Grayson." "Okay Mr. Grayson, I'll do all I can to get you on a flight to Miami tonight." I looked around and I took a piece of paper from my cash drawer. On it was written a supervisor's sign. All the agents were given their coded signs as to sign into the computers. Everyone had their own and were told not to give it out to anyone. I had my own sign as well as a supervisor's sign which no other agent had. I had gotten this when I worked as a gate agent.

One of the supervisors was being transferred and said to me, "I know that you are and always will be a terrific worker as you found a home here, and I can see what kind of a worker you are." I will never forget his words to me. Now was my chance to help a fellow human being in need. I signed out of my regular sign and used the supervisor's sign. I immediately signed in with the supervisor's sign and put Mr. Grayson on the non-stop to Miami departing at 8:40pm and gave him an aisle seat. I looked up at him and said, "okay Mr. Grayson, you are all set, and I gave you an aisle seat." He could not thank me enough. I wished him well and he left the ticket counter to go to the gate, which was gate 6. The rest of the evening went by very fast. So the ticket line was short as I could see the end of the line. I had started at 3:00pm and it would be 11:00pm when my shift would end. Thursday was Thanksgiving and I would work on the holiday, as it wasn't one of my days off. I would work a morning shift and would go to my fiancée's brother's house, as he would have everyone there for Thanksgiving. I had been going with my girlfriend for a number of years and now it was entering the fourth year of our relationship. I had proposed to her and next year in the fall of 1972 would be a good time to get married. The Thanksgiving Day feast included lamb, and pasticcio and many other dishes as well as many Greek pastries. It was a good time to relax as the first three days of this holiday week were extremely hectic and you had to keep your cool as passengers could be very obnoxious and you had to take it with a grain of salt. The rest of the week went by quietly as compared to Tuesday and Wednesday. I would now be refreshed but Sunday lay ahead when again it would be very busy. Sunday came and it was but not as I thought it would be. At the ticket counter we had a rolodex, which had all names of people who had passed bad checks. Sure enough I came across a name that rang a bell and this person came into my line. He was paying for his ticket with his check and I needed two forms of identification; he could not produce two forms and I ran his check into a machine which we had acquired recently that helped to stop the amount of bad checks which we had acquired. It said to call for an authorization. I called for an authorization and the voice told me on the other end that this bank account was closed. I looked at the passenger and said, "This account is closed. Unless you can pay by another means I can't sell you this ticket."

He gave me a credit card and I ran it through the machine to see if it was okay and it was rejected as it said to call for authorization. I called and the credit card company told me to pick up the card. I told the passenger this as I had the credit card company on the telephone. I turned to the passenger and told him that I had to keep the credit card and return it to the credit card company. I thanked them and hung up the telephone. I then told the passenger that he would have to pay cash in order for me to sell him a ticket. He turned and walked away.

Time passed, and I was again planning another trip abroad. This time, I would go back to Greece to stay for a few days and then fly to Istanbul. I started to ask my fellow workers to swap days with me, as I would be away for about twelve days. One person who I knew would swap with me, would be Richey who had never said no to me, as I would always pay back the days I owed my fellow workers. This particular day that I had spoken to my friend Richey something happened that was to change things forever. Eastern Airlines had trained its employees for cross utilization. If the airline needed more ticket agents at the ticket counter the supervisor on duty that day would ask you to work at the ticket counter instead of being a gate agent. So my friend Richey was asked to work at the ticket counter. I was going to lunch when I saw a state police cruiser outside of the terminal. I walked towards the ticket counter and I was shocked at what I saw before me. The state police had Richey in handcuffs. He put his face down so as not to look at me as we passed each other with the state police accompanying him to the cruiser outside of the terminal. I immediately asked another fellow worker, Myra Gorman what happened. A passenger complained that Richey was trying to sell marijuana to him out of his cash drawer. When the supervisor found out, someone called the state police. I felt very sad for we had been friends for a long time. This would be talked about for a long time.

I would now ask other fellow workers to work for me. They were Myra Gorman, Rafaela Carsone, and Jack McGonagle, and John Simpson and two other employees so this would make up for the time that I would be away plus my four days off for working vacation relief. It was nearing spring and the weather would be warmer in Greece and Turkey.

CHAPTER FIFTY-FIVE

My Trip to Constantinople

On Saturday March 17 my fiancée, Betsy took me to the airport with her mother to see me off. I flew out of Logan Airport on Alitalia Airlines non-stop to Rome.

I would connect with another Alitalia flight to Athens. When I arrived in Rome my connecting flight to Athens was on time so I only had fifty minutes between flights. At the gate more people showed up for the flight. While waiting for the flight to Athens, a man and his son came and sat two seats away from me.They spoke Greek. I pretended not to listen but I could not help but hear them. They were a father and son returning home for Pascha (Easter). They had a lot of carry-ons. The time came for all the passengers to board the flight, and we had been given seat assignments. When all the passengers sat down I found that this father and son sat across from me on the aisle. Again, I heard Greek spoken. I was now tempted to speak, but I would hold my tongue. Then I heard something that bothered me. As I understood them they were bringing gifts back to their family, and knew that they would have to pay duty tax. This would amount to quite a bit of money, and I heared him say to his son that the money that he had worked for would be nearly gone. It was now that I turned and excused myself for interrupting. The father turned to me and said, "Are you Greek?" "Yes, I am," I said. "Well," he continued, "I see that you have a lot of things that you are bringing into the country." I answered, "Yes."

"You will have to pay heavy duty on those items." I answered and said, "No I won't."

He answered back, "Yes, you will." "I am an American and have an American passport." I could see by telling him that, he would ask me a favor. "Would you, could you, help me?" "What can I do for you?" "Please, could you pretend that these things that I have belong to you, as they will tax us a lot of money and these are for my family for Pascha (Easter)." I said, "Give them to me, and I will take them through customs for you." "I cannot thank you enough for your kindness," he said. It was only an hour and half flight to Athens, and Valentina and George would be meeting me at the airport as I had sent them a telegram before leaving Boston I finally introduced myself. "My name is Anastasi in Greek." "My, it is your name day, and the holiest day of the year," he said. "My name is Stavros and my son's name is Alexandros."

The plane landed and we continued talking to each other. I said, "Let everyone get off first, then we will get off. I will take everything from you and we will deplane." He agreed and I told him that after going through customs they should go outside and I would meet them there. The bus took us to the terminal and we got off the bus to collect our baggage and proceed through customs. I had told him not to look at me at all. The Greek nationals had to go in a different line going through customs. The tourists went to another line. I went through customs very quickly and proceeded to go outside. Valentina and George were waiting for me. I approached them, greeted them and asked them to wait a minute. Across the street, I could see Stavros, and Alexandros. I walked to them, and gave them their things. His eyes got teary, and he said to me. "You are what people should be, a very, very special human being. Words will never be enough for what you did for me." I was glad to help in the small way that I could. "Happy Pascha to you and your family." "Yiasas," I said, and we parted. I turned and walked towards Valentina and George. They asked me and I told them what I had done.

She said, "That was a wonderful thing you did. I doubt if counting on my hand I could find five people to do what you did. You are like Diogenes who with his lamp was looking for an honest man." We hailed a cab and went to my hotel where I stayed before, the King's Place in Constitution Square.

I checked in, and then went and had something to eat with Valentina and George. I then suggested that we meet tomorrow in the morning. The next day was Sunday and it was quiet, as people were not working. We decided to go to the plaka district. This was the oldest part of Athens. Nearby was a square named Monosteraki. On Sunday there was a huge flea market, where you could pick up some treasures at reasonable prices, and then have a gyro for fifty cents, about 15 drachmas. I met them in the lobby of the hotel at 9:00 a.m. We walked toward the Plaka district, but avoided it, as crowds would swell and there would be hundreds of people. In a crowd of this size the men would pinch the women on their bottoms. So we decided instead to head for the Dora Stratou Theatre on Philopapou hill, where Greek dances were held. We relaxed and enjoyed the music. I told them that I would go to Constantinople, because I wanted to see the Hajia Sofia church. "Aren't you afraid going there?" Valli asked me. "No" I said. "I may never have this chance again," I blurted out. "I leave tomorrow and will be gone for three days." "You don't know anyone there. You are taking a big chance." George, Valli's husband said.

"Okay, if that is what you want to do. Only be very careful."

We talked for a while and watched the dances, very colorful. It was dinnertime and we headed for the Plaka district to enjoy the food and the bouzouki music. We reached the Plaka district and a place called The Paradise.

Here the motion picture "Stella" was made with Melina Mercuri, and Sofia Vembo. We decided to have our dinner there. It was a dinner theater. We were seated by the maitre di' and we faced the stage. There was a famous singer performing here. Her name was Poly Panou. She had come to the United States years ago and I had remembered her. She had a terrific voice and had a string of hits. This was a great night. We could enjoy music and our dinner at the same time. We had a wonderful night. The night passed too fast as far as I was concerned.

The evening ended and I wish that it had lasted longer as I enjoyed it very much. I actually got up and danced the hasapico and I had an audience. We walked back to the hotel and I said I would call them when I returned from Constantinople.

When I got to the airport the next morning, I paid the cab driver, and went to the Olympic Airways ticket counter and said to the ticket agent, "I am on the 1:00 p.m. fight to Constantinople." He said, "They don't allow you to go to Constantinople as they don't want Greeks. They hate the Greeks.

You are a Greek national and they will refuse your entry." "No, I am not, I am an American and I have an American passport. I was born in the United States," I said. "I am awfully sorry, I should have asked you for your passport. You will have no difficulty. I have checked your baggage to Constantinople and you're all set."

There were not many people at the gate, and somehow it would not be a full flight. I noticed two men at the gate area. One was a middle-aged man who had a moustache that looked like something out of the Gay Nineties when men waxed their moustaches. The other gentleman was older. I looked at the middle- aged gentleman who was frantic because he had misplaced his passport. He was going through his carry-on as well as emptying his pockets to find that all-important document. He started talking to himself and, finally, he found it. It was in a hidden pocket in a carry-on. I went and sat near this older gentleman. I struck up a conversation with him asking him if this was his first time traveling to Constantinople. He said that he lived there. I then asked him if he knew of a hotel where I could stay and be comfortable as it was my first time traveling to Constantinople. He was glad to help me. Although he was a Greek national, he was also a British citizen, so he traveled with a British passport so he could leave Turkey and return to Turkey. He said he would be happy to take me to a hotel that was owned by Greeks. I would enjoy my trip now, I thought. The time came to board the flight. As we boarded the bus that was to take us to the airplane, he spoke to me. We had introduced ourselves and now I was calling him by his first name, which was Ianni or John.

He warned me that when we landed at Yeskoy airport in Constantinople not to speak Greek at all. The Turks hated the Greeks. He said, "Speak any other language, but not Greek." I now felt more comfortable for this kindly older gentleman to help me, as it was my first time going there. We boarded the flight, and I sat in first class and he in coach. Working for an airline, first class was not expensive, and Olympic Airways gave us airline employees 75 percent off the fare. This was the first time I sat in first class on Olympic Airways. Flight time was about one hour and twenty minutes.

The surprise that I got during this flight was having a glass of champagne and having caviar for the first time. I don't care if I never have caviar again. I can't see what the fuss is all about having this delicacy. I tried to read but the excitement of traveling to Constantinople was too much as now I would visit a place that I was told about "The Mother of Churches," the Haiia Sofia, which in Greek means The Holy Wisdom.

After deplaning I saw Ianni and went over to him. "Now remember not a single word in Greek going through customs. We will meet afterward, when we board the bus to go into the city." I claimed my luggage, and went immediately to a line that said in English, foreigners only to pass through customs. I opened my baggage as the customs officer looked in my luggage and at me. He put a chalk mark on my suitcase and then said, "Move on." I did and met Ianni at the bus. We boarded the bus, and sat toward the middle. There were few people on the bus, and they sat up front. No one would hear us speak where we sat. It was midafternoon so I would be able to see out the window of the bus as we traveled into the city. The next thing he told me was not to look around. I had noticed a gentleman with worry beads in his hand looking at everyone on the bus. He sat in the last seat. "He is a policeman and he is noticing all of us," Ianni said. "As we travel into the city you will see a lot of ruins. This is where the Turks fought the Greeks in 1922. There are some that go back a few thousand years farther up on this road. The last stop will be at the Olympic Airways office near Plateia Taksim. Plateia Taksim is a big square and you will see many cars going here and there." We arrived at the Olympic Airways office and got off the bus. We claimed our luggage and as we started to walk he explained to me about this huge monument around the square. "You see this? It was erected here for the victory over the Greeks in the disaster of 1922."

It was huge. We continued to walk up a street away from the square and came to his house. He rang the bell and a friend came to the door. He told him, "I'll be back in a few minutes. I am going to the Plaza Hotel with this fellow."

We walked up another street from his house and turned to the right to see the Plaza Hotel. We went in and he spoke to the desk clerk. "This is a gentleman who came from Athens to visit here in Constantinople for a few days." With that Ianni excused himself, and I turned and thanked him very much for assisting me. I said goodnight to him and he left. The desk clerk turned to me and said, "I will give you a room for tonight; it is small, and I will change your room tomorrow. Okay," he said. I followed the bellhop to my room. I showered and went to bed.

CHAPTER FIFTY-SIX

The Hajia Sofia, The Holy Wisdom

The next morning, I came down to the lobby. I saw in a far corner two young men who appeared to be visitors. Then I turned and noticed a woman near the entrance to the hotel. I went to her instead of the two young men. I greeted her, "Good morning, madam." She returned the greeting by asking in English, "Do you wish to have some breakfast?" I answered, "Yes." Just then a woman came into the lobby and spoke quietly to this woman who had greeted me. She spoke in Greek. I immediately excused myself and spoke to them in Greek.

"You are Greek, how wonderful, so nice to make your acquaintance." "My name in Greek is Anastasi." The woman who had just come in said, "My name is Fotini Pantelis," and the woman who sat behind a desk and had asked me if I wanted breakfast, said that her name was Demetra.

As we were talking, Demetra told me to be careful. "You see, even if Greek people own property here, we have to employ some Turkish people. It is the law."

"Those two young men who are waiters are Turkish," said Demetra. Mrs. Pantelis then spoke to me, "You have no idea what they did to the Greek community here in Constantinople.

My family owns a restaurant and they the Turks smashed windows, chairs, dishes and anything that they could get their hands on, because of the dispute over Cyprus." I looked on in amazement as the expressions in her face changed from smiles to tears. "We worked so hard," she continued. "Excuse me" Demetra said, "I have a headache." "Okay, I will get you Tylenol." I went straight to my room and came back in a flash with a few Tylenol tablets. Demetra could not thank me enough. "I'll bet that before I leave here this morning your headache will be gone." She smiled as she got a glass of water and took the two Tylenol tablets. Fotini said, "Look, why don't you save a girl from this life, and marry her." "I did not come here to get married." I said.

With that I said good-bye and went to have breakfast.

After breakfast I then walked to the Olympic Airways office. I went in, and there was this woman sitting behind a desk, talking on the telephone. I understood her as she was speaking in Greek. I thought to myself how great. She hung up the telephone. "Thank goodness you're Greek," I said. She did not respond. Instead, she stared at me as if to want to harm me in some way. She was Turkish. Then she said, "What do you wish?" "I would like to go to the Hajia Sofia church." I said. "You can take a dolmush," she said. I asked, "What's a dolmush?" "It is a shared taxi that stops quite often to pick up passengers and let off passengers." I did not take a dulmush. I asked her if she would call me a taxicab. She did, and it came right away. I thanked her and went outside and got into the cab. "Do you speak English?" I asked the driver. "Yes" he said. "I would like to go the Hajia Sofia Church." "You are Greek?" I fired back, "I was born in the United States, of Greek descent." We went around Taksim Square and took a left; I thought we would go by the Galata Bridge and I would get to see the Bosporus, but that did not happen. We approached the Church of the Holy Wisdom. What a magnificent sight. I could not get over how big it is. The cab driver said, "Look, I will wait for you." No, that is all right," I said. He insisted and I went inside. At the entrance the great bronze doors were heavy. I had heard that you could come in here riding your horse. As I continued walking inside this magnificent structure and looking around, I was so amazed at how the dome for which it is known was placed there, as this was built in the sixth century. I could see where the altar was built. The original stairs were outside as the Moslems put another set in the church. In 1453 when the Turks captured Constantinople, they rode into the church on their horses. Terrible, as Mass was being said. It is said the patriarch took the holy vestments and hid behind a door. The Turks decided to seal him up in that room. This is where I looked up and saw to my astonishment a hand in the cement. This hand was way up and you could not touch it. The church is said to have one hundred doors with one that is sealed up that would make ninety-nine doors that are still open. I could not find any stairs to go up to the second level. I did find an incline that brought me to the second level. Here restoration was done, and all the Arabic script was removed and the icons that were underneath were at last revealed. Gold was used unsparingly especially on one icon of the Christ Pantocrator. Just in front of this icon are two colorful spots where the emperor and the empress stood during church services. I walked down the incline and heard two men talking in Greek, and went closer. Just then an old man came into view and also spoke Greek approaching the other men to say that he knew something about the history of the Holy Wisdom Church.

I excused myself and also spoke about knowing something about what happened in 1453. The Turks have been here for about five hundred years as opposed to the Greeks who have been there for three thousand years. The Greeks founded Byzantium as it was called before the Emperor Constantine moved the capital from Rome to Byzantium and then it was renamed Constantinople. We all contributed to the story of this great Mother of Churches. I stayed a little longer, and I have wished that camcorders had been invented then, as I certainly would have been taping the interior of this structure. I said my good-byes to the three men that I met there, and went outside where the taxicab driver, was waiting for me.

I asked him to go to the Fanar district, a Greek district. "Okay, get in and we will be on our way." We reached the Church of Saint George and the nearby residence of the patriarch. The cab driver said he would wait. I opened the gate, and went into the church and lit a few candles.

Here was another church with much history connected to it. I went up toward the altar to see the old icons. After spending some time up at the altar, I turned to exit the same door that I had come in. I went out into the courtyard and up the stairs where the patriarch might be. I opened the door and saw a man, who said to me in Greek, "Can I help you?" "Yes you can, I would like to see Patriarch Athenagoras." I said. "He is a very busy man," was the response, "I came all the way from America," I continued. "I am from Boston, Massachusetts. I know that the Patriarch went to school in Boston." It was Boston University. The man who was talking to me suddenly disappeared. I then saw this giant of man coming toward me. "Good morning, your Excellency," I uttered.

"So you are from America," he said. "I come from Boston, Massachusetts, and I know that you went Boston University." "I am honored to meet you, and to speak with you." "I came to Constantinople to see the Hajia Sofia and to meet you." "What is your name?" he asked. "My name is Anastasi in Greek and in English it is Ernest," I said. He asked, "How long are you staying in Constantinople?" "I'll be here for another day, returning to Athens the day after tomorrow." "Please come for lunch tomorrow, and we can talk some more." Just then a bus pulled up and a deacon came up to tell the patriarch that the people on the bus were from Epirus, Greece. They had come by bus to Constantinople to visit the patriarchate and of course to see Athenagoras. I felt I was in the way and wanted to excuse myself when they started taking pictures. Someone grabbed me and said, "We want you in the picture." "I am not from Epirus," I said. "We want to show different people from different parts of the world," someone said. "You see we have people from different parts of the world and that is what is important. The Patriarchate is recognized all around the world. The Turks are very prejudiced, which I found out, coming here for the first time and speaking to people. They are self-centered with no respect for anyone that is not Turkish." I spoke again to the patriarch and wished him well and I left. The taxi took me back to the Hotel Plaza. The taxi driver asked me, "Are you leaving tomorrow?" I said, "Yes." but I did not want him to know that I was going to have lunch with Patriarch Athenagoras. I ate at the hotel before I retired for the night, as I wasn't about to explore Constantinople at night. I would not like to get mugged or killed by these barbarians.

The next morning, I took another taxicab to the Fanar District to once again visit Patriarch Athenagoras. At 1:00 p.m. I climbed the stairs, and someone asked me what I wanted. I told him I was invited to have lunch with the patriarch. I approached the top of the stairs and was ready to open the doors to the Patriarchate. I again spoke in Greek not fearing retribution as it was forbidden to speak Greek in public. Here I was comfortable, and just as I was about to sit down in a waiting area, a deacon came out and asked me to follow him to the dining room. From the other side of the dining room, Patriarch Athenagoras approached and greeted me. Then we were seated. We all prayed and asked for God's blessing for the food He had given us, and for human beings to help and forgive one another. This was a beautiful prayer, especially knowing what was going on outside in this country of Turkey, where minorities were persecuted and could not live in peace with their fellow human beings. I asked the patriarch how everything was, and he said, "We are no better or worse. The authorities are not treating us better. Let us forget about this for the moment and enjoy our lunch. I hope you like mousaka and grape leaves for that is the menu for today." "Oh, I love what you are serving. I haven't had this food since I left America. I am enjoying this very much." We spoke of the Cyprus problem. President Nixon and Henry Kissinger were no friends of Cyprus, and allowed Turkey to invade the island and cause the further decay in relations, where the minority was trying to rule the majority. I told him in the United States the majority rules. I told him that I had gone to Israel. He asked me about Israel, and I told him that land belongs to the Hebrew people as it was given to them by God. If only the Jews had listened to God down through the ages but they are a stubborn people. They should not be called Jews, as there is no such thing. Moses was not a Jew; he was a Levite, the protector of the twelve tribes. I told him of a person who teaches at Harvard University and the conversation that I had with her. I told him when I met her I realized from her name that she was Jewish. I said to her, "You should not be called Jewish." Instead of biting my head off, and saying yes we are. she answered me by asking, "What should we be called?" I said, "you are Hebrew, part of the twelve tribes."

She said, "You are a very educated human being." I continued speaking to Patriarch Athenagoras, and he marveled at my knowing of many things. I finally had to excuse myself as the time was getting late, and I wanted to be at the airport early to check in for my flight to Athens. "It has been a most interesting afternoon with you my young man. I wish you from my heart all the best to you in your life. I thank the good God that allowed us to meet, and my blessings to you, and have a safe trip back to the United States." I responded, "Your Excellency, I am very happy to have had this chance in my life to meet you, and talk with you. You are an inspiration to all the Hellenic people the world over. I wish continued good health to you and God's Grace upon you."

I took his hand and kissed it out of respect for him, and said, good-bye. I got a taxicab just outside the entrance of the Patriarchate, and told him I wanted to go to the Plaza Hotel near Taksim Square. When I arrived back at the hotel, I told him to wait, as I would be back in a few minutes as I was going to the airport. I went directly to my room, and took my luggage, and checked to make sure I had taken all my belongings. I came down to the lobby as fast as I could and paid my bill at the desk. I turned, and away I went down the few steps to the street and the taxicab that was waiting for me just in front of the door. It was now 4:45 p.m. and my flight was at 7:30 p.m. I was off to the airport. It would take about fifteen minutes to get there so I was doing all right. I arrived about 5:05 p.m. paid the cab driver, and went in to Olympic Airways ticket counter and checked in. I could now relax by going to the gate and waiting until they announced the boarding of the flight to Athens. I bought myself some loukoumi at the airport but it was not as good as when I bought it in Greece. It is made on the island of Siros. There is none better than the loukoumi from this Greek Island of Siros. Well the time came for boarding the flight back to Athens. I would stay and see my cousins for a few days and then leave for the States. In a little more than an hour, I arrived back in Athens. I took a cab to the Kings Palace Hotel and called my cousins. I told them I would wait for them to come to Athens from Piraeus, and meet them here at the hotel. In about an hour they arrived, and we decided to go out for a few hours to listen to bouzouki music in the Plaka District. I told them that I would be leaving on tomorrow's flight back to America. So this would be my last evening in Athens.

Valli and George were sad that I could not stay longer in Greece. We stayed out till about midnight enjoying the music and performers. We returned to my hotel in Constitution Square. Here I said good-bye to them and that I hoped to return in the future but I gave them no date. In the morning, I decided to take a walk around Athens since my flight was not until 2:00 p.m. I had remembered passing a music store the night before and wanted to see if I could purchase a record album titled Zorba the Greek. In 1968 on my first trip to Greece, the country was under a dictatorship. Mikis Theodorakis had written the music and because of affiliation with the Communist Party his music was banned in Greece. I finally came to the street where the music store was located and went in. I inquired about this album, and the proprietor said, "Yes, I have it." So for one hundred and fifty drachmas I purchased it. Next I came to a little Byzantine church named Kapnikarea. I went in, and lit a few candles and left. I returned to the hotel and left for the airport.

CHAPTER FIFTY-SEVEN

Back in Boston

After landing in Boston, I collected my luggage, and headed for a telephone to call my fiancée, Betsy, to tell her that I was home. Betsy and her mother came to the airport and took me home to Malden. When I got home, I asked them if they wanted to come up the house for a while. They said, "no" as they knew I would be tired after a long trip. I said, "Thanks for bringing me home. I'll call you tomorrow." The next morning, on Friday, I started to unpack my clothes when the phone rang and it was Betsy asking me about our wedding plans. We had been engaged for four years and planned to marry in the fall of 1972. We had reserved the hall where the reception was to be held. It was like a hole in the wall, but inside it was beautiful. We had met the manager named, Ernie, and chosen the menu with my fiancée. That evening we got together to talk about the music we would have at the wedding. We chose the Trio Moderno. They were the most popular band at that time, and we had gone to some dances where they played. We would try to book them well in advance hoping that they would be available. I had to talk to Arthur Marathas, who was the leader of the band. We called him that evening, and asked him if he could play on the twenty first of October." He said, "Wait a minute I'll look at my calendar." We crossed our fingers and hoped for the best. I could hear him moving something around, and then he came back on the telephone.

"It's fine. It's okay for the twenty first of October." I looked at my fiancée and we both were smiling from ear to ear. "Mr. Marathas, thank you very much."

We now had everything except the photographer. I remembered going over to one of Betsy's friend's house and noticing her wedding album on the coffee table. I asked her, "Dina, who did your wedding album?" "Why it was Ciro's of Boston," she said. "I can't get over how it was done. It was very unusual. The photographs are full pages. They are washable. Plus, it has a gold edge on all the pages and it was bound in leather."

"Yes," Dina said, "it was pretty expensive." I would call Ciro's tomorrow. I was working the morning shift on Saturday and I waited till the afternoon when I had finished my shift. So when Betsy picked me up, we went straight to her house and I called Ciro's of Boston but there was no answer. I figured they were closed for the weekend. Monday came and, just as soon as I got off work, I called Ciro's.

Ciro's was in Dorchester, which is a part of Boston. I called him, and sure enough, he told me that he is closed on Saturdays. He asked me to come to his studio. I asked him, "How about a week from Monday? I have to be out of town for about a week, because of my job." "Sure," he said. "I want my fiancée to come with me. All right if we are there at 7:00pm?" I said to him, on the phone. "That's fine," he said. This was done and we would meet with the photographer the following Monday after my return from Miami.

My next day at work was not an easy one as we had flights to Washington National Airport the first one departing at 7:00a.m. I got a real winner at seven in the morning. A passenger was mad as hell when he approached the ticket counter.

He flung his ticket at me, and yelled, "Here is my goddam ticket!" I simply said, "Good morning. Would you like a window or an aisle seat in the smoking or non-smoking section?" He fired back, "Give me an aisle seat." I gave him seat 25c on the aisle, and checked his one piece of luggage for Washington D.C. He proceeded to Gate 5. I had told my supervisor, John Kroeger, what had happened. "Ernie, this is one of the toughest jobs working with the public." John said, "I know, John," I replied. Just then an amazing thing happened. The passenger came back to the ticket counter and saw me, and my supervisor talking. He came right up to me, excusing himself. "I came to apologize for being very harsh, and impolite to you. I've wronged you, and I feel very bad. It is just that I've had a bad morning. My car would not start, and I had to make this flight. I have an important meeting in Washington this morning." I replied, "You have made my day, and I can't thank you enough for coming back. I hope and pray that everything goes well for you at your meeting, and have a great day. Please, I don't want you to miss your flight. "Okay," he said, and he left. My supervisor stood motionless looking at me. "Ernie, that is the first time I have actually seen a passenger return to say he was sorry for the way he behaved.

You are a great worker, and a credit to this airline," John said. I felt on top of the world, and I guess I could take anything that would come along today.

My fiancé had arrived to pick me up, and we headed to the Sumner Tunnel, connecting East Boston with Boston proper, then toward Cambridge where my fiancée lived. We had to decide on the wedding guest list. There were at least fifty people from the airport that I had in mind to invite. Then there were my mother's friends who I had worked with years before. How could I not invite them? They were a part of my life since I worked at Dave's place during my teenage years when my mother was alive. I now cherished those days without regret.

I can remember after my mother died, I was walking down my street, and my mother's boss, Dave Pressman happen to be walking by Clark Street going to visit his brother Izzy. I called out to him, "Dave," he turned and looked. "Sonny, oh Sonny," he sighed and said my mother's name. "Mary, how I miss her." "Where are you?" Betsy said, as I looked at her in amazement. "Oh, I was thinking out loud about my mother's boss years ago. I won't leave him and the others out of my wedding. I can't. I would rather leave out some of my family than leave out these wonderful people." "All right don't worry, Sonny; they will be invited to our wedding." It brought back memories of when my mother was alive, and I knew these wonderful people.

Meanwhile I had to decide who I was going to invite from my job. There were a lot of people there that I thought I wanted to have at my wedding, but I knew that I might offend others. Our wedding list would exceed two hundred people, so the expense had to be taken in to account.

The next thing I had to think about was who would stand in for my parents, as both of them were dead. I was very close to my Uncle Louis and Aunt Penny, so I asked them if they would stand in for my parents. They were both thrilled to do so. Almost everything was done and now, my fiancée Betsy and I could relax, as the wedding was a year away.

Betsy drove me home. The next day at work it was not a quiet day at the airport. The shuttle flights were delayed. It was foggy. As I looked out the window I could see fire apparatus and police cruisers traveling on a private road beyond the terminal and I knew that something was dreadfully wrong. There had been a crash. I called the control center and asked Joe what happened. "Ernie, there has been a bad accident. A Delta airlines flight has crashed into a wall," he said. I ran down the jetway, and opened the door to take a better look, as I could not see anything, as my view was obstructed. When I finally was able to see something I saw a huge ball of fire that had engulfed everything around it. More fire apparatus was called. The flames rose above the terminal building and now you could see these flames even with the fog. I returned to the gate area and passengers' asking me what is going on? All I said is there has been a plane crash. I called the control center, and asked Joe what was going on? Joe knew more than I knew because of talking to the controllers in the tower. Joe said, "I don't think there were any survivors, as I understand from what is going on. The plane is completely engulfed in flames," he said. "Oh my God," I exclaimed.

At the end of my shift I was stressed. When Betsy came to take me home she saw my face, and asked, "Sonny what is it? You look terrible."

"Well, I am shaking from this mentally painful experience that occurred today. It will be all over the T.V. tonight, and the newspapers tomorrow. There was a terrible accident. A plane crashed this afternoon and I just can't stop thinking of it, and the passengers on that Delta flight. It was awful. The flames, the smoke, people running around the plane trying to save passengers from this terrible accident." "Sonny, take it easy." "I am trying, and I just want to go home. I need a good stiff drink, but I don't drink. That's the trouble." Betsy drove me home and I kissed her, and said, "I'll call you in a little while, okay?

As long I live in this life I will never forget, what I have seen today. I have flown all over the world, and I know that I have been in some near mishaps but to witness this tragedy firsthand is too much."

The next day the newspapers had the airplane crash all over their front pages. Every passenger had died except one. Charles Lundren had survived the crash. He had been taken to the Massachusetts General Hospital in Boston. The Shriners Burns Hospital is right next door. Here they could do wonders for people who were badly burned. I would now follow this story to its conclusion. Each day I would read the paper to see what was happening with this person. I read where his fiancée, Cheryl Langton came from Vermont, and would stay in Boston and visit him daily. Then one day I read where he had to have his legs amputated, as they were too far burned to save them. No sooner had the doctors performed this amputation then he passed away two days later. Although my fiancée followed this tragedy with me, we never talked about it again.

CHAPTER FIFTY-EIGHT

Zurich and Vienna

Some months passed and I decided to take my last trip as a bachelor.

Swiss Air had an interline trip in conjunction with Austrian Airlines and it was only ninety-nine dollars. I decided to take trip this as a way of relaxing and I wanted to visit and do some shopping for my fiancée. I would be away for nine days. This included two days in Switzerland and the rest of the time it would be visiting Austria. I told my fiancée, and she agreed that it was good to get away for a while. I made all the arrangements. I was to leave the following Saturday on Swiss Air.

On Saturday I departed from Logan Airport, and arrived the next day in Zurich, which is closer to the German border. I found out that in Switzerland, five languages are spoken. If you live close to the French side, they speak French. If you live near the Italian border, they speak Italian. Swiss Air landed in Zurich and German was spoken here. The other two languages are old Romanish.

Zurich is a very clean city and I enjoyed the sights. I was taken to the Rhine fall and here this sight is very beautiful. Here I purchased a handbag for my fiancée and a demitasse teacup.

The next morning, we were off to Vienna, the capital of Austria. This country, as well as Germany, was divided among the four major powers. It was only fifteen years before that under a strict agreement, Austria finally gained its freedom and was now once again a nation.

The next five days would be spent in Vienna. What a beautiful city. When checking in at the hotel, I met two other people from my party. One was named Jack from Mexicana Airlines, and the other person was Al from U.S. Air. Hanna Mueller had been a ground hostess with Eastern Airlines and was now returning to visit her father who lived in Vienna. When we were assigned our rooms I had to share my room with the two fellows who I met at the airport when we collected our luggage. We tossed a coin to see who would get the single bed. I won. We settled in. We would not do any sightseeing until tomorrow. I decided to go out on my own, and explore Vienna. I did, and came upon St. Stephens Church. What a magnificent cathedral. Luckily it escaped the bombing so it seemed. I went to a pastry shop and bought some strudel. Oh boy, was it ever so good. I next went to a jewelry store, to buy a charm for my fiancée's charm bracelet. It was just like the coach that Cinderella rode in to the ball. I then visited a music store, and purchased a long-playing album. I loved all of the Strauss Waltzes. Later I found out that the waltzes are played in the park every Sunday.

After exploring a little of Vienna on my own, Hanna called the hotel, and left me a message. I was to meet her in the lobby of the hotel, at 7:00 p.m. and she was to take me to meet her father. I met Hanna at 7:00 p.m. and she took me to meet her father and have supper with them. We took the tram and on the way she started to tell me about some of the employees at Eastern. I was not shocked, as I knew that some were gay, and I would try to pretend I did not know anything about that. "You know Ernie, that Richey is one, and there are about another eight people that you work with." "Look, Hanna, I don't bother with any of them outside of working at the airport. I never really knew how naïve I was until coming to work for an airline. I have had such an awakening." I said goodnight to Hanna and wished her well, for she told me she would not be returning to America as her husband had completed his studies in Boston.

That night, I returned to the hotel. It was dark when I entered my room, and not wanting to disturb my roommates I did not put any lights on, and felt my around the room. Suddenly, I heard voices, "oh that feels good, did you get your climax?" Oh my God, they were in bed having sex. I went to bed and made sure that I pretended that I did not hear anything that was going on. The next morning, I got up and left, as I did not want to disturb these two lovers. I had breakfast, and joined the tour to go off to Schonbrunn, the palace of the Hapsburgs. This palace is not very far from Vienna and has forty rooms. I came upon the grand ballroom, and thought of the Emperor's Waltz being played here by Johann Strauss. I saw the bedroom of the Emperor Franz Joseph and where he died. The grounds are beautiful, with many flowers. The afternoon I was free to do some exploring of my own.

That evening with the tour group I went to a beer garden in the Vienna Woods. The food was very good. We enjoyed the music, and I avoided my two roommates like the plague. We had two more nights in Vienna, and my next to the last night, I went to a place called the Greichen Spiegel, meaning "Greek house". It was founded and owned by Greeks. Upon entering it seemed kind of dim and I realized it wasn't that dark. The ceiling was lit with a pastel color.

Another strange thing was on the ceiling there were all signatures. Now these were not ordinary signatures. They were signatures of all the famous people who had visited this Greek house. All the famous composers of years gone by were here. I was amazed. I walked up to the bar, and asked the bartender if he spoke English. He did. I ordered a beer, and he brought it in a glass stein. I never drank beer before. This was Austrian beer, and it was strong.

I asked the bartender if I could purchase this glass stein, and he said I could. When I returned to the hotel I asked the hotel clerk if I could change rooms. He asked, "What is wrong with the room?" I did not mention anything that went on there the night, before, just that I wanted peace and quiet. He accommodated me, and I thanked him since it was only for two nights, tonight and tomorrow night.

The last day in Vienna was spent at an amusement park. I saw the biggest Ferris wheel in the world. It is called the Wonder Wheel. The seats are enclosed, so that when you are on it you felt secure. The surprise was that each car would slide so you were in motion at all times besides riding in a circular motion. This was not something we had back in America. I returned to the hotel, and packed for my departure the next day for Boston. I returned home, and told my fiancée Betsy what had happened. She like me was naïve.

CHAPTER FIFTY-FOUR

The Shower & The Wedding

My fiancée's sisters-in-law and girlfriends were planning a wedding shower, and of course took me into their confidence. It would be held in Revere, at the Disabled Americans Hall in August. I wrote the list of names with the help of my fiancée's sisters-in-laws. The night of the shower was beautiful, with a clear starry sky. I told her we were going to a Greek-American dance and the orchestra that we liked so much, the Trio Moderno, would be playing. My fiancée didn't have a clue as to what was really going on. On August the 16th 1972, Saturday, I opened the door to the hall and heard everyone yell surprise.

She cried and cried. It was a wonderful night. We thanked everyone for coming. We talked about our honeymoon and planned to go to Israel and Greece. My fiancée had never been farther than New York City. She was really excited, and I told her she would have the time of her life. She went with her mother to choose her wedding gown. I could not see the wedding gown until the day of our wedding. The bridesmaids' gowns were red velvet with gold trim.

The tuxedos were black. I would wear a white shirt and the best man and ushers would wear pink shirts. The important day came Saturday, October 21. I had a two-week vacation. We had sent out two hundred invitations, and they all replied in the affirmative. This was going to be some wedding. Many people had never been to a Greek wedding and it was something to see.

My Aunt Penny and Uncle Louis came by two o'clock to get dressed at my house. My Aunt Penny's gown was beautiful, taffeta brocade with a jacket. She looked so stunning in it. We had to be at the church. The wedding was at 5 p.m. The wedding ceremony was at the church of Saints Constantine and Helen in Cambridge.

Meanwhile, at the church, people had arrived for the wedding ceremony, and the bridal party was there including my brother Johnny. Everyone started wondering where the groom was. People started saying maybe he got cold feet, and won't show up, which would be very embarrassing for the bride and her family. I parked the car, and ran through to the side entrance of the church, and I suddenly appeared at the altar. Father Metaxas said, "Bravo, glad you could make it."

The wedding party was being escorted into the church. I could now see my Aunt Penny and Uncle Louis waiting to be escorted down to the pew on the groom's side.

There were seven bridesmaids and seven ushers, plus a ring bearer and flower girl. They had all come down the aisle, and were now at the altar as the wedding march played. I turned to my best man, Jimmy, who was laughing as he said to me, "I will remember this always." "I know," I said.

I looked up, and there before me was my wife-to-be, with her father. He lifted her veil, and kissed her, and then turned to me and shook my hand and went to the first pew where his wife was. Father Metaxas opened the ceremony saying in Greek, "Blessed is the name of the Lord." He later repeated in English for the guests who did not understand Greek.

The ceremony was more than hour. It was a double-ring ceremony and the best man exchanged the stephana, or crowns, on our heads three times, signifying the Father and the Son and the Holy Ghost. We walked around a ceremonial table three times while the best man held the stephana. The crowns symbolized the crown of thorns Christ wore on his head, placed there by the Roman soldiers who scourged him before his crucifixion. We also drank wine, the wine at the Passover, which Christ and his apostles celebrated. When the ceremony was nearly over, Father Metaxas spoke to the guests and explained about the wedding ceremony, which had taken place. The wedding rings were placed on our fingers and exchanged three times to signify the Father, the Son, and the Holy Ghost. After the priest's speech he continued to finish the ceremony, pronouncing us man and wife.

I turned, and kissed my wife, and there was such an uproar and clapping of hands as we turned and were congratulated by our families. We then proceeded up the aisle to the limousine. Of course all this time the photographer was taking many pictures.

We did not have video cameras back then. At the limousine more pictures were taken as we prepared to leave for the Tremont Villa in Everett for the reception. When we arrived at the Tremont Villa the orchestra was already there playing music as we entered the hall. The dance music would come later. There was an open bar for about two hours. The guests were finding their place cards and taking their seats. The wedding party was introduced and seated, then the bride and groom were introduced, and a thunderous applause burst forth from the guests. The best man toasted us, and an announcement was made for all to go to the receiving line. When my brother Nicky came into the line, I suddenly broke down, and could not stop crying. "Sonny, what are you crying for?" he asked. If he only knew for a few moments that my mind took me out of where I was and brought me back to a time when our mother was alive. I remembered what she did for so many people. The pain of not having her here would never leave me as long as I lived. Just then a voice called me, "Sonny, Sonny come out of it. Where are you?" "I am sorry. For a few brief moments I was transported back to the West End, and the wonderful person that we had for too short time our mother." It was my Aunt Stella, my mother's sister, who called me out of my trance. She was in the receiving line right after my brother Nicky. As she kissed me on my cheek, she said, "Of the four boys, you are most like your mother. I could never be like her. She was my older sister and I always wanted to have her personality and imitate her ways. She always cared for me even when I didn't deserve it. She helped me out many times and, yes, Sonny, I miss her too, very much. Now look, this is your wedding day, and it is supposed to be a very happy occasion." With a sigh, I said, "I know, and I am trying, Aunt Stella." "Good, now dry those tears, and smile because there are a lot of people in this receiving line who want to congratulate you and your wife." "Thanks, Aunt Stella, I love you." "I love you too," she said.

After the receiving line was over, we took our seats for the fine cuisine. First was the pastene soup with a little grated cheese to top it off. Then came the antipasto, followed by ziti macaroni in marinara sauce, followed by the filet mignon in its own juice served with garlic mashed potatoes and string beans hollandaise. The dessert was Baked Alaska.

As the meal was winding down, the emcee asked for the bride and groom to come to the dance floor for the first dance. Then my in-laws came up to dance along with Aunt Penny, and Uncle Louis, then the rest of the wedding party. We all had our time on the dance floor, as this was regular dancing. Arthur Marathas started to play Greek music and the first dance was the kalamatiano.

The dance floor was suddenly alive with everyone out on the dance floor. The kalamatiano emptied the tables. People who did not know how to dance this went up to learn, as the music was so intoxicating. My wife and I were in the first line of dance as the emcee had asked everyone to come up and dance. With everyone dancing no one wanted to sit down. The Greek dances are varied with as many as 10 different dances.

My mother-in-law was beaming with happiness. Betsy and I put her to lead

the kalamatiano. She looked terrific in her gown, as I could see the photographer taking her picture.

This would go on all evening, and there was American music too. The garter was taken off and the bridal bouquet was tossed. It was a wonderful time. As we left, my brother in law said, "Go on. Get out of here." We took his advice. As the wedding came to a close, I would be on to new and exciting chapters in my life.

CPSIA information can be obtained
at www.ICGtesting.com
Printed in the USA
BVOW04s0200210317
479026BV00001B/37/P

9 781457 551758